June 15, 2003

HAPPY FATHER'S DAY

LOVE FROM

Peter & Carmen

Janis & Jamie

Steve & Beth

100 Years of Change

snapshots
in time

With grateful thanks to Frances Banfield, Helen
Courtney, Lucinda Hawksley, Helen Johnson, Lee
Matthews, Sonya Newland, Martin Noble, Ian
Powling, Susan Thompson, Nick Wells and Dr
Frances Wood.

ISBN 1 55110 734 1

First published in 1998 by
DEMPSEY PARR
13 Whiteladies Road
Clifton
Bristol
BS8 1PB

This edition published in 1998 by
WHITECAP BOOKS LTD
351 Lynn Avenue
North Vancouver, BC
Canada
V7J 2C4

Created and produced for Dempsey Parr by
FOUNDRY DESIGN & PRODUCTION
a part of The Foundry Creative Media Company Ltd
Crabtree Hall
Crabtree Lane
Fulham, London
SW6 6TY

Printed in Italy

100 Years of Change

snapshots in time

Eithne Farry, Karen Hurrell, and Jon Sutherland

Introduction by
Brian Moynahan

WHITECAP BOOKS

Contents

Introduction   *9*

From kings to political heroes, rebel leaders to entrepreneurs, the rise and fall of the twentieth century's most powerful and influential figures and institutions are charted in stories that have hit the world's headlines since the turn of the century.

1. *World in Action*   *13*

2. *Power & Politics*   *41*

3. *Business & Economics*   *67*

The twentieth century has seen incredible changes in cultures and lifestyles all over the world. Through the entertainment media, in the arts, and through their unshakable beliefs, people have endeavored to improve the quality of their lives and their environment.

4. *Arts, Entertainment & Culture*   *75*

5. *Human Rights & Society*   *97*

6. *Religion & Cults*   *111*

Some entries that cover events of particular significance have been selected as milestones and are indicated by this symbol.

The past one hundred years have seen some of the most dramatic breakthroughs in mankind's never-ending quest for new knowledge and discoveries.

7. *Exploration & Discovery*   *117*

8. *Transport*   *129*

9. *Science & Technology*   *143*

10. *Medicine & Health*   *153*

Through the despair and bravery of two World Wars, numerous internal conflicts and international disasters, the world's most turbulent century has witnessed its darkest hours and finest moments.

11. *War & Peace*   *161*

12. *Natural & Environmental Disasters*   *183*

    Bibliography   *196*

    Author Biographies & Picture Credits   *197*

    Subject Index   *198*

    Index of Names   *199*

Introduction

It has, by any standards, been a big century. Flight has been mastered: the first heavier-than-air machine limped briefly into the air over North Carolina in 1903; less than 70 years later—the blink of an eye in terms of history—Neil Armstrong walked on the moon. Two World Wars have been fought, with unparalleled butchery; the second of them was brought to a close by a new weapon, the atom bomb, which had been developed in five years.

Social behavior has been revolutionized by the perfection of the female contraceptive pill; and political behavior by the totalitarian embrace of fascist and communist ideologies. Travel has been transformed by mass-produced cars, jet planes, and more frequent vacations; leisure by the movies, radio, television, cassette tapes and CDs, and the new breed of global superstars and pop artists who appear on them. Computers have changed the way we work, and faxes, portable telephones and the Internet the way we keep in touch.

But, for all the grand scale of its advance, the century has also been more intimate than any that went before. No part of the world is obscure, and neither is any individual in whom the world decides to take an interest. The immense progress in communications—cameras, microphones, satellite links, instant news—means that we know much more about each other. Or we think we do; and the great value of the snapshots in time in this book is to remind us how far we have traveled—backwards as well as forwards, for one of the by-products of scientific progress has been to multiply the horrors we can inflict on each other—and how much we have forgotten.

The mosaic of the century is built here through major events and milestones in the lives of individuals. Great themes emerge—the retreat from empire, for instance, or the advance of women's rights from a voteless start—and so do the people who make them. There are, too, now-dimly remembered events that made headlines at the time—Bonnie and Clyde go bank-robbing, Winston Churchill marries Clementine, Terry Waite is kidnapped—and that help give the century its flavor.

It is startling to be reminded—as the reader is here—that a breakthrough as fundamental as the discovery of blood groups dates from only 1903, the same year that the Wright brothers got airborne, or that antibiotics only came into use from 1941. Yet the dramatic fall in infant mortality, new drugs and vaccines for great killer diseases—TB, cholera, typhoid, polio—have changed the scale of human existence; more people have lived this century than in all the millennia that have gone before.

Technology has made millions of people richer and their homes more comfortable; they are employed in scores of new industries; life expectancy has greatly increased. Less of their lives are consumed in routine

drudgery and more time is available for new pleasures: a spin in the car, the computer game, the vacation escape.

From the Boer War to Chechnya, the evidence is here that human affairs have failed utterly to match this scientific enlightenment. People may be a lot smarter, but their inhumanity is magnified by their instinct to convert new knowledge into new weapons of destruction. The *Dreadnought* of the beginning of the century soon enough becomes the nuclear-powered submarine. Mass media are used for mass propaganda by modern dictators—and the cast list is long, Stalin, Hitler, Mao, Ceausescu—to enslave the mind in ways beyond the capacity of their predecessors.

Old catastrophes of nature—earthquakes, volcanic eruptions, typhoons—are joined by new manmade disasters: the Chernobyl nuclear accident, stricken tankers, and chemical spills. New countries are formed; some, like Yugoslavia and the Soviet Union, are born and die within the century itself.

Henry Ford may have thought that "history is more or less bunk," but the progress of his brain child—the affordable motor car—is traced here via his

Tin Lizzie and the Beetle and the Mini to an era in which oil wars are fought to keep it in gasoline. Express trains reach a peak with the British *Flying Scotsman* in 1928, appear to be doomed by jet airliners and the end of the Orient Express in 1962, but launch a stunning comeback with France's TGV (*Train à Grande Vitesse*—"High Speed Train") in 1981. A Channel tunnel, mooted since the pre-railway time of Napoleon, finally joins Britain to the Continent by rail.

Styles—Art Nouveau, the New Look—come, go and come back. Winnie the Pooh and Mickey Mouse start their long-lasting careers; Bill Haley introduces rock and roll, Marilyn Monroe flits across the screen and *Jurassic Park* takes half a billion dollars at the global box office. The last remote places are reached, the South Pole in 1912, the top of Everest in 1953, the deepest point of the ocean in 1960. The exploration of space begins; by 1997, pictures of the surface of Mars are being sent 310 million miles back to Earth.

The century has been filled with innovations and events. That makes it doubly interesting to go back through it. What happens within our lifetimes tends now, more than ever, to pass out of memory because the mind is bombarded with so much new material. It takes an effort to think of a world without television, traffic jams and airports—or to remember when a quarter of the world was British and the arrest of Dr Crippen through radio messages was thought to be a hi-tech miracle. But that is the reward of the many hindsights in this book.

Brian Moynahan

World in Action

1

History is more or less bunk. It's tradition.
We don't want tradition. We want to live in
the present and the only history that's
worth a tinker's damn is the history
we make today.

Henry Ford, 1916

1900 Boxer rebellion in China

Overleaf: *the celebrations as Britain hands Hong Kong back to China in 1997 (see page 38).* Below: *Boxer rebels besieged the city of Peking, having slaughtered thousands of foreigners and Chinese Christians.* Right: *the Australian flag showing the British Union Jack and the Commonwealth star.*

FOLLOWING AN ULTIMATUM to the Chinese government to suppress the activities of the Boxers (a group of rebels who began as peaceful patriots and became murderous xenophobes), the major world powers sent detachments of troops to Peking to protect their nationals. The Boxers, calling themselves the "Fists of Righteous Harmony," stormed across China slaughtering all foreigners on sight. After fierce fighting around Tianjin, allied troops stormed the city in the face of over 100,000 Boxers to find that 1500 foreigners had been massacred. Despite the defeat, over 300,000 Boxers supported by Chinese imperial troops massed around Peking. The Boxers did not restrict their attentions to foreigners but also slaughtered many thousands of Chinese Christians. After an epic 56-day siege of the capital, an allied column of 10,000 battled their way from Tianjin, relieving the beleaguered legations that had taken refuge around the British

Embassy. The joint force, commanded by the German Count von Waldersee, arrived in time to save the besieged foreigners who had only one week's food and supplies left. Implicated in the plot to oust all foreigners from Chinese soil, the Emperor and the Dowager Empress fled Peking just two days before the relief force arrived, carrying with them a vast amount of treasure. As a result of the rising, Russia annexed Manchuria, the Chang Jiang (Yangtse River) was declared an international waterway and China was forced to pay £65 million in reparations.

1900 Britain annexes Tonga Islands and Orange Free State

AFTER JUST A YEAR, the Boers under Paul Kruger were defeated by Lord Roberts—resistance had been reduced to a handful of Boer raiding parties. However many of the key Boer leaders were still at large and in possession of gold bullion to the value of £500,000. The British narrowly missed capturing President Marthinus Steyn of the Orange Free State as they marched triumphantly into the state capital, Bloemfontein. Despite the partial success of his mission, Roberts annexed the Transvaal and the Orange Free State in September. It was during the siege of Mafeking that Baden-Powell created the Scouts in imitation of military principles. Meanwhile, in May, the British annexed Tonga, formerly the Friendly Islands. In the previous month, the British Sandwich Islands had become US territory and been renamed Hawaii.

1901 Birth of the Commonwealth of Australia

ROYAL ASSENT WAS GIVEN to the act that created the Commonwealth of Australia in July 1900. The first prime minister, Edmund Barton, formally took his place in history in January 1901. The Governor-General, Lord Hopetoun, presided over the ceremony in front of 50,000 people from the four corners of the continent. A two-mile-long procession of British, Australian, and Empire troops paraded through Sydney in celebration of the new Commonwealth. By May, the first Australian Federal Parliament had met in Melbourne, the state capital, but Australia would still continue to support the UK through the difficult times in the future.

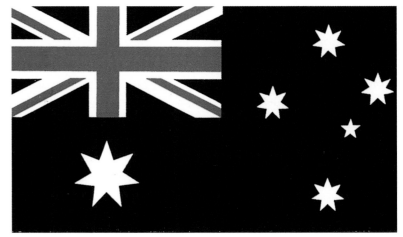

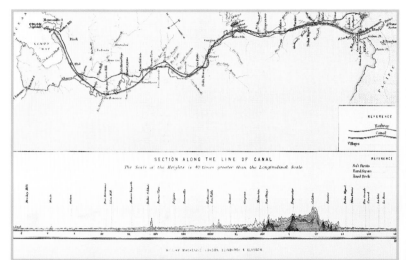

SECTION ALONG THE LINE OF CANAL
The Scale of the Heights is 40 times greater than the Longitudinal Scale

1905 Russia's Bloody Sunday

IN AN ATTEMPT TO DELIVER a petition to Czar Nicholas II, 500 loyal strikers led by Father George Gapon were gunned down outside the Winter Palace in St. Petersburg. The Czar had promised an urgent examination of the plight of the peasantry following a spate of rioting in most of the major cities. Although the strikers were led by a priest carrying a cross, and pictures of the Czar were displayed prominently to reinforce their loyalty, their progress was barred by lines of infantry who fired on them without warning at just 30 yards. Russia rapidly fell into chaos, with key figures like Leon Trotsky demanding a revolution to sweep away the Czars.

Left: *map showing the Panama Canal during its construction.*
Below: *Father George Gapon leading the workers to the Winter Palace, where they were killed – an act that led to widespread revolution.*

1902 US Commission chooses Panama as site of canal

AFTER A LONG BATTLE IN CONGRESS between two rival groups of senators, the Americans finally decided to build a canal linking the Pacific and Atlantic Oceans across Panama. A French company, led by the engineer Ferdinand de Lesseps, had been trying to build such a canal since the late 1870s. After skilful negotiations by the New York lawyer William Nelson Cromwell, the French company agreed to be bought out for $40 million. The alternative route through Nicaragua was finally put aside when eruptions from Mount Pelée on Martinique cost 30,000 lives. The pro-Panama group sent Nicaraguan stamps to each Senator showing an erupting volcano. The canal project would shorten the route between the two US coasts by 8000 miles.

1903 British capture Kano from Nigerian rebels

FOLLOWING THE FULMANIS' JIHAD (holy war) at the beginning of the eighteenth century, Kano was chosen as the capital of the emirate. It became the center of trade in silk, spices, and slaves for the area. The empire based on the city reached its height under Muhammad Bello who administered it under strict Muslim rules. As the empire began to decay as the new century dawned, the British, eager to extend their influence in the area and rid themselves of the troublesome rebels, captured the city. This opened the way to the establishment of a railway from Lagos and a direct link to the trade coming from the Sahara region.

1905 Norway attains independence

IN JUNE 1905, the Norwegian parliament refused to recognize the Swedish monarchy and declared its independence from Sweden. A split in the union had been expected for some time. A referendum of the Norwegian people in August showed 80 per cent support for the dissolution of the union with Sweden. The terms of Norwegian independence were announced in Stockholm the following month, forcing the Swedish king, Oscar II, to abdicate formally from the Norwegian throne in October. A second referendum in Norway followed in November revealing 78 per cent support for the second son of the Danish King Frederick VII. Prince Carl formally accepted the throne of Norway on November 18th and was duly crowned as Haakon VII.

1907 Germany's fleet building brings about the Triple Entente

IN RESPONSE TO THE GROWTH of the German military machine at the beginning of the century, the other major European powers realized that they would have to work together in order to restrain the ambitions of the united Germany. Great Britain, France, and Russia, who would be

Gatun Lock on the Panama Canal, which was completed in 1913 after over ten years of construction. It provided the first direct route between the Pacific and Atlantic Oceans.

at the heart of the allied cause in 1914, had already signed independent treaties. The Triple Entente built upon the Franco-Russian Alliance (1894) and the Anglo-French Cordiale (1904). With Germany attempting to build ever more powerful *Dreadnoughts* (warships), the response had to be a concerted one if the allies were to thwart Germany's ambitions. Each of the allied nations had, in its own way, things to fear from Germany, as they would soon discover in 1914.

1908 Winston Churchill marries Clementine

1908 PROVED to be an important year for Winston Churchill in a number of ways. Following the resignation of Sir Henry Campbell-Bannerman, Asquith took over as Prime Minister. Churchill joined the cabinet as President of the Board of Trade and David Lloyd George as Chancellor of the Exchequer. In September Churchill married Clementine Hozier, who would be his closest friend and companion until his death in 1965. For Churchill the pre-war years would be of intense activity: often the only voice in government that alerted the country to Germany's ambitions and always in the right place to keep himself in the public eye. These formative years would prepare him well for his role in the future.

1913 Panama Canal completed

PRESIDENT WILSON finally opened the Panama Canal in October. It was completed at a cost of £60 million and was described at the time as "the greatest liberty man has ever taken with nature." The project was managed by the autocratic engineer Colonel George Goethals. The US president formally completed the canal himself by detonating a 40-ton charge of explosives from the White House, some 4000 miles away. This charge removed the last obstacle. On November 17th, the steamship *Louise* successfully navigated the canal, passing into history as the first vessel to use the waterway. In January, in recognition of Goethals's contribution to the canal project, President Wilson offered the engineer the post of first governor of the Canal Zone.

1914 Great War (World War I) begins

WITH JUST TWO pistol shots Gavrilo Princip would send millions to their deaths. He assassinated the heir to the Austro-Hungarian throne as he rode through Sarajevo in an open carriage. The first bullet hit Archduke Franz Ferdinand and the second struck his wife. It was obvious that the plot had been well planned: earlier a bomb had been thrown at the couple. The assassin was aided by a secret Serbian group calling itself the "Black Hand." It was this connection that would lead Austria to take the most aggressive steps against Serbia. The "Serbian wasp nest," as Count Leopold von Berchtold described it, had to be dealt with. The Serbians had already expressed satisfaction at the death of Franz Ferdinand. Vienna cut off diplomatic relations with Serbia in July and both sides mobilized. Meanwhile, the Russians pledged their support to the Serbians. Austria declared war and invaded Serbia, causing the mobilization of 1,200,000 Russians. Germany had already pledged its allegiance to Austria and warned Russia that it would mobilize if the Russians did not back down. The Germans declared war on the Russians (the Kaiser and the Czar were cousins). Britain and France mobilized, stating that they would protect neutral Belgian soil if they needed to. When Germany invaded Belgium in August a rash of war declarations ensued.

1916 Death of Yuan Shikai begins Chinese Civil War

YUAN WAS THE FIRST president of the Republic of China (1912–16), a former military leader and reformist minister for the Manchu dynasty. After the destruction of the Chinese army by the Japanese in 1895, he was instrumental in rebuilding the army. Yuan was finally chosen by the Emperor and the provisional government to become president. Beset with opposition to his attempts to secure a foreign loan, he had the chairman of the National Assembly murdered. He beat off a revolt in 1913, but widespread opposition (backed by Japan) challenged his authority. His European friends, preoccupied with the war in Europe, deserted him; his death plunged China back into chaos and civil war.

1917 Russian Revolution begins

THE WAR against Germany had not gone well for the Russians; over two million had died in 1915 alone. The government continually ignored the popular calls for peace and the Czar had taken personal command of the conflict. The Russian economy was in ruins, and revolts, strikes, and factory closures were widespread. Massive defections from the army began to undermine Russia's ability to withstand the Germans. In March the Czar suspended the Duma, but when the Winter Palace fell to the mob the Czar had no other choice but to abdicate. He passed his throne first to his son and then to his brother, Grand Duke Michael. Bolshevik agitation would soon destroy the chance of stability and Czarist Russia would be extinguished.

Left: *a British recruiting poster from World War I*. Below: *soldiers from the Russian Revolution with the red flag fixed to their bayonets*.

1921 Mysterious footsteps in the Himalayas start Yeti rumors

THE TIBETAN YETI is a mythical creature said to inhabit the mountainous regions well above the snow line. There have been numerous sightings of the "Abominable Snowman," said to be very similar in appearance to the North American Big Foot. Yeti is the Sherpa name for "bear man" and this may be the true nature of the beast. Apparently, when a bear moves along at a certain speed the hindfoot overprints the forefoot, making a large impression in the snow. The result looks like a large human footprint. Other prints have been attributed to snowfalls, but no one can explain the occasional sightings of the beast.

1923 Lady Elizabeth Bowes-Lyon marries Prince Albert Frederick

Below: Lady Elizabeth Bowes-Lyon leaving her parents' house in London for her marriage to Prince Albert. Right: the gangster victims of the St Valentine's Day Massacre.

LADY ELIZABETH BOWES-LYON was the youngest daughter of the 14th Earl of Strathmore and Kinghorne. The family can trace its descent right back to Robert the Bruce. Elizabeth married Albert, the Duke of York, on April 26, 1923. On December 11, 1936 Edward VIII abdicated and her husband became King George VI, while Elizabeth became the Queen Consort. She had two daughters: Elizabeth—the future Queen—and Margaret. When her husband died in 1952 their daughter ascended to the throne, and the Queen Consort became known as the Queen Mother. She is one of the most popular members of the Royal Family. Elizabeth never forgave Edward VIII for having abandoned the throne without giving her husband adequate warning.

1928 Serious floods in London

IN JANUARY THE RIVER THAMES burst its banks, drowning 14 people including four young sisters. The tragedy, caused by a sudden thaw and a high tide, engulfed low-lying areas of the capital. Hundreds were made homeless as properties beside the river were flooded. The dry moat of the Tower of London was filled, as were the vaults of the Palace of Westminster. Priceless Landseer paintings were damaged as the Tate Gallery succumbed to the flooding, although many of the paintings were evacuated in time. The capital was virtually cut off from the rest of the country when the telephone lines were water-damaged. In the following month 11 were killed as gales swept the country.

1929 St Valentine's Day Massacre, Chicago

GANGSTER AL CAPONE, in an attempt to protect his stake in illegal alcohol, extortion, and prostitution rackets, had seven men gunned down, all members of a gang led by George "Bugsy" Moran. This incident was the latest in what Police Commissioner William F. Russell described as "a war to the finish." Men dressed as police officers successfully passing themselves off as a raiding party killed the seven victims. The men, armed with tommy-guns, lined their victims up against a wall at the back of a beer-house in Chicago before murdering them with a hail of bullets. The Police Commissioner was furious that the gangsters chose to dress up as policemen, particularly since half of his force was under investigation for corruption.

1932 Lindbergh baby kidnapped

THE KIDNAPPING of 20-month-old Charles A. Lindbergh Jr triggered the most intensive manhunt in history, with 100,000 involved in the search. The child was taken while his mother and father (the aviator) were eating their evening meal. A note was left on the windowsill demanding $50,000. Even Al Capone offered $10,000 reward for the child's safe return, so great was the nation's concern and shock at the crime. Further ransom notes were delivered throughout March. The ransom was paid, but the battered body of the child was later found just 5 miles from the Lindberghs' home. Bruno Hauptmann was later arrested, tried, and found guilty of the crime but he successfully appealed.

1934 Strikes in Spain

COINCIDING WITH A VIOLENT national strike in Spain called for by socialists and the trade union movement, Catalonia attempted to declare itself an independent state. The strikes were in response to the appointment of three Catholic Popular Actionist ministers to the right-wing government. Martial law was pronounced and government troops clashed with strikers across the country. Troops were brought in from Morocco to quell the uprisings; garrisons were mobilized and the civil guard reinforced. For several days the fighting continued; shots were even fired at the home of the premier, Señor Lerroux. The smouldering discontent would soon ignite once more into full-scale civil war.

The violent acts of Bonnie and Clyde included armed robbery and murder. They have become legendary and somewhat romantic figures since their deaths in 1934.

1934 Bonnie and Clyde die in Louisiana

THE INCREDIBLE four-year career of Bonnie Parker and Clyde Barrow ended in the most dramatic of ways in Louisiana. Apparently working on a tip-off, Texas Rangers ambushed the pair, riddling their bodies with over 50 bullets. They died as they lived, with shotguns and revolvers in their hands, but there was little they could do against the immense fire-power directed against them. The criminal duo left a trail of murders and robberies across the south-west of America. They are credited with the murder of at least 12 people and numerous woundings. Both were still in their mid-twenties when they were killed. Their exploits have passed into folklore around the world.

1934–35 Mao Zedong marches 6,200 miles across China

IN A DESPERATE ATTEMPT to elude the 700,000-strong Chinese Nationalists commanded by General Jiang Jieshi (Chiang Kai-Shek), the communist rebels began a 12-month march across China. The First Front Army, outnumbered seven to one, was expertly commanded by Mao Zedong. It broke out of Jiangxi Province, crossing the Yangtse with just 30,000 troops intact. Harassed along their route by the Nationalists, warlords, and bandits, desperately short of ammunition and supplies, Mao regrouped 6,000 miles away in Yan'an. In comparative safety in Shaanxi Province, Mao forged a movement that would sweep the Nationalists away and create Communist China, although this goal was many years away.

1936 Crystal Palace burns down

FLAMES WERE SPOTTED at 8 P.M. on November 30th and by 8:30 P.M. the whole of the great pavilion was alight. Despite the efforts of 500 firemen, the structure could not be saved. It had been designed in 1851 by Sir Joseph Paxton for Britain's Great Exhibition in Hyde Park. It was then re-erected in Sydenham. Millions of people viewed the spectacle, which could be seen as far away as Margate and Brighton. An incoming Imperial Airways flight from Paris reported seeing the blaze mid-Channel. The birds in the aviary were released in an attempt to save them but many of them perished in the smoke and flames.

1937 The "Hindenburg" tragedy

ON MAY 6th, the giant dirigible *Hindenburg*, which had cost £380,000 to build, exploded in flames, killing 33 people. The *Hindenburg* had already made ten successful trips across the Atlantic when it came to grief in New Jersey. The most plausible reason for the explosion seems to be the fact that a thunderstorm had placed static electricity in the mooring mast and when the *Hindenburg* came alongside it ignited the hydrogen gas. The *Hindenburg* had come from Frankfurt and had been delayed by strong headwinds over Canada. It had been circling the mast waiting for a lull in the storm, and was at about 300 ft when the disaster occurred.

1938 Bombing of Guangzhou

IN LATE MAY and early June 1938 the Japanese began a ten-day bombing of the Chinese city of Guangzhou (Canton). The death toll ran into tens of thousands as the Japanese attempted to bomb the Chinese into submission. With few anti-aircraft guns and no fighter aircraft, the Chinese could only hope for salvation. Even when an unarmed passenger aircraft attempted to leave the city it was shot down. By October 21st the city had been occupied. Some 3000 Japanese, led by tanks, moved in after a 100-mile push through Chinese lines. The Chinese, led by Jiang Jieshi, fled inland, attempting to destroy anything that was of use to the Japanese before the city was occupied.

1944 Glenn Miller disappears on flight to France

ON DECEMBER 16, en route to a concert date in France, the aircraft carrying the world-renowned band leader Colonel Miller went missing. There was no sign of the wreckage and the pilot had not signalled that there was a problem. Miller had volunteered for service in 1941, but had been persuaded that the morale value of his music would be of more use to the war effort. From 1941 to 1944 his band played in almost every war zone in the world from the Pacific to Europe. His music dominated broadcasting during the latter part of the war. The crew and two of Miller's companions were also lost.

1946 Riots in Calcutta

THREE DAYS OF FIGHTING rocked the city of Calcutta in August. Over 3000 people were killed and 10,000 injured as Muslims and Hindus clashed over the British plans on India's constitution. The Muslim League, angry at the proposals to create an all-India government, wished to establish its own state of Pakistan. Two battalions of British troops were forced to fire on rioters who disobeyed the curfew that had been imposed. The government in Bengal seemed powerless to stop the violence, which cut off Calcutta from the rest of India. Starvation threatened as the unrest still boiled when Nehru was appointed head of the provisional government.

1947 Lord and Lady Mountbatten become the last Viceroy and Vicerene of India

LORD LOUIS MOUNTBATTEN was appointed on February 20 as the Viceroy of India with a brief to manage the handover of power to the Indian people. Lord Wavell, later Earl Wavell, had been the previous Viceroy. England's prime minister Clement Attlee had decided that it was the right time to change the Viceroy in the light of the fact that Indian independence was looming. There had been a number of dis-agreements between the government and Wavell and this had hastened his removal from the post. Even when Mountbatten had taken up his post, the violence still claimed lives. In March, 293 people died in the Punjab and another 147 in Bombay.

1947 Wedding of Princess Elizabeth and Prince Philip

ON NOVEMBER 20th the heir to the British throne married the Corfu-born son of the late Prince Andrew of Greece. The crowd was 50 deep in places along the route of the wedding procession between Buckingham Palace and Westminster Abbey. The congregation of 2,500 was sprinkled with dignitaries from around the world. The couple's 500-lb wedding cake was cut by the sword of Prince Louis of Battenberg, the bridegroom's grandfather. They honeymooned in Hampshire before moving into their new home, Clarence House. The government agreed to give the Princess extra ration coupons so that she could have a new wedding dress, but she did not have a trousseau because of clothes rationing.

Above: the front cover of The Illustrated London News *depicting Princess Elizabeth and Prince Philip. Right: the Jewish Star of David was adopted for the flag of Israel when the state was founded in 1948.*

1948 Berlin airlift

AFTER WALKING OUT of the Allied Control Council meeting in March, the Russians clearly intended to make a military move against Berlin. In the following month the Russians began checking all rail and road movements into Berlin. By June, over 200 aircraft a day were flying into Berlin to prevent the city's population from starving. It was estimated that around 2,500 of food a day was required. In September this had risen to 895 aircraft per day carrying over 7,000 tons. On September 18th US pilots flew in 651 times carrying over 5,000 tons of coal. The Berlin blockade ended in May 1949, after costing the allies $200 million. The Russians had installed a communist government in the east of Germany and had accepted the creation of West Germany.

1948 Israel founded

THE NEW INDEPENDENT STATE of Israel came into being at 4 P.M. on May 14th. The former Jewish Agency leader, David Ben-Gurion, became the first prime minister. The Jewish leaders had finally agreed to a ceasefire in April after the Palestinian government had threatened them with military action by the British. It was this act that temporarily defused the situation. The fact that the new state of Israel did not have clearly defined borders was to be the cause of many conflicts in the future. It was hoped that the Israelis and the Arabs could agree. The reaction to the forming of the new state was somewhat predictable; the Israelis mobilized their Haganah army of 30,000, while the Egyptians massed on the southern border. Meanwhile in Amman, the King of Transjordan pledged to support any Arab move with his own troops, the Arab Legion. The rest of the year saw conflict on all fronts, with the UN and the British getting involved. Despite the shooting down of five RAF reconnaissance aircraft in January 1949, the British government recognized the state of Israel on the 29th. After 42 days of talks a truce was signed between Israel and Egypt on February 24th.

1952 Mau Mau freedom movement

THE SECRET AND SINISTER Mau Mau movement began to assert itself in 1951, but little was known about its purpose or origins. By April 1952, Kenya was on the verge of chaos as the Mau Mau openly intimidated and murdered people who refused to support them. In

November the movement began an open rebellion against the British. Murdering and intimidation intensified, white settlers began to arm themselves and the British sent in troops. Many Mau Mau were killed and thousands of suspects rounded up. Jomo "Burning Spear" Kenyatta was jailed for seven years in April 1953 for masterminding the Mau Mau plot. He would later become the leader of his country.

1953 Jacqueline Bouvier marries John Kennedy

ON SEPTEMBER 14th John Fitzgerald Kennedy married Jacqueline Lee Bouvier. Kennedy had been a PT boat commander during World War II, and had survived the boat's sinking by the Japanese in 1943. JFK had traded his naval career for politics in 1946 when he won a seat in the House of Representatives. A Harvard graduate, JFK was the son of the former US ambassador to London. By the time he married he had just won a Senate seat in Massachusetts after beating Henry Cabot Lodge. He would die tragically in Dallas in 1963 at the hands of an assassin, after becoming president in 1960.

1954 Outbreak of anti-French violence in Algeria

ALGERIAN NATIONALISTS orchestrated an effective series of attacks against key French targets in the Aurès district of the country on November 1st. The Nationalist leader, Ahmed Ben Bella, had begun his campaign to rid the country of the French. For their part, the French were seriously under-manned in the country as military and police targets were hit and were powerless to respond. On the 12th the French Interior Minister, François Mitterrand, decided to send French troops to Algeria later proposed integrating Algeria with France. The writing was on the wall for the French colonial possessions in Africa. Within ten years little would be left.

1956 Hungarian  uprising

ON OCTOBER 23rd demonstrations called for Hungarian independence and a withdrawal of Russian forces from the country. Within three days, the demonstrations had developed into full-scale revolt, with Hungarian nationalists openly defying the Russians and engaging in running battles in the cities. In the first few days an estimated 3000 people died in their attempts to fight the tanks of the Soviet army. The prime minister, Imre Nagy, promised that once the revolt had been suppressed he would enter into negotiations with the Russians for a withdrawal of troops. His words fell on deaf ears and it was the Russian troops who would settle the situation. By November 5th the Soviets had crushed the rebellion with a concerted operation against key points in the country. Hungarian soldiers had vainly attempted to bar the way into Budapest but against thousands of troops backed by over 1000 tanks they had little hope. The Defence Ministry and the Parliament fell at 9:00 A.M. and the last words heard from the prime minister over Radio Budapest were at 5:15 P.M. At 8:10 P.M. the radio station fell silent after desperate cries of "Help Hungary." The West, despite their concerns, seemed unwilling or unable to assist the Hungarians or stop the Russians. The Russians would not allow dissent at any cost in their eastern European possessions.

Above: *John F. Kennedy with his wife Jacqueline following their marriage on Rhode Island in 1953.* Below: *wrecked tanks in the streets of Budapest after the Hungarian uprising.*

1957 Dutch nationals expelled from Indonesia

Below: national flags from the member countries of the European Economic Community. Right: the Malay armoured car regiment on parade during the celebrations of Malayan independence.

IN DECEMBER 1949 Ahmed Sukarno became the first President of Indonesia. The former Dutch East Indies cut diplomatic ties with Holland in August 1954. After surviving an assassination attempt in November 1957, Sukarno called for a 24-hour boycott of Dutch businesses as a protest against continued Dutch rule. The Dutch responded on the 2nd by barring Indonesians from entering Holland. Sukarno's reprisal was swift. On the 5th he expelled all Dutch nationals from the country. Sukarno continued to be a thorn in the sides of the Dutch and the UN for a number of years. Another failed attempt on his life was made in 1962 and in 1965 he survived a coup attempt. He died in 1970.

1957 The founding of the EEC

THE TREATY OF ROME was signed on March 25th by six European nations with a total population of 160 million. France, Italy, West Germany, Belgium, Holland, and Luxembourg agreed to a 15-year development of the European Economic Community. The aim of the Treaty was to allow the free movement of people, trade, and funds. At a stroke all tariffs and duties were abolished. Then, as now, the British were sceptical about total involvement with the EEC. The prime minister, Harold Macmillan, felt that there was a place for Britain in such an organization,

but the Commonwealth ties were still too strong to allow inclusion at that time. In many respects, the British government should have realized the inevitability of joining with Europe. Being an outsider meant that many of the benefits of membership could not be enjoyed and that the large trading bloc that the EEC represented was a severe threat to British businesses and trade. Britain's policy of the time was the establishment of a European Free Trade Area that would include all western Europe. The subject of sovereignty was an issue that would have to wait. While the French thought this policy irrelevant compared to the benefits of membership of the EEC, it later transpired that Macmillan was pro-EEC.

1957 Malayan independence

AFTER 170 YEARS of British rule the largest of the Asian colonies gained its independence on August 30th. In the capital, Kuala Lumpur, the chief minister Tunku Abdul Rahman, proclaimed that this was the greatest day in the history of Malaya. The country had a rich ethnic mix of native Malays, Chinese, Indians, Eurasians, and Europeans. He went on to praise the efforts of the British in suppressing the communist uprising that so nearly tore the country apart. Since the nineteenth century Malay had occupied a key position in the British Empire. It was a dangerous battleground during World War II, but the Japanese were finally defeated by the British, ably assisted by loyal Malays.

1957 Rebellion in Cuba

PRESIDENT BATISTA'S claims that Fidel Castro had been killed in December 1956 were proved inaccurate when it was revealed that the rebel leader was alive and personally directing the guerrilla war against the regime. Batista's army, which numbered many thousands, was bled dry throughout the year by well-timed attacks on key positions around the island. With a few hundred guerrillas, one of the arch exponents of jungle warfare was beginning to make parts of the country untenable. In the cities, pro-Castro activists sabotaged essential services and bombed buildings at great risk to themselves. The Batista regime simply responded with torture and repression.

1958 Escalation of violence in Cyprus

SMOULDERING DISCONTENT flared into violent rioting in Cyprus in January. On the 28th, a British army vehicle drove through a Turkish demonstration and sparked off a series of riots that would leave seven dead and hundreds injured. The leader of the minority Turkish community, Rauf Denktash, managed to defuse the situation after a public appeal. Two Turks were killed and over 100 injured during the rioting. Violence flared again in June, claiming four more lives. A curfew was imposed on the 20th after Archbishop Makarios, the leader of the Greek-Cypriot community, rejected a peace plan. A further week of violence in July led to 31 more deaths.

1958 Munich air crash

ARGUABLY ONE OF THE best football teams of the decade was decimated in a tragic air crash on February 6th. The Manchester United squad, on their way home from a successful quarter-final game with Belgrade, were on a BEA flight to Munich when the pilot lost control while landing.

The aircraft ploughed into an airport building, killing seven players outright along with eight journalists and three Manchester United employees. Matt Busby (later Sir) survived the crash, but five of the dead were internationals including Roger Byrne, Tommy Taylor, David Pegg, Bill Whelan, and Duncan Edwards. Three months after the crash Manchester United met Bolton at Wembley in the FA Cup Final. The depleted squad lost 2–0.

Members of Matt Busby's Manchester United team boarding the plane to Belgrade. On the return flight, the plane crashed destroying one of the best football teams of the era.

1961 Berlin Wall erected

THE COMMUNIST German Democratic Republic came into existence in 1949. By 1961 over 2.5 million people had left the country, most entering West Berlin. On the night of August 13, 1961 temporary fortifications were erected around West Berlin. From 1961 to 1989, 70 or more people were killed trying to escape into West Berlin. There were only two very heavily guarded checkpoints (the most famous of which was Checkpoint Charlie) between East and West Berlin and the 13-ft high wall stretching some 29 miles became the symbol of the puppet East German state. Even the buildings on the East German side of the wall were demolished for several hundred yards, others had their west-facing windows bricked up.

Armed guards patrolling the Berlin Wall, the barrier which divided Germany into East and West. It became one of the greatest symbols of political segregation of the twentieth century.

1962 Cuban missile crisis

ON APRIL 8th the 1179 members of the abortive Bay of Pigs invasion were sentenced to 30 years imprisonment each by a Cuban court. Fidel Castro offered to release them for $62 million. In August another sea raid was undertaken by US-backed Cuban exiles. Reactions to this event and the gathering crisis over the status of Cuba fuelled US claims that Cuba was a threat to their safety. Russia pledged that a US attack on Cuba would mean nuclear war. Krushchev's threats were amplified when it was discovered that there were Soviet nuclear missiles in Cuba. President Kennedy responded by obtaining powers to call up 150,000

1961 Dag Hammarskjöld dies

DAG HJALMAR AGNE CARL HAMMARSKJÖLD was born in Zambia in 1905, son of the prime minister of Sweden (1914–17). Hammarskjöld was an economist, statesman, and later the second Secretary-General of the UN. He was active throughout the 1950s and to his death in 1961 in a variety of peace talks and mediations. He helped resolve the Suez Canal crisis, mediated in the 1958 Lebanon and Jordan problems and sent a UN force into the Congo in 1960 to suppress the civil disorders. He supported an independent UN free to deal with international challenges. Unfortunately, he died in a plane crash while on a peace mission to President Tshombe of the Congo on September 18, 1961.

reservists if he needed to. The US Secretary of State Dean Rusk immediately briefed South American allies on the missile crisis. The world appeared to be on the brink of nuclear war. During mid-October the two superpowers traded political blows and tit-for-tat accusations and demands. Finally, the Russians gave in and agreed to dismantle the missiles. The exact agreements may never be known, but what is clear is that the missiles had been proved to be offensive rather than defensive and that the US naval blockade could not be challenged by the Russians or the Cubans. Because Fidel Castro was not consulted regarding the Soviet decision to withdraw the missiles, the Cubans subsequently drew closer to the Chinese instead of their former allies.

1963 Great Train Robbery

THE RIPPLES OF the Great Train Robbery still touch politics and crime today; with the the request for Ronnie Biggs's extradition from Brazil. Yet he was a small player in an audacious crime that allegedly netted around £1 million. Faking a stop light on a line in Buckinghamshire, the gang intercepted a Royal Mail train at about 3:00 A.M. on August 8th. With military precision, they took 120 mailbags stuffed with notes. The driver later died, arguably from injuries sustained that night, but this has never been proven. Several of the gang were caught, convicted, and sentenced and have retained their notoriety, including Buster Edwards, the flower-seller, whose life was turned into a hit film.

1963 Profumo affair

THE BRITISH SECRETARY OF STATE for War, John Profumo, admitted to having lied to the House of Commons regarding his relationship with Christine Keeler. He had no option but to resign. Keeler was known to have had an affair with the Russian Naval Attaché, Eugene Ivanov. The situation almost brought down the government when 30 Tory MPs refused to back Harold Macmillan's battle against an opposition vote to censure the government. Other links in the scandal were Dr Stephen Ward, who arranged the party where Profumo met Keeler, and Mandy Rice-Davis, who was Ward's lover and former girlfriend of slum property boss Peter Rachman. Ward later committed suicide.

1963 Protests in Saigon

QUANG DOC, a Buddhist monk, committed ritual suicide by burning himself alive in Saigon on June 13th. Extremist Buddhists rocked the capital with rioting and protests against the maltreatment they received at the hands of President Diem's regime. The Vietnamese government was losing a war against the Vietcong; the government's position was not helped by its indifference and outright violence towards its own people. In August the army arrested 100 monks and 600 students who had been protesting. By September they were arresting civilian leaders at will. The US seriously considered a radical reappraisal of their role in the country and threatened a reduction in military and economic aid to Diem.

Jack Mills, driver of the Royal Mail train infamously held up and robbed by Ronnie Biggs and his accomplices. Today Biggs is still in exile in Brazil.

1963 The winds of change in Africa

ON DECEMBER 12th Kenya became the 34th African state to gain its independence. European rule of the continent was on the wane, reduced to a handful of countries in the south. Libya, Tunisia, Morocco, Guinea, and Ghana had gained their independence in the 1950s, but the 1960s had experienced a flood of independence celebrations. Harold Macmillan coined the phrase "the winds of change." At the beginning of the decade Chad, Niger, Mali, Mauritania, Senegal, Ivory Coast, Nigeria, Cameroon, Central African Republic, Gabon, Zaire, Congo, Togo, Dahomey, and Madagascar had all severed their links with their colonial masters. By the end of the decade only 15 countries had maintained some links with Europe.

Spectators look at the car driven off a bridge in Massachusetts by Senator Edward Kennedy, killing his friend Mary Jo Kopechne. The incident incited the infamous Chappaquiddick inquest.

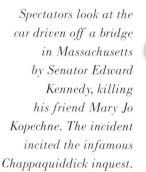

1968 Invasion of Czechoslovakia by Russia

THE PRAGUE SPRING of 1968 turned into a Russian winter as hundreds of thousands of Soviet troops brutally crushed the revolt in Czechoslovakia. Desperate Czechs attempted to stem the tide of tanks and troops with their bare hands as Alexander Dubcek, the reformist leader, was taken away in an armored personnel carrier. Dubcek had hoped that the threat of invasion would not be carried out, but his beliefs were rapidly dispelled as the Russian tanks rolled across the border. As the invasion seemed imminent, prominent individuals switched sides and the Communist Party newspaper suddenly denounced the very reforms it had supported in previous weeks. According to the Soviet press agency TASS, the Czechs

welcomed the Russians with open arms, but pictures and reports from the country told a very different story. A one-hour strike was called on August 23rd to protest against the invasion. On the following day Dubcek began a series of discussions with the Soviet leadership. Even when the tanks disappeared in September the curfews and censorship stayed in place. More protests occurred in October when it was revealed that the Warsaw Pact troops would remain in the country for the foreseeable future. Desperate disobedience continued into November, with students occupying Prague University in protest against government repression.

1969 Edward Kennedy involved in Chappaquiddick inquest

FOLLOWING AN ACCIDENT in which his friend Mary Jo Kopechne died, presidential candidate Edward Kennedy appeared in court on July 20th. The car carrying the senator and Kopechne crashed on Chappaquiddick island, but eight hours lapsed before Kennedy reported the incident. He pleaded guilty to the charge of failing to report an accident and announced at the end of the month that he would not be standing for president in 1972. The exact details of the case may never be known, but why Kennedy took so long to tell the police about the incident is still one of the most perplexing issues surrounding the case. It certainly ruined his political career.

1973 Ben-Gurion dies

DAVID BEN-GURION was born in Poland in 1886. Attracted to the Zionist Socialist movement he emigrated to Palestine (1906) where he worked as a farm laborer and formed the first Jewish trade union in

1915. From 1921 to 1933 he was general secretary of the General Foundation of Jewish Labour and in 1930 he became leader of the Mapai party. As defense minister he presided over the Israeli army's development into one of the Middle East's strongest. A founder of the state of Israel in 1948, he became the country's first prime minister 1948–53 and again 1955–63. On retiring from politics he remained a symbol of the Israeli state until his death.

1973 Student riots in Athens

THE GOVERNMENT OF George Papadopoulos was overthrown on 28 November by the Greek militia. The rhetoric and approach were very similar to those of 1967 when the colonels, who staged a coup, accused the government of weakness for believing that they would retain power only until the situation had been stabilized. The coup ended a week of violence in which 10 people died. Tanks were used against the students of Athens Polytechnic where 5000 were protesting against the lack of political and academic freedom. The martial law that had been declared by Papadopoulos had triggered the coup, with the Greek troops taking up strategic positions around the capital in the early hours of the morning.

1974 Patti Hearst kidnapped

THE 19-YEAR-OLD HEIRESS Patti Hearst was taken by the shadowy Symbionese Liberation Army on February 22nd. She was the daughter of the millionaire publisher Randolph Hearst. A series of ransom notes were received and Patti was described as a "prisoner of war." On April 15th Patti re-emerged as an armed accomplice in a SLA bank raid. Despite the fact that Patti may well have been "covered" by another armed SLA terrorist, the FBI had no other option but to issue a warrant for the arrest of all the bank robbers. Subsequent SLA messages revealed that Patti had become one of the gang, assuming the name Tania.

1979 Airey Neave murdered

AIREY NEAVE WAS BORN IN 1916. During World War II he worked as a British intelligence officer and, although caught, he escaped from Colditz, the famous high-security German prison camp. Becoming interested in politics, he first entered parliament as a Conservative in 1953 and served in a variety of posts. He was a close adviser and friend of Margaret Thatcher during the years running up to her election as prime minister. From September 1975 he was shadow under-secretary of state for Northern Ireland and consequently became a target for extremist groups and terrorist organizations. In 1979 he was killed by an Irish terrorist bomb planted beneath his car.

1979 Earl Mountbatten murdered

LOUIS, 1ST EARL MOUNTBATTEN of Burma, was born in Windsor in 1900. The great-grandson of Queen Victoria, he served at sea in World War I and during World War II was chief of combined operations in 1942 and commander-in-chief in South-East Asia in 1943. As the last viceroy of India (1947) and first governor-general of India until 1948, he oversaw the country's transition to independence. He returned to service at sea as 4th sea lord (1952–55) and was later appointed 1st sea lord (1955–59). He was murdered by an IRA bomb aboard his yacht while sailing near his holiday home in County Sligo in the Republic of Ireland.

Patti Hearst in front of the Symbionese Liberation Army insignia, the group who kidnapped her and who she later joined.

1979 Vietnamese invade Cambodia

A VICIOUS SERIES of border clashes between Vietnam and Cambodia erupted into full-scale war when the Vietnamese deposed the Cambodian dictator, Pol Pot. The new Vietnamese-backed administration was quick to distance itself from the excesses of Pol Pot. Within days of the administration's taking control thousands of skeletons had been uncovered as mute testimony of the "killing fields" of Cambodia and the "Year Zero" policy of the old regime. Systematically, the Khmer Rouge had slaughtered all "intellectuals" and opponents of their rule. Whole villages had been wiped out and the country was in a state of terror. Despite attempts to bring Pol Pot to justice, he managed to retain a degree of control in certain parts of the country for many years.

Below: *Iranian hostages after their release.* Right: *Prince Charles and Princess Diana after their wedding in St Paul's Cathedral.*

1980 Iranian hostage crisis

PROMPTED BY THE SPEECHES and action of Ayatollah Khomeini, fanatical followers stormed the US embassy in Tehran, taking nearly 100 staff and marines hostage. On the day of the attack, 4 November, the hostages were blindfolded and handcuffed before being taken down into the basement. On the 17th the Iranians set the women and black hostages free, warning that any attack would result in the execution of the remaining hostages. In desperation President Carter authorized a hostage rescue that ended in disaster and eight US deaths. After 444 days in captivity the hostages were finally released. Khomeini had the last laugh by delaying the release until Carter had been replaced by Reagan as President.

1981 Prince Charles and Lady Diana marry

CHARLES PHILIP ARTHUR GEORGE is the eldest son of Queen Elizabeth II and Prince Philip and heir to the British throne. He became Prince of Wales in 1958 and was invested at Caernarvon in 1969. He served in the RAF and the Royal Navy (1971–76). In July 1981 he married Lady Diana Frances Spencer, the younger daughter of the 7th Earl Spencer, at St Paul's Cathedral, the first English bride of a royal heir since 1659. Their first child was Prince William Arthur Philip Louis who was born in 1982 and their second son, Prince Henry Charles Albert David, was born in 1984. The couple were separated in 1992, amid much publicity.

1983 Harrods bombed by the IRA

ON DECEMBER 17th at the height of London's Christmas shopping period, the IRA set off a bomb outside Harrods. Given the size of the crowds in Knightsbridge that day, thousands of people could have been caught in the attack, as a result the number of casualties seemed relatively light, but five people died (four British and one American) and 80 were wounded. This attack showed a marked departure from earlier IRA targets of the armed forces or the police. In July of the previous year the IRA had killed seven bandsmen and four troopers of the Household Cavalry. The next attack would aim to hit the very center of the government.

1983 Massacres in Assam

ON FEBRUARY 20th over 600 Muslims were massacred in one of the worst cases of sectarian violence since India and Pakistan became separate countries. Indira Gandhi sacked the state government of the Punjab in October for failing to deal with continued religious and political unrest. In the following year, the violence flared up again. Throughout May Hindus and Muslims clashed in the Bombay area, resulting in the deaths of another 100 people. In June, the Indian military launched Operation Blue Star to storm the Golden Temple of Amritsar that had been held by militants. Ninety soldiers and 712 extremists died. In October Indira Gandhi was murdered by her own Sikh guards.

1984 Libyans expelled from the UK

FOLLOWING THE MURDER of policewoman Yvonne Fletcher outside the Libyan Embassy in St James's Square in London, the Libyans were given seven days to leave the country. The policewoman was apparently shot from one of the rooms of the embassy, which led to a siege of the building. The officer was on duty during an anti-Gaddafi demonstration outside the embassy. Britain broke off diplomatic relations with Libya in protest at the fact that the embassy had been used as a base for terrorist activity in the capital. On April 22nd, 30 Libyan diplomats left the country. In June prime minister Margaret Thatcher called on the West for "relentless action" against terrorists.

1984 Brighton bombing

AN IRA BOMB that was designed to murder the majority of the British cabinet blew apart the Grand Hotel in the early hours of October 12th. The 20-lb bomb killed three people and injured at least another 30. Prime Minister Margaret Thatcher survived the blast, but others were not so lucky. This was, by far, the most audacious attack by the IRA on the British mainland. Four floors of the hotel were wrecked and it was fortunate that more people were not killed or injured by the blast. Mrs. Thatcher was quoted as saying at the time, "Life must go on." Neighboring hotels were evacuated in case other devices were present.

1985 Heysel stadium disaster

BRITISH FOOTBALL HOOLIGANS were blamed for the deaths of 41 Italian and Belgian supporters. Some 350 people were also injured as Liverpool fans charged Juventus supporters in the Belgian stadium in Brussels. The European Cup Final game ended in tragedy when a safety fence collapsed, crushing fans and causing several deaths from trampling. Mounted riot police were needed to quell the fighting. Britain's Prime Minister Thatcher was quoted as saying that the fans had brought "shame and dishonour" to the country and to football. This event brought English clubs a period of absence from European competitions. Belgium banned English clubs from playing on their soil after this incident.

The Grand Hotel in Brighton—seen after an IRA bomb tore through it during a Conservative Party conference, killing three and injuring over 30 people.

1987 IRA bomb at Enniskillen

DURING THE REMEMBRANCE DAY service on November 11, 1987 the Provisional wing of the Irish Republican Army set off a bomb that they had planted earlier. The devastating blast killed 11 people and injured 61. Enniskillen is a garrison town and has been a Protestant stronghold since the seventeenth century. The bombing incident outraged the country and led to accusations of police and military negligence: for not making sure that the area had been checked before the crowds arrived at the memorial for the out-of-door service. The inhabitants of Enniskillen still mourn the slaughter of November 11th, making the Remembrance Day services that are held there all the more poignant.

1987 Terry Waite kidnapped

TERRY WAITE WAS BORN IN CHESHIRE (1939) and educated in London and the US. He was appointed lay training adviser to the bishop of Bristol (1964–68) and the archbishop of Uganda, Rwanda, and Burundi (1968–71), and consultant with the Roman Catholic Church (1972–79). From 1980 he worked as religious adviser on Anglican

Above: *Prince Andrew and Sarah Ferguson on their wedding day.*
Right: *the anti-Semitic Klaus Barbie during World War II—he was later convicted of crimes against humanity.*

1986 Prince Andrew marries Sarah Ferguson

ANDREW ALBERT CHRISTIAN EDWARD is the second son of Britain's Queen Elizabeth II and Prince Philip. He was commissioned in the Royal Navy, qualifying as a helicopter pilot, and served in the Falklands War (1982). In 1986 he married Sarah Margaret Ferguson, and they were made Duke and Duchess of York. Their first daughter, Princess Beatrice Elizabeth Mary, was born in 1988 and their second, Princess Eugenie Victoria Helena, was born in 1990. Sarah began to write and has had several of her *Budgie the Helicopter* books published and made into a TV series. She also became a firm friend of the Princess of Wales. Andrew and Sarah separated in 1992 but have remained friends.

1987 Klaus Barbie arrested

GERMAN NAZI KLAUS BARBIE was a member of the SS from 1936. He was known as the "Butcher of Lyon:" as SS commander in Lyon his crimes included rounding up Jewish children from an orphanage and torturing Resistance leader, Jean Moulin. He was involved in deporting Jews from Holland (1940) and in tracking down Jews and the Resistance in France (1942–45). He escaped capture in 1945 and was employed by US intelligence services in Germany before moving to Bolivia with his family in 1951 and working as a businessman. Barbie was expelled from Bolivia (1983) and was arrested and convicted of crimes against humanity in France in 1987.

Communion affairs to the then archbishop of Canterbury, Dr Robert Runcie. Possessing great diplomatic skills, Waite undertook many overseas assignments and on January 20, 1987 he was seized in Beirut, Lebanon, while seeking to negotiate the release of European hostages. Taken hostage himself, Terry Waite was captive from 1987 until his final release on November 18, 1991.

1988 Australia's Bicentenary

CAPTAIN JAMES COOK discovered Australia in 1770, but it was not until 1787 that the British decided that it would be an ideal place for a penal colony. On January 26th of the following year 736 convicts were landed at Sydney Cove, New South Wales, under the control of Governor Arthur Phillip. As far as Australians are concerned, January 26th marks the birth of their nation. When the Bicentenary fell in 1988 the event was celebrated throughout the country with a huge range of civic and ceremonial activities. One of the youngest developed countries in the world and the only single-state continent had come of age. The events attracted thousands of visitors and dignitaries.

Ⓜ *1989 Berlin Wall torn down*

WHEN THE EAST GERMAN state collapsed in 1989, the Berlin Wall was swept away with it. Officials, ably assisted by the crowds, tore down the symbol of the Iron Curtain on November 9th. A few sections still remain, but the majority has either disappeared or been sold to collectors. Although the unification of Germany was a dream come true to the German people, it was not without severe dangers and dissent. The new Germany inherited many of the problems that had beset the last leaders of East Germany and had brought about its downfall. Housing shortages, unemployment, crime, racial violence, strikes, and demonstrations threatened to sour the joy of the unification. Faced with immense changes for the east of Germany, coupled with the fact that there was a worldwide recession, the German government battled to cope. It was forced to close a large proportion of the eastern factories because of their inefficiencies, privatize those that were left and cut social services. The medicine was unpalatable but necessary if the German economy was to survive the shock of absorbing the under-funded former East Germany. While the former East Germans complained about their second-class status, the affluent West Germans complained about their

In November 1989 the Berlin Wall was torn down, marking the beginning of a long process of reunification between East and West Germany.

falling standards of living. Industrial performance and living standards have vastly improved in the last few years.

1990 German unification

THE RUSSIAN-DOMINATED states of Eastern Europe began to break away from their wartime liberator as the policies of Mikhail Gorbachev permeated the region. When East Germany collapsed more than 200,000 of the citizens moved into West Germany. By July 1990 the two parts of Germany were financially bound together; in October East and West Germany ceased to exist. All citizens were inhabitants of the Federal Republic. Berlin was made the capital of the country and Helmut Kohl was returned as leader of the reunified state. Germans call reunification *die Wende*, which means "the change." Despite a number of social and economic problems Germany is set to be the major force behind European affairs in the next century.

DEM DEUTSCHEN VOLKE

1991 Robert Maxwell dies

JAN LUDVIK HOCH was born in Slatina-Selo in Czechoslovakia in 1923. He managed to escape the Holocaust and fled to France and then to Britain where he changed his name to Ian Robert Maxwell. After the war he obtained German academic and scientific papers and published them all over the world. He founded the Pergamon Press in 1951 and by the 1960s he was a major force in publishing. He also served as a Labour MP until 1970. In 1981 he bought the British Printing Corporation, selling it in 1987. He then purchased the Mirror Group, using it as a foundation to create Maxwell Communications. He secretly siphoned off $1.2 billion to support his shaky empire. Faced with exposure, he died after falling off his yacht in 1991.

1990 Brian Keenan released

BRIAN KEENAN taught English at the American University in Beirut before he was abducted and taken hostage at gunpoint by militant Muslims. He would be held for four and a half years. Keenan was subjected to periodic beatings by his captives but was clearly supported through the ordeal by his fellow captives, including John McCarthy. When Keenan was taken, the city of Beirut had already become a battlefield and the dangers to foreign citizens were well known. He also spent some of his time in captivity with Terry Anderson and Tom Sutherland who had been abducted before him. Brian Keenan is now an accomplished writer.

1991 John McCarthy released

JOHN McCARTHY was released in August 1991. He had been a journalist working in the Lebanon when he was abducted by Fundamentalists. He spent some of his time in captivity with Brian Keenan, and later the two men were also held with Tom Sutherland, Frank Reed and Terry Anderson, all American prisoners. McCarthy was deeply affected by the ordeal, suffering beatings and solitary confinement. He obviously played a great role in helping his fellow captives survive the years of imprisonment. McCarthy was one of the last hostages to be released. After he was released, the West continued their pressure on the Fundamentalists to release the remaining captives.

Opposite: *Middle East hostage John McCarthy talking about his ordeal under the Lebanese Fundamentalists after his release in 1991.*
Left: *the German flag flying outside the Reichstag building—a symbol of* die Wende, *the act that saw East and West Germany reunified as one political state.*

1991 Unrest in Albania

ALBANIA BEGAN RESPONDING to the wave of democratization in 1991 by opening diplomatic dialogue with the West and the US in particular. Albania had been an all-but-closed society since the end of World War II. Under extreme pressure from the people, the Communist Party began a series of reforms that would lead to a change in their name and a complete rethink of their policies. Despite hanging on to power in the 1991 elections and appearing to be secure, they were thrown out of office in March 1992. Subsequently, the Communist Party was banned and many of the Communist leaders were convicted of embezzlement and imprisoned in 1993.

1991 End of the Cold War

LITTLE BY LITTLE the Russians had begun to distance themselves from political, social, and economic decisions in Eastern Europe from 1989. Even when pro-democracy governments swept to power in Poland, Hungary, Czechoslovakia, and East Germany, they refused to become involved. Inevitably, the Warsaw Pact dissolved and the Council for Mutual Economic Assistance withered away. The dagger at the West's heart was now rusty and bent. The Russian economy had been deteriorating for several years, but when Gorbachev became President the call for drastic changes in the domestic situation could be heard across Russia. Nationalist and independence movements had sprung up in almost every part of Russia. They were becoming more audacious and forthright. Ultimately, the hard-liners decided enough was enough and struck against Gorbachev in August 1991, placing him under house arrest. Boris Yeltsin at the head of the reformers crushed the coup, which was short-lived. By September 5th a new transitional government had been established, immediately

recognizing the independence of the Baltic states of Lithuania, Latvia, and Estonia. Yeltsin was gradually becoming the predominant political figure and was instrumental in dissolving the USSR on December 21st. The new Commonwealth of Independent States replaced the USSR or the Soviet Union. Gorbachev resigned on December 25th and on the 26th the Soviet parliament was dissolved forever.

1992 Palestinians deported from Israel

WAR AND DISSENT had torn the Holy Land apart for centuries. The Palestinians, stateless and in their eyes living in an occupied land, had suffered deportations on several occasions. In 1948, directly after the war and the founding of the state of Israel, 780,000 Palestinians were forced out to make room for Jewish immigrants from Europe and from the Arab

world. The plans for Palestinian self-rule on the Gaza Strip and the West Bank meant that more Palestinians would be displaced and deported to these areas. The new zones, economically weak and reliant on Israel, have become new hotbeds of dissent and fundamentalism. Yasir Arafat remains the nominal leader of the Palestinian people.

1992 Queen Elizabeth's "annus horribilis"

1992 SAW A SERIES of family crises and other unfortunate occurrences for the British Royal Family. The separation and subsequent divorce of the Prince of Wales and Diana, Princess of Wales, was just the beginning. Later in the year, Prince Andrew and his wife Sarah Ferguson separated. There was also a terrible fire in the apartments of Windsor Castle, which added to the Queen's distress. Her obvious concern for the events was crystallized in the Queen's Speech at Christmas when she referred to the year as being one of the worst that she had experienced. She knew that the Royal Family had to make many changes and their tax status would be the first of these.

1993 World Trade Center bombed in New York

ON FEBRUARY 26th a 1210-lb bomb was packed in a van and detonated inside the garage of the World Trade Center. It ripped a 200-ft crater in the basement of the world's second tallest building. The explosion killed six and injured over 1,000. At the time it was believed to be the most destructive terrorist attack in the history of the USA. The mastermind behind the bomb was Sheikh Omar Abdel-Rahman, a fundamentalist Muslim leader. In the days following the explosion US investigators discovered that this attack was just the first of a series that had been planned by an Islamic group.

1993 IRA bomb the City of London

ON APRIL 24th another huge bomb went off to rival the World Trade Center outrage. A truck packed full of explosives was used by the IRA to devastate the financial center of the City of London. Only one person was killed, but another 44 were injured. It was the damage to the properties around the site of the explosion that will be most remembered. Estimates in excess of $1 billion have been quoted as the final repair figures. One of the buildings to suffer the most damage was a thirteenth-century church. This event was the precursor of yet another horrific IRA attack on Docklands' Canary Wharf in 1996.

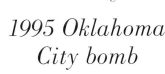

1994 Plane crash kills Rwandan president, triggering tidal wave of violence

CERTAINLY THE WORST instance of genocide in Africa's history occurred in Rwanda from April to August 1994. On April 6th a plane carrying President Habyarimana of Rwanda and neighboring Burundi's President Ntaryarima was shot down near Kigali airport by Hutu extremists. A planned massacre of the Tutsi minority ensued, with killer squads of Hutu slaughtering indiscriminately. They had already murdered over 2,000 before the death of the President; now they were unchecked. On the 7th, Prime Minister Uwilingiyimana was murdered. The UN arrived in May and attempted to establish safe areas. The Tutsi Rwandan Patriotic Front was particularly active by now, taking control of the country by August. In all, one million were killed and millions became refugees.

1995 Oklahoma City bomb

ON APRIL 19th a bomb placed in a truck outside a federal office building went off, killing 169 and wounding over 500. Ex-US army friends Timothy McVeigh and Terry Nichols were indicted. A third man, Michael Fortier, turned state's witness. The participants were members of a right-wing paramilitary group. The act occurred on the

The aftermath of the IRA bomb that exploded in the City of London, injuring 44 people and killing one.

second anniversary of the end of the Waco siege in Texas. If nothing else, this event shattered the American people's view that they were immune from terrorist actions. Later in the year an Amtrak passenger train was deliberately derailed, killing one and injuring 100. A note at the scene was signed by a group calling itself the Sons of the Gestapo. References were also made to Waco.

1995 Quebec says "Non" to separation from Canada

THE SEPARATIST GROUP Parti Québécois (QC) agitated for a referendum to push forward a separation of the province from the rest of Canada. When it came in October 1995, they were narrowly beaten. They lost by

Above: the victory speech at the Quebec referendum after a close-run campaign ended in a "no" vote for separation from Canada.
Right: the Prince of Wales and governor of Hong Kong watching the handover celebrations.

just 54,000 votes, with 50.6 per cent of the Quebec electorate voting to remain part of Canada and 49.4 per cent voting for sovereignty. The situation was further complicated by the claims of the native Canadian Indians that 10 nations plus the Inuit (Eskimo) lay claim to 580,000 sq. miles of Quebec. It was clear that the claims of the French-speaking separatists were but one of the major considerations regarding the future of the province.

1997 British return Hong Kong to China

BRITAIN FIRST USED HONG KONG as a naval base in the nineteenth century. It was ceded to Britain forever in 1842 after the end of the Opium Wars. The New Territories were leased to Britain in 1898 on a 99-year lease. Talks regarding the return of Hong Kong and the other territories began in 1982. The Sino-British Joint Declaration of 1984 was signed in Beijing and bound Britain to return the territories in 1997. Under this agreement Hong Kong would become known as the Hong

Kong Special Administrative Region of China and be allowed to retain many of its own social, legal, and economic systems for another 50 years after the handover. The Tiananmen Square massacre in 1989 threatened to derail the negotiations and by the early 1990s emigration from Hong Kong had reached an average of 60,000 per year, the majority of the emigrants leaving for Canada and other Commonwealth countries. In July 1993 China established a Hong Kong government in waiting, but Hong Kong government elections in March 1995 showed that the majority of the people were against pro-mainland candidates. The convincing victories in both the local elections and those for the Hong Kong Legislative Council caused China to think again. Now that the handover has been completed, the region has suffered periodic economic and political uncertainties, culminating in the halving of the share values of companies traded on the Hong Kong stock exchange.

1997 Diana, Princess of Wales, killed in Paris

THE YOUNGEST DAUGHTER of the 7th Earl Spencer married Prince Charles in 1981. They had two sons, William and Harry, but the couple separated in 1992. They were divorced in 1996. Although linked with other suitors, Diana appeared to be interested in supporting causes as diverse as the arts, children's charities, AIDS and the campaign to eradicate the use of land mines. Since her marriage to Charles she had been the target of the media who had relentlessly pursued her since the engagement was announced. In the last few months of her life she was linked to Dodi Al Fayed, the son of the owner of Harrods. Rumors of an engagement spread, renewing media interest. She died in controversial and, as yet, unresolved circumstances in an underpass in Paris in 1997. The world was shaken by her death and her funeral received unprecedented coverage.

Diana, Princess of Wales, a few months before she was tragically killed in a Paris car crash with Dodi Al Fayed.

Power & Politics

2

It would be a great reform in politics if wisdom could be made to spread as easily and as rapidly as folly.

Winston Churchill, 1947

1900 King Umberto of Italy assassinated

UMBERTO I HAD been king of Italy since 1878, when he succeeded his father, Victor Emmanuel II, the first king of Italy. He joined the Triple Alliance with Germany and Austria-Hungary in 1882, a pact intended to offset the power of Russia and France. His colonial exploits included the defeat at Aduwa, Abyssinia, in 1896. He was assassinated by an anarchist in July 1900, a month after the defeat of the Pelloux government. The alliance was last renewed in 1912 but during World War I Italy's initial neutrality changed and it denounced the alliance in 1915. Umberto was succeeded by Victor Emmanuel III.

1900 UK Labour Party founded

THE LABOUR PARTY is the UK political party based on socialist principles; it was originally formed to represent workers. A Scottish socialist, Keir Hardie, and a workers' leader, John Burns, had already entered Parliament independently as Labour members in 1892, but it was in 1900 that a conference representing the trade unions, the Independent Labour Party (ILP) and the Fabian Society founded the Labour Party. It was known until 1906 as the Labour Representation Committee, when 29 seats were gained in Parliament. By 1922 the Labour Party was recognized as the official opposition and in 1924 it formed a minority government for a few months under party secretary Ramsay MacDonald.

Overleaf: cartoon showing the public's admiration for Mao Zedong.
(see page 50).
Right: Queen Victoria, four years before her death in 1901.
Opposite: as Prince of Wales, Edward VII enjoyed a somewhat frivolous lifestyle, and this love of social and sporting life continued into his reign as King.

1901 Queen Victoria dies

VICTORIA, THE ONLY CHILD OF EDWARD, Duke of Kent, the fourth son of George III, was born on May 24, 1819 at Kensington Palace, London. She succeeded her Uncle, William IV, becoming Queen of Britain in 1837. In 1840 she married Prince Albert of Saxe-Coburg and Gotha. She soon demonstrated a good grasp of constitutional principles, a surprising maturity, a firm will and a conservative nature. When Melbourne's government fell in 1839 she exercised her prerogative and refused to dismiss the ladies of the bedchamber. Peel then resigned, enabling her to prolong the preferred Melbourne administration until 1841. Her relations with her prime ministers were either stormy (Peel, Palmerston, Gladstone) or affectionate (Melbourne, Disraeli). She had four sons and five daughters: Victoria, the Princess Royal; Albert Edward, later Edward VII; Alice; Alfred, Duke of Edinburgh and of Saxe-Coburg-Gotha; Helena; Louise; Arthur; Leopold; and Beatrice. Always strongly influenced by her husband, she went into seclusion after his death from typhoid in 1861, which brought her temporary unpopularity. With Disraeli's administration she rose again in the public's favor, becoming Empress of India in 1876. From 1848 she regularly visited the Scottish Highlands, where she had a house at Balmoral built to Albert's designs. She died at Osborne House on the Isle of Wight on January 22, 1901.

1901 President McKinley shot by anarchist

WILLIAM McKINLEY WAS the 25th president of the US, a Republican elected in 1896. He went to Congress in 1876 and was repeatedly re-elected. In 1892 he was made governor of Ohio, his name being identified with the high protective tariff carried in the McKinley Bill of 1890. His term as president was marked by the US's adoption of an imperialist policy, as shown by the Spanish-American War in 1898 and the annexation of Cuba and the Philippines. In November 1900, as in 1896, he secured a large majority and was re-elected. He was shot by anarchist Leon Czolgosz in 1901 in Buffalo, New York, and died eight days later.

1902 King Edward VII crowned in Westminster Abbey

EDWARD VII (1841–1910) became King of Britain in 1901 after the death of Queen Victoria, and was crowned in 1902. As Prince of Wales he was a well-known social figure but Queen Victoria considered him too frivolous to take part in political life. In 1860 he made the first tour of the US and Canada ever undertaken by a British prince, and after his father died (1861) he undertook many public duties, taking a close interest in politics. He married Princess Alexandra of Denmark in 1863 and they had six children. As King he contributed to the Entente Cordiale with France in 1904 and the Anglo-Russian Agreement (1907).

1903 Army officers kill King and Queen in Serbia

SINCE 1459 SERBIA had been under the domination of the Turks. Uprisings in 1804–16, led by Kara George and Milosh Obrenovich, forced the Turks to recognize Serbia as an autonomous principality under Obrenovich. The assassination of George on Obrenovich's orders gave rise to a long feud between the two houses. Following a war with Turkey (1876–78), Serbia became an independent kingdom. On the assassination of the last king, King Obrenovich, in 1903 by army officers, the Karageorgevich dynasty was able to seize the throne. The restoration of this dynasty gave rise to a new pro-Russian orientation for Serbia, which brought it into conflict with Austria-Hungary, which in turn contributed to World War I.

1904 Russian Minister of the Interior assassinated

VYACHESLAV KONSTANTINOVICH PLEHVE was a Russian imperialist statesman who endeavored to uphold autocracy and police-run government. He was appointed director of the police department in the Ministry of the Interior in 1881, becoming Minister of the Interior in 1902. He zealously obstructed liberal local government activity, harshly pursued Russification policies, particularly against the Armenians and the Finns, and encouraged anti-Semitic propaganda, which led to a violent pogrom at Kishinev in Moldova in 1903. To soothe labor discontent, he backed police-controlled patriotic labor unions. He actively supported the Russian policy in Korea which provoked conflict with Japan. Plehve was assassinated in 1904 by a member of the Socialist Revolutionary party.

The last Emperor of China was crowned in 1908 at the age of just two years. He was deposed three years later in favor of a republic.

1905 October manifesto announced by Czar of Russia

ON JANUARY 22, 1905 thousands of striking, unarmed workers marched to Czar Nicholas II's palace in St Petersburg asking for reforms. Government troops fired on the crowd, killing many people. After this "Bloody Sunday" slaughter the revolution gained strength, resulting in a general strike, which crippled the country in October. Revolutionaries in St Petersburg formed a council called the Soviet of Workers' Deputies. The Czar announced a manifesto, which granted the Duma (parliament) the power to pass or reject proposed laws. These measures satisfied a few of the liberal elements but the revolution continued to gain ground, coming to a head when the army crushed a serious uprising in December.

1907 Gandhi speaks with Churchill

MOHANDAS KARAMCHAND GANDHI, later known as Mahatma, was born in India in 1869. He studied law in London, and in 1893 he gave up a Bombay legal practice to live in South Africa where he spent the next 21 years opposing discriminatory legislation against Indians, instigating a campaign of civil disobedience. On March 22, 1907 he pleaded the Indians' case to Winston Churchill, at the time colonial secretary, against incoming legislation that required that all Indians would be fingerprinted and forced to carry registration documents. Although Churchill lent a sympathetic ear, some of the legislation still went through and Gandhi again had to return to a campaign of non-violent non-cooperation.

1908 Pu Yi becomes Emperor of China at age two

PU YI WAS CROWNED as Emperor in 1908 at the age of only two years but he was to be the last Emperor of China. In 1911 revolution broke out and imperial rule ended with the infant being deposed. In 1912 a republic was formed and the ex-emperor was pensioned and sent to a summer palace near Beijing. He became known in the West as Henry Pu Yi, and in 1932 the Japanese set him up as a provincial dictator in Manzhouguo; he later held the title of Emperor Kangde from 1934 to 1945. In 1945 civil war resumed in China and he was imprisoned by the Russians and then the Chinese Communists. In 1949 the People's Republic of China was formed.

1908 Portuguese King Carlos I and Crown Prince Luis assassinated

KING CARLOS I was King of Portugal from 1889. In 1906 João Franco, a monarchist sympathizer, was appointed premier and was later accused of illegal money transfers to Carlos. Carlos was assassinated in Lisbon with his elder son, Luis. It is not known who killed them but the deed was applauded by republicans. He was succeeded by his younger son, Manuel, who was only 18 and unable to cope with the republican attacks on the monarchy. After the murder of a leading republican a revolution began, succeeding in taking over control in October 1910. Manuel fled the country, settling in England where he remained an exile until his death in 1932.

1914 Archduke Franz Ferdinand of Austria assassinated

IN 1867 EMPEROR FRANZ JOSEPH had established the dual monarchy of Austria-Hungary. The Treaty of Berlin in 1878 gave Austria the administration of Bosnia and Herzegovina, which Austria annexed in 1908. On June 28, 1914 the heir to the Austrian throne, Archduke Franz Ferdinand, and his wife were assassinated in Sarajevo, Serbia, by a Serbian nationalist.

On July 28th Austria declared war on and invaded Serbia, precipitating World War I. As Russia began to mobilize, Germany declared war on Russia and France, cutting through to the west and invading Belgium. On August 4th Britain declared war on Germany. World War I lasted until 1918, with the US entering to aid Britain, France, Russia, and their allies in 1917. In all, an estimated 10 million people died with double that number injured. Austria was defeated in 1918, the last Habsburg emperor was overthrown and Austria became a republic, which comprised only Vienna and its immediate provinces. The peace Treaty of Versailles was signed on June 28, 1919 between the Allies and Germany, which established the League of Nations. German rearmament was restricted, and Germany agreed to pay for war damage. The US never ratified the treaty and made a separate peace accord with Germany and Austria in 1921.

1916 The Easter Rising in Dublin

REBELS PROCLAIMING an Irish Republic rose up against the British in Dublin on April 25th. While rebels shot at sentries guarding Dublin Castle, others seized strategic parts of the city. The British responded by pouring troops into Dublin, led by General Sir John Maxwell, swiftly regaining control and seizing key leaders. By May 11th 794 civilians had been killed along with 521 police and soldiers. Padraic Pearse, the rebel leader, was also dead along with five of the other seven rebel leaders. James Connolly, the last surviving rebel leader, was shot by a firing squad. Meanwhile, Sir Roger Casement, the former diplomat, was tried and executed for treason after attempting to smuggle German arms into Ireland.

1919 League of Nations formed

THE LEAGUE OF NATIONS was suggested by US president Woodrow Wilson in 1917 as part of the peace settlement for World War I. The League covenant was drawn up by the Paris peace conference in 1919 and was incorporated in the Versailles and other peace treaties. Its member states undertook to preserve the territorial rights of all and to put international disputes before the League. It was established in Geneva, Switzerland, in 1920 and included representatives from states throughout the world. Its status was undermined, however, by the US decision not to join the League and because it had no power to enforce its decisions. It was dissolved in 1946.

Recruitment poster from World War I; the war which was largely instigated by the assassination of Archduke Franz Ferdinand on a visit to Serbia.

*Joseph Stalin (right)
and Vladimir Ilyich
Lenin (left), two of
the most prominent
leaders in Russian
political history.*

1921 Irish Free State established

ON DECEMBER 7TH, after Britain's Lloyd George threatened to put down the Irish rebellion by force, a treaty was signed. The 26 southern counties became independent, the six Ulster counties remaining part of the UK. A boundary commission was set up to establish the dividing line between north and south. The Irish Free State was seen as the end of "700 years of repression" by the Irish leaders. It was hoped that differences regarding the status of some of the areas close to the new border could be settled and that a new parliament, based in Dublin, would take over control of the Free State in the near future. With this agreement, it was hoped that the violence and disagreements would end.

1928 Hoover becomes president

HERBERT HOOVER, born in 1874 to Quaker parents in Iowa, became the 31st US president. Supporting his family from an early age, following his father's premature death, he initially trained in mining. During World War I he was closely associated with relief of distress in Europe. He became secretary of commerce under Harding. A Republican candidate, he defeated "Al" Smith in the presidential election of 1928, but his opposition to direct government assistance for the unemployed after the world slump of 1929 made him unpopular and he lost to Roosevelt in 1932. He assisted President Truman with the various American European economic relief programs that followed World War II.

1924 Death of Lenin

VLADIMIR ILYCH LENIN was born in 1870. He was active in the 1905 revolution and had to leave Russia when it failed, settling in Switzerland in 1914. He returned to Russia after the February revolution of 1917 and led the Bolshevik revolution in November of that year. From the overthrow of the provisional government at that time until his death in 1924, he effectively controlled the Soviet Union. He concluded the peace agreement with Germany, and organized a successful resistance to the pro-Czarist uprisings and foreign intervention in 1918–20. His modification of Marxist doctrines to fit the Russian conditions became known as Marxism-Leninism and became the basis of communist ideology.

1929 Stalin comes to power

JOSEPH STALIN was born in 1879 and was educated to become a priest, but was expelled for Marxist propaganda. He joined the Social Democratic party in 1898 and then Lenin and the Bolsheviks in 1903. He was repeatedly exiled to Siberia during 1903–13. He became a member of the Communist Party's Politburo and sat on the October revolution committee. Stalin soon consolidated a powerful following and was appointed general secretary of the Communist Party in 1922. After Lenin died in 1924, Stalin sought to take over the reins and to create "Socialism in one country," often clashing with Trotsky who thought Socialism in Russia impossible until there was revolution in western Europe. After the argument was won in 1927 a series of five-year plans was launched to collectivize industry and agriculture and Trotsky was banished in 1928. Stalin controlled the USSR from 1929. As a dictator he soon disposed of all real and imagined enemies and he eliminated all opposition in the Great Purge 1936–38. During World War II, Stalin intervened in the military direction of the campaigns against the Nazis, his role being denounced after his death by Krushchev and others in the Soviet regime. After the war Stalin maintained autocratic rule until his death in 1953.

1930 Gandhi arrested

AFTER RETURNING TO INDIA in 1914, Gandhi took an increasing interest in the home rule movement (Swaraj), becoming master of the congress organization. He ran a civil disobedience campaign in 1920 which involved many violent disputes. From 1922 to 1924 he was jailed for conspiracy and then in 1930 he led a 200-mile march to the sea to collect salt in symbolic defiance of the government monopoly. He was re-arrested, but on his release in 1931 he negotiated a truce between congress and the government and attended the London Round Table Conference on Indian constitutional reform. Once back in India, however, he renewed the civil disobedience campaign and was arrested yet again.

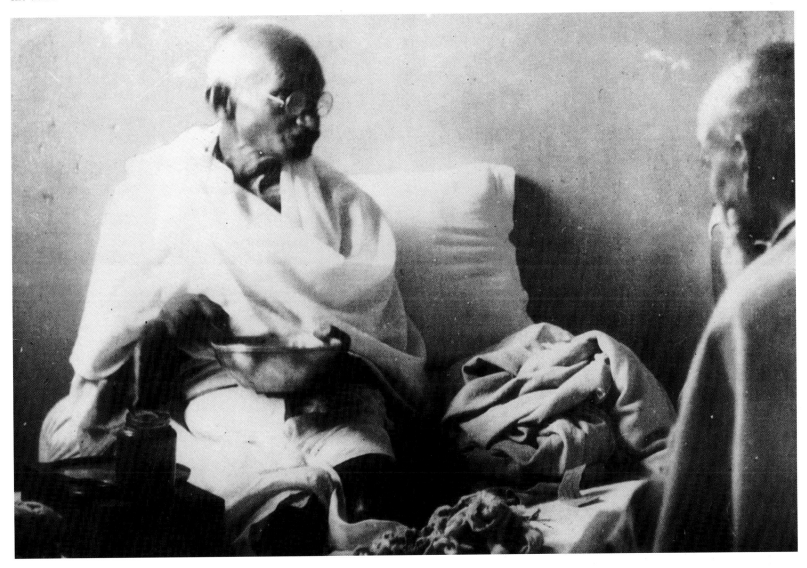

Mahatma Gandhi was released from Yerowada Jail in January 1931 and shortly after attended the Round Table Conference in London to discuss Indian constitutional reform.

Above: *parade of officers of the Third Reich at the Nurnberg Party Day Rally in 1933. Right: Edward VIII, who abdicated when the government would not allow him to marry twice-divorced Wallis Simpson.*

1932 Hitler seizes full power in Germany

ADOLF HITLER was born in 1889 in Austria and lived poorly for many years, dodging military service and emigrating to Munich in 1913. He volunteered for war service in 1914 and rose to the rank of corporal. In 1919, while spying on the activities of small political parties, he joined one of them, changing its name to National Socialist German Workers' Party (Nazi Party), and provided it with a manifesto of nationalism and anti-Semitism. The party achieved little importance until the 1930 election; but by 1932, although Hitler was defeated by Hindenburg in the presidential elections, it formed the largest group in the Reichstag. Hitler became chancellor in a Nazi-Nationalist coalition in 1933.

Ⓜ 1936 Edward VIII abandons the throne

EDWARD VIII was born in 1894. He was the eldest son of George V and was appointed Prince of Wales in 1910. During World War I, he served in the navy and the army and achieved considerable popularity. He became King Edward VIII when he succeeded to the throne following the death of his father on January 20, 1936. On November 16th, however, a constitutional crisis arose when Edward declared that he wished to marry Mrs. Wallis Warfield Simpson, an American divorcee he had met in 1930. Mrs. Simpson had already been divorced from her first husband, US Navy Lieutenant E. Spencer, in 1927, and the divorce from her second

husband, Ernest Simpson, an American-born Englishman, came through during 1936. The king made it clear to Stanley Baldwin and his government that he was determined to marry her even if it meant giving up his title. The marriage of the "Supreme Governor" of the Church of England to a divorced person was considered totally unacceptable and so the king renounced the throne and was finally forced to abdicate on December 11th. He left for voluntary exile in France where he married Mrs. Simpson on June 3, 1937. He was created Duke of Windsor and was governor of the Bahamas between 1940 and 1945.

1938 Chamberlain—peace in our time

ON SEPTEMBER 29, 1938 the Munich Agreement was signed by the leaders of the UK (Neville Chamberlain), France (Edouard Daladier), Germany (Adolf Hitler) and Italy (Benito Mussolini), under which Czechoslovakia was ordered to surrender the Sudetenland to Germany. Chamberlain claimed it would guarantee "peace in our time" and

received a tremendous reception on his return to the UK. Unfortunately it did not prevent Hitler from taking the rest of Czechoslovakia in March 1939 and within the year Britain was at war with Germany. He became prime minister in 1937, criticism of his war leadership accompanied military reverses and in 1940 he handed the premiership to Churchill. He died within the year.

1940 Churchill takes over

WINSTON CHURCHILL had been in parliament since 1900. A Liberal until 1923, he held the posts of Home Secretary in 1910, Lord of the Admiralty 1911–15 and Secretary of War 1918–21 and then became Colonial Secretary, playing a leading role in establishing the Irish Free State. He joined the Conservatives in 1923 and was made Chancellor of the Exchequer (1924). At the start of World War II he was again Lord of the Admiralty until May 1940 when he was called to the premiership as head of an all-party administration, it was then that he made his now-famous "blood, sweat and tears" speech. He led Britain for the remainder of the war.

 ## 1945 Mussolini and Hitler die

BY 1945 things were falling apart for Mussolini and Hitler. Italian leader Benito Mussolini had resigned on July 25, 1943 and had been arrested, only to be rescued by German parachutists in September 1943. Vainly seeking to regain what he had lost, he set up a "Republican Fascist" government in Northern Italy. Mussolini, his mistress Clara Petacci and other Fascists were caught by Italians at Dongo on Lake Como trying to head for the Swiss border. After some form of trial they were shot on April 28, 1945 and their bodies were taken to Milan and hung upside-down in a public square. In Germany, Rundstedt's counter-offensive against the allies in the Ardennes in December 1944 under Hitler's direction had failed and Germany had been invaded. Hitler was living out his fantasies commanding non-existent armies from his bunker, the air-raid shelter beneath the chancellery building in Berlin. On April 29, 1945, with the Russians only several hundred yards away, he married his mistress Eva Braun in the presence of the Goebbels family, who then poisoned themselves. All available evidence suggests that Hitler and Braun committed suicide on April 30th and had their bodies cremated. Hitler's beloved Third Reich, which was to have endured forever, had ended ingloriously.

1945 Labour sweeps to power

BRITAIN'S WARTIME coalition government was dissolved on May 23, 1945. Churchill formed a caretaker government until a general election was held in July of that year. Labour swept to power with a huge electoral victory and Clement Attlee became prime minister. Attlee had actually paved the way for Churchill's wartime success by refusing to let Labour join the coalition under Chamberlain. During his six years in office he instigated a huge program of reform under which the Bank of England, the coal mines, civil aviation, cable and wireless services, railways, road transport, and steel were nationalized, the National Health Service was introduced and independence was granted to India and Burma.

1946 Paul Henri Spaak elected president of United Nations

THE UNITED NATIONS (UN), an association of states for international peace, security and cooperation, was established in 1945 as a successor to the League of Nations. The UN charter was drawn up at the San Francisco Conference in 1945. The original intention was that the UN's Security Council would preserve the wartime alliance between the US, USSR, and Britain (with France and China as permanent members) in order to maintain peace. This did not happen because of the Cold War. Paul Henri Spaak, Belgium's first socialist premier (1938), was elected president of the first General Assembly of the UN in 1946. He also became Belgian premier again in that year.

Two of the most notorious political leaders of the first half of the century, Benito Mussolini and Adolf Hitler, both died ignominiously in 1945.

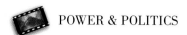
1948 `Mahatma Gandhi assassinated

IN MAY 1947 Gandhi had at last realized his dream. Since 1946 he had been negotiating with the British government over constitutional reform, and finally India had been granted independence. He hailed the decision as "the noblest act of the British nation." Things were darkened in his last few months by communal strife between Hindus and Muslims, but his fasts to shame the instigators helped to avert the situation to some extent. He was assassinated in Delhi by a Hindu fanatic on January 30, 1948, just ten days after a previous attempt on his life. He is now venerated as a moral teacher, a pacifist reformer, and a dedicated patriot.

1949 Mao Zedong proclaims the People's Republic of China

Cartoon showing the public's admiration for Mao Zedong, after he had formed the People's Republic of China.

WHEN THE WAR with Japan, where Chinese nationals and communists had both fought, ended in 1945, civil war resumed in China. In 1949, following the elimination of nationalist resistance on the mainland, the People's Republic of China was proclaimed by Mao Zedong (Mao Tse-

tung) in Beijing. Initially, the Communist regime concentrated on economic reconstruction. Mao had helped found the Chinese Communist Party (CCP) in 1921. Mao's thoughts and writings, detailed in *New Democracy* and his *Little Red Book*, dominated the functioning of the Republic between 1949 and 1970. Mao resigned the chairmanship of the Republic in 1959 but remained chairman of the CCP's politburo until his death (1976).

1951 Churchill wins election

DURING ATTLEE'S government Churchill proved himself a strong leader of Britain's opposition party, speaking out in international speeches against the tyranny behind the Iron Curtain (his own phrase) and fostering the idea of European and Atlantic unity, later to come together as NATO. In 1951 he came to power again at the age of 77 and was prime minister until 1955, when he resigned. During this period he still found time to publish his six-volume *History of World War II* (1948–54) and a four volume *History of the English Speaking Peoples* (1956–58). He remained in old age a back-bencher and was regarded with veneration. He died in 1965.

from the army in 1952 to campaign for president, where the popularity he had gained in Europe swept him to nomination and ultimate victory. In power he promoted business interests at home, during an era of post-war prosperity, and conducted the Cold War abroad. His vice-president was Richard Nixon. A popular politician, he was re-elected by a wide margin in 1956.

1952 Evita dies

DURING PERÓN'S rule, Evita campaigned for women's suffrage and acquired control of newspapers and business companies. She also founded the Eva Perón Foundation for the promotion of social welfare. In 1952 she died of cancer and the nation mourned. After her death Perón lost popularity and was deposed in a coup in 1955, after which civilian rule was restored. Perón continued to direct the Peronista movement from exile in Spain. Another coup in 1966 restored military rule, and a later Peronist party successfully brought Hector Campora to the presidency in 1973. Campora soon resigned to make way for Perón, with his third wife Isabel as vice-president. Perón died in 1974.

Left: Evita Perón addresses the crowds celebrating Labour Day in Buenos Aires.
Below: King George VI, who ascended the throne after the abdication of his brother, died suddenly in 1952.

1951 Evita Perón promises to stand as vice-president

SINCE 1930 Argentina had been run by alternate civilian and military rule. The Radical Civic Union Party held power from 1916 until the first military coup in 1930. Civilian government returned (1932) until a second military coup in 1943 paved the way for the rise of Lieutenant-General Juan Domingo Perón. In 1945 he married radio actress Evita (Eva) Duarte. Strengthened by Evita's popularity, Perón created the Peronista party based on extreme nationalism and social improvement and became dictator in 1946. After that, Evita virtually ran the health and labor ministries and in 1951 she stood for the post of vice-president but was opposed by the army and withdrew.

1952 Eisenhower wins presidential election

DWIGHT ('IKE') Eisenhower (1890–1969), a Republican, became the 34th US president in 1952. A general in World War II, he commanded the Allied forces in Italy in 1943, then the Allied invasion of Europe and from October 1944 all the Allied armies in the West. He resigned

1952 George VI dies

GEORGE VI, king of the UK from 1936, when he succeeded after the abdication of his brother, Edward VIII, died suddenly of coronary thrombosis in 1952, having suffered from cancer for several years. He had been created Duke of York in 1920 and married Lady Elizabeth Bowes-Lyon in 1923. They had two children, Elizabeth and Margaret. During the Blitz of World War II he remained in London at Buckingham Palace to help create a feeling of solidarity among the people of Britain. He and his family toured bombed areas and inspected mines and munitions factories to help maintain morale. In 1947 he toured South Africa with his family; the same year in which India gained independence from Britain.

1952 Prince Hussein pronounced King of Jordan

HUSSEIN IBN TALAL became King of Jordan in 1952, succeeding his father, King Talal, who was deposed because of mental illness. The king struggled to maintain rule despite political upheavals inside and outside his country. His federation of Jordan with Iraq in 1958 came to an end with the Iraqi military coup d'état in July. By 1967 he had lost all his kingdom west of the river Jordan in the Arab-Israeli wars. In 1970 he suppressed the Palestine Liberation Organization, which was acting as a guerrilla force against his rule on the East Bank territories. Subsequently he became a moderator in Middle Eastern politics, signing a peace agreement with Israel in 1994.

1953 Queen Elizabeth II crowned

PRINCESS ELIZABETH was born in London on April 21, 1926. During World War II she served in the Auxiliary Territorial Service and by an amendment to the Regency Act she became a state counselor at 18. She married her third cousin, Philip, Duke of Edinburgh, in November 1947. She was proclaimed Elizabeth II when her father, George VI, died on February 6, 1952 and was crowned on June 2, 1953 with millions watching the televised coronation. Philip became Prince Philip in 1957 and together they had four children, Charles, Anne, Andrew, and Edward. Despite recent criticisms of the monarchy she has maintained her position as a powerful ambassador for the UK.

Queen Elizabeth II being crowned in Westminster Abbey in 1953, following the death of her father King George VI.

1957 Olav V crowned king after the death of Haakon VII

OLAV V was the son and successor of Haakon VII of Norway and Maud, daughter of Edward VII of Britain. Born in England he was educated in Norway and at Oxford. In his youth he was an outstanding sportsman and an Olympic yachtsman. In 1929 he married Princess Martha of Sweden. He stayed in Norway with his father, who refused to abdicate when it was invaded by Germany in 1940, and was appointed head of the Norwegian armed forces. Later he escaped with Haakon to England, returning in 1945. He became Olav V when his father died in 1957. His son Harald succeeded to the Norwegian throne as Harald V in 1991.

1958 Charles de Gaulle becomes prime minister of France

FRENCH GENERAL CHARLES DE GAULLE organized the Free French troops fighting the Nazis during World War II, becoming head of the provisional French government in 1944–46. When national bankruptcy and civil war in Algeria loomed in 1958, de Gaulle was called on to form a government. As prime minister he changed the constitution to make a presidential system and became the first president of the Fifth Republic in 1959. He was re-elected in 1965. A staunch nationalist, he opposed British entry to the EEC, withdrew French forces from NATO in 1966 and pursued development of a French nuclear deterrent. He resigned (1969) after defeat in a referendum on constitutional reform.

1959 Harold Macmillan visits Soviet Union on voyage of discovery

HAROLD MACMILLAN became prime minister of Britain on January 10, 1957 after Eden resigned in the wake of the Suez crisis. Macmillan worked hard to restore British–US relations which had been strained by the Suez crisis. In February 1959 he visited Nikita Krushchev in Moscow on what he called his "voyage of discovery." Despite rumors of a snub by Krushchev, who stopped talks because of a toothache, the meeting led to the signing of a five-year trade pact between Britain and the USSR in May. He led the Conservatives to a resounding victory in 1959 by highlighting post-war full employment under the slogan "You've never had it so good."

1963 JFK shot in Dallas, Texas

ON NOVEMBER 22, 1963 J. F. Kennedy was assassinated while on a state visit to Dallas, Texas. He was shot several times by rifle fire while being driven in an open-top car through the streets of Dallas with his wife Jackie sitting beside him. A gunman, Lee Harvey Oswald, was arrested shortly after and was named as the assassin. Oswald himself was shot and killed at point-blank range by Jack Ruby two days later while under heavy police escort on a jail transfer. Oswald was an ex-marine who had gone to live in the USSR in 1959 and had returned when he could not become a Soviet citizen. Jack Ruby was a Dallas nightclub owner, associated with both the underworld and the police. A number of conspiracy theories have been woven around the Kennedy assassination, which was investigated by a special commission headed by Chief Justice Earl Warren. The commission determined that Oswald operated as a lone assassin. It is, however, often speculated that Oswald was a "patsy," someone set up to take the blame for the shooting. A later congressional report re-examined the evidence and determined that Kennedy "was probably assassinated as a result of a conspiracy" though it did not venture into what that conspiracy was.

1960 JFK becomes president of the US

JOHN FITZGERALD KENNEDY was born in Massachusetts in 1917, served in the navy in World War II, was elected to Congress in 1946 and to the Senate in 1952. He married Jacqueline Lee Bouvier in 1953. In 1960 he defeated Nixon and became the 35th US president, the first Roman Catholic and the youngest person to be elected president. His policies included the unsuccessful Bay of Pigs invasion of Cuba, but in 1963 he secured the withdrawal of Soviet missiles from the island. At home he brought academics into Washington as advisers and set out a reform program, "New Frontiers," which was implemented by Lyndon Johnson after his death.

1964 Death of Nehru

JAWAHARLAL NEHRU, an Indian nationalist politician, became prime minister of India in 1947. Prior to the partition, the split of British India into India and Pakistan, he had led the socialist wing of the Nationalist Congress Party and he was second only to Mohandas Gandhi in his influence. Between 1921 and 1945 he was imprisoned nine times by

Left: John F. Kennedy became the 35th president of the United States in 1960. His youth and enthusiasm endeared him to the American people. Above: JFK is shot in Dallas while driving through the streets with his wife.

the British for political activities. As prime minister from the creation of the dominion of India he conceived the idea of neutrality and peacemaking towards the major powers. He committed India to a policy of industrialization. He died in 1964 and his daughter Indira Gandhi later became prime minister too.

1964 Nelson Mandela imprisoned

AFRICAN NATIONALIST leader Nelson Mandela was a successful lawyer in Johannesburg before joining the banned African National Congress (ANC) in 1944. For the next twenty years he led a campaign of defiance against the South African government and its racist policies, and in 1961 he organized a three-day national strike. Despite giving a memorable four-hour defense speech at his trial in 1964, he was sentenced to life imprisonment for political offences. He continued to be a powerful symbol of unity for the anti-apartheid movement and an international campaign for his release was launched, led by his wife, Winnie, who was herself continually subjected to restrictions on her own personal freedom.

Nelson Mandela after being tried and convicted of political offences. He was later sentenced to life imprisonment.

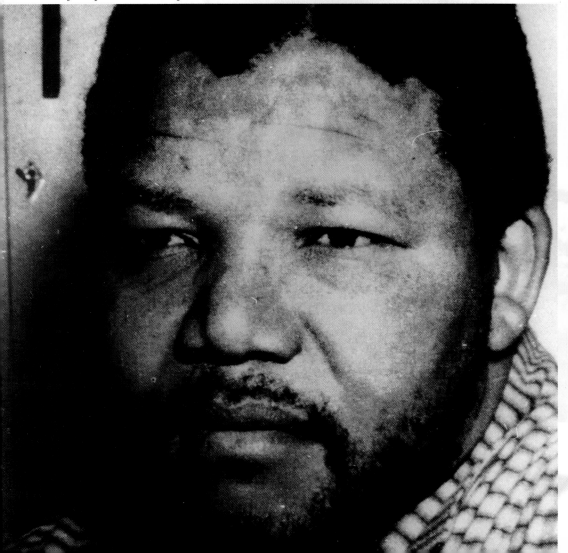

1966 Verwoerd assassinated

HENDRIK VERWOERD, the South African right-wing politician, became vice-chairman of the National party in 1946 and was elected senator in 1948. He was the chief promoter of apartheid legislation (segregation by race) during his time as minister of native affairs from 1950 to 1958. In 1958 he was elected national leader by the Nationalist party and as prime minister of South Africa he dedicated himself to the founding of a republic. After strong opposition to his apartheid policies South Africa finally left the commonwealth and became a republic in 1962. Verwoerd continued with a strict apartheid policy. He was stabbed to death on the floor of parliament by Dimitrios Tsafendas in 1966.

1967 Che Guevara executed

THE ARGENTINIAN communist revolutionary leader Che Guevara was born in 1928. He graduated in medicine at the university of Buenos Aires in 1953 but left Argentina soon after because of his opposition to Perón's government. He then joined Fidel Castro's revolutionary movement in Mexico in 1955 and played a significant role in the Cuban revolution in 1956–59. Following this he held government posts under Castro. An activist of revolution elsewhere, he became a hero of left-wing youth in the 1960s. After leaving Cuba in 1965 to become a guerrilla leader in South America, he was captured by government troops while trying to stage a revolt and was executed in 1967.

1968 Robert Kennedy assassinated

ROBERT KENNEDY was presidential campaign manager for his brother John F. Kennedy during 1960. He became attorney-general in 1961 and promoted the Civil Rights Act of 1964 as well as following a racket-busting policy. He was a key aide to his brother but when JFK's successor, Lyndon Johnson, preferred Hubert Humphrey for the vice-presidential nomination he resigned and was elected senator for New York. In 1968 he campaigned for the Democratic party's presidential nomination but on June 5th, after winning the Californian primary election, he was shot and died the following day. His assassin, Sirhan Sirhan, a Jordanian-born immigrant, was sentenced to the gas chamber in 1969.

1969 Nixon becomes president

TRAINED AS A lawyer, Republican Richard Milhous Nixon first entered Congress in 1947 and in 1948, as a member of the Un-American Activities Committee, pressed for the investigation on Alger Hiss, accused of being a spy. Nixon was senator for California from 1951 until he was elected vice-president under Eisenhower. He lost the presidential election in 1960 to John F. Kennedy, partly because televised electoral debates put him at a disadvantage. He did not seek presidential election in 1964, but tried again in 1968. His campaign based on "law and order" defeated vice-president Humphrey in one of the most closely contested elections in US history, becoming the 37th president in 1969.

1970 Gamal Abdel Nasser dies

Egyptian general, Gamal Abdel Nasser was born in 1918. In 1952 he was the driving force behind the Neguib coup, which ended the Egyptian monarchy. Nasser became prime minister (1954) and then president of Egypt from 1956 (president of the United Arab Republic from 1958). His nationalization of the Suez Canal in 1956 led to an Anglo-French invasion and the Suez crisis. Nasser had ambitions for an Egyptian-led union of Arab states and this resulted in disquiet in the Middle East. Although a strong advocate of Arab unity towards the end of his presidency, he became increasingly dependent on arms and aid from the USSR. He died in 1970.

1971 Idi Amin
seizes control of Uganda

UGANDAN SOLDIER and politician Idi Amin was born in 1925. He joined the British (later to become Ugandan) army and rose through the ranks, becoming a colonel in 1964. A friend of the prime minister, Milton Obote, he was made commander-in-chief of the army and air force, but when relations between them worsened, Amin staged a coup in 1971, dissolving the parliament and establishing a military dictatorship, taking legislative and executive powers into his own hands. Amin then proceeded to expel all Ugandan Asians and many Israelis in 1972, seized foreign-owned businesses and estates, and ordered the execution of thousands of his opponents, making his bloodthirsty regime notorious worldwide.

Left: scenes of grief in Beirut as President Nasser is mourned.
Above: Richard Nixon became one of the most controversial figures in American political history.

1973 Spanish premier assassinated

IN DECEMBER 1973 Spanish premier Admiral Luis Carrero Blanco was traveling to mass in his car when a bomb blasted it 65 ft into the air. The car was hurled over the church and landed on the second-floor balcony of a nearby building. Blanco was pulled out alive from the wreckage but died shortly after. The bomb was planted by the terrorist organization

Basque Homeland and Liberty (known as ETA). Blanco was General Franco's handpicked successor as head of government and effectively the man in power owing to Franco's ailing health. Franco relinquished the premiership to Prince Juan Carlos in 1973, but remained head of state until his death (1975).

Above: *the* New York Post *headlines the Nixon Watergate scandal.* Right: *US president Jimmy Carter, whose term was characterized by efforts to establish peace in the Middle East.*

1974 *Nixon resigns after Watergate*

RICHARD NIXON was re-elected as president in 1972 in a landslide victory over George McGovern. He resigned in controversy in 1974 over the Watergate affair. Watergate, the US political scandal, was named after the building in Washington, DC, which housed the Democrats' campaign in the 1972 presidential elections. Five men, hired by the Republican Committee to Re-elect the President (CREEP), were caught after breaking into the Watergate with electronic surveillance equipment. For two years, investigations were run by the media and a Senate committee and it was revealed that the White House was implicated in the break-in, and that there was a "slush fund" used to finance unethical activities. In August 1974 President Nixon was forced by the Supreme Court to surrender to Congress tape-recordings of conversations he had held with administration officials, and these indicated his involvement in a cover-up. Nixon resigned rather than face impeachment charges on three counts: for obstruction of the administration of justice in the investigation of Watergate; attempting to use the IRS (Internal Revenue Service), FBI, and CIA as weapons against political opponents; and failure to produce "papers and things" as ordered to the Judiciary Committee. The only US president to have left office by resignation, he was granted a pardon later in 1974 by President Ford.

1976 *Jimmy Carter becomes president*

DEMOCRAT JIMMY Carter became the 39th US president, narrowly winning victory over Gerald Ford. Carter was concerned with the establishment of peace in the Middle East, and he organized the Camp David peace agreements. Other features of his presidency were the return of the Panama Canal Zone to Panama and the Iranian seizure of

US Embassy hostages. In 1980, prompted by the Soviet invasion of Afghanistan and instability in Iran, he issued a doctrine stating that any outside attempt at control in the Persian Gulf would be met by military force if necessary. Defeated by Reagan in 1980, he emerged during the 1990s as a mediator and peace negotiator.

1977 *Bokassa crowned*

JEAN-BEDEL BOKASSA was commander-in-chief of the Central African Republic from 1963 until, in December 1965, he led the military coup that gave him the presidency. On December 4, 1976 he proclaimed the Central African Empire and one year later crowned himself emperor for life. In all, £30 million was spent on his coronation, with £2 million spent on the crown alone, paid for by his patron, the president of the French Republic. His regime was characterized by state violence and cruelty. Overthrown in 1979, he was in exile until 1986. Upon his return, he was sentenced to death but this was commuted to life imprisonment in 1988.

1978 Aldo Moro murdered

ALDO MORO, an Italian Christian Democrat politician, was prime minister in 1963–68 and again, with a coalition government, in 1974–76. After this government fell in January, Moro became premier again between February and July as head of a caretaker government. In October 1976 he became president of the Christian Democrats, remaining a powerful influence on Italian politics even though he held no public office. On March 16, 1978, Moro was kidnapped in Rome by Red Brigade terrorists while on his way to attend a special parliament session. After government officials repeatedly refused to release 13 members of the Red Brigade on trial in Turin, Moro was murdered by the kidnappers.

Ⓜ 1979 Ayatollah Khomeini returns to Iran

IRANIAN SHI'ITE Muslim leader Ruhollah Khomeini was born in 1900. He held the title Ayatollah, which means "sign of Allah," when he became the chief teacher of Islamic philosophy and law. He was exiled from Iran (1964) for opposition to the pro-western regime of the Shah. Ayatollah Khomeini continued to campaign against the Shah from his exile in France, demanding a return to the principles of Islam. The pressure on the Shah became so great that he left the country in 1979 and the Ayatollah made a triumphant return and became virtual head of state. Iran underwent an "Islamic Revolution" involving a return to strict observance of Muslim principles. Relations with the US worsened when a group of Iranian students took 63 Americans hostage in Tehran, demanding the Shah's return to face trial. The Shah's death in 1980 did little to alleviate the crisis, the hostages finally being released in 1981. In 1980 war broke out between Iran and Iraq over a border dispute. The war escalated throughout the 1980s until 1988, when Iran accepted the provisions for a UN-sponsored ceasefire. Relations with the UK were restored in December 1988 but the death threat issued to author Salman Rushdie over *The Satanic Verses* caused a severance in March 1989. Khomeini died in June 1989.

1979 Fall of Idi Amin

IN 1978 Idi Amin made a decision to annex the Kagera area of Tanzania, near the Ugandan border. This gave President Julius Nyerere of Tanzania the opportunity to send his troops into Uganda to support the Uganda National Liberation Army which had been formed to fight Amin. Within six months Tanzanian troops had entered the Ugandan capital Kampala and Amin was defeated. He fled to Libya in 1979 but later made attempts to make his home in several countries, including Saudi Arabia, Zaire, Senegal, and Nigeria. He was not wanted in any of them and in 1989 he was reported to have tried to return to Saudi Arabia from Zaire.

Ayatollah Ruhollah Khomeini, who inspired great adulation in Iran, returns home after being exiled in France.

Above: *Margaret Thatcher and her son Mark celebrate her first election victory in 1979. She became the first female prime minister of Britain.*
Opposite: *President Reagan makes an address at a Washington Fund-raiser—the former movie star became the 40th US president in 1980.*

1979 Margaret Thatcher wins election and becomes first female prime minister

MARGARET THATCHER had trained as a barrister before joining politics. In 1970 she became Britain's education minister under Edward Heath. She was the unexpected victor in the 1975 Conservative leadership election when she defeated Heath. Building up support for the party, she won the election in 1979 and became Britain's first female prime minister. During her first term she sent British troops out to recapture the Falkland Islands from Argentina. Following victory in the Falklands her popularity soared and she was re-elected. Her second term was marked by the miners' strike (1984-85), which ended in the miners' defeat and with power shifted away from the unions. She narrowly avoided the IRA bomb in October 1984 at the Conservative conference. Victory again in 1987 made her the first prime minister in 160 years to be elected for a third term but she became increasingly isolated by her autocratic stance. In 1989 she introduced the unpopular community charge or "poll tax," which caused violent protest marches on Britain's streets. In 1990 splits in the Cabinet over Europe and consensus government led to a leadership challenge. Thatcher resolutely stood in the first round before resigning and giving her support to John Major, who replaced her as prime minister and Conservative party leader.

1980 Princess Beatrix becomes Queen of the Netherlands

THE ELDEST OF four daughters of Queen Juliana and Prince Bernhard Leopold, Beatrix went into exile with her family when the Germans overran the Netherlands in World War II and she spent the war years in Britain and Canada. In 1965 her betrothal to German Diplomat Claus von Amsberg caused a furore because of his past membership of the Hitler Youth and German army, though he had been cleared by an allied court. They married in 1966 and the hostility dimmed at the birth of Willem-Alexander (1967), the first male heir to the Dutch throne in over a century. Beatrix succeeded to the throne following her mother's abdication in 1980.

1980 Ronald Reagan becomes president

RONALD REAGAN was born in Illinois in 1911 and became a Hollywood actor in 1937. He appeared in over 50 films including *Bedtime for Bonzo* in 1951 and *The Killers* in 1964. As president of the Screen Actors Guild 1947-52 he became a conservative, was critical of bureaucracy that stifled free enterprise and he named names before the House Un-American Activities Committee. He joined the Republican party in 1962 and his term as governor of California (1966-74) was marked by battles with students. He lost the Republican presidential nominations in 1968 and 1976 to Nixon and Ford respectively. He won it in 1980 and became 40th US president, beating Jimmy Carter.

1981 Ronald Reagan shot

ON MARCH 30, 1981 Ronald Reagan was shot and wounded by a 25-year-old drifter, John W. Hinckley, but he made a speedy recovery. Following a coup in Grenada (1983) he sent US troops in; a surge of patriotism followed and his re-election in 1984 was by a landslide. His Strategic Defence Initiative (Star Wars), involving militarizing space, prevented a disarmament agreement with Gorbachev in 1985 and 1986, but a 4 per cent reduction in nuclear weapons was agreed in 1987. Also in 1987 an arms scandal, known as Irangate, was investigated by the Tower Commission. Reagan persistently said that he had no recollection of the events in question and no firm evidence was found against him.

1981 President Sadat assassinated

ANWAR SADAT succeeded Nasser as Egyptian president in 1970. He helped to restore Egyptian morale by his handling of the campaign in the 1973 war against Israel. In 1974 his plan for social, economic, and political reform in Egypt was unanimously accepted in a referendum. In 1977 he visited Israel at Camp David, to lay plans for a reconciliation between the two countries and he shared the Nobel Peace Prize with Israeli prime minister Menachem Begin in 1978. The only Arab leader to sign a peace treaty with Israel during this period, he was criticized by other Arab statesmen and hard-line Muslims. While reviewing troops in 1981, he was assassinated by Muslim extremists.

1984 Indira Gandhi killed

NEHRU'S DAUGHTER, Indira Gandhi, joined the central committee of Indian Congress in 1950, becoming president (1959) and prime minister in 1966. After her conviction for election malpractices (1975) she declared a "state of emergency," with civil liberties curtailed and censorship imposed, until she lost the 1977 election. Acquitted from a corruption charge (1978), she resigned from the Congress party, becoming leader of the new Indian National Congress. After becoming prime minister again in 1980, she was assassinated in October 1984 by members of her Sikh bodyguard, resentful of her employment of troops to storm the Golden Temple at Amritsar and dislodge dissenters. Her murder provoked a Hindu backlash and 3,000 Sikhs were massacred.

Indira Gandhi, Indian prime minister, is mourned by the people after she was assassinated by members of her own bodyguard.

1986 Swedish prime minister assassinated

OLOF PALME was an active member of the Swedish Social Democrats from the 1950s and joined the government in 1963 as minister without portfolio. He succeeded Tage Erlander as party secretary and prime minister in 1969. Soon afterwards his attacks on US war policy in Vietnam and his acceptance of US Army deserters who sought refuge in Sweden strained relations with the US, and he lost the 1976 election. In 1989 he acted as UN special envoy to mediate in the Iran-Iraq war. Elected again in 1982, he tried to reinstate Socialist economic policies in Sweden. He was assassinated by a lone gunman in 1986 and his murder remains unsolved.

1987 The Irangate scandal

IRANGATE was the 1987 US political scandal over the sale of arms to Iran via Israel. This broke the law prohibiting the sale of US weapons for resale to a country listed as a "terrorist nation," and the law requiring sales above $14 million to be reported to Congress. Lieutenant-Colonel Oliver North, a military aide to the National Security Council, and security adviser John Poindexter were both tried in 1987 on charges of obstructing congress and unlawfully destroying government documents and found guilty in 1989–90. The Congressional Joint Investigative Committee reported that the president bore 'ultimate responsibility' but found no firm evidence that Reagan had been aware of the deal.

Bottom left: *Lieutenant-Colonel Oliver North is sworn-in before he gives evidence at the Irangate trial.*
Left: *Mikhail Gorbachev was awarded the Nobel Peace Prize for his reforms in the USSR.*

1988 Gorbachev becomes president of USSR

MIKHAIL GORBACHEV was a member of the Politburo from 1980, general secretary of the Communist party (1985–91), becoming president of the Supreme Soviet from 1988. He introduced liberal reforms in the USSR such as *perestroika* and *glasnost*. He was awarded the Nobel Peace Prize in 1990 for his attempts to halt the arms race but early in 1991 he tried to placate the right wing of his party and produced a plan for a reformed union treaty. Alarmed hard-liners staged a coup in late summer but he was he rescued by Boris Yeltsin. His power was weakened by then, though, and he resigned in December 1991, yielding power to Yeltsin.

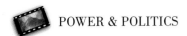

1989 Ceausescu murdered

NICOLAE CEAUSESCU was imprisoned in 1936 for communist activities; it was in prison that he met the communist leader, Gheorghe Gheorghiu-Dej, who became leader of Romania in 1952. When the Communists came to power (1947) he worked his way up until, under Gheorghiu-Dej, he was second-in-command. When Gheorghiu-Dej died (1965) he became leader and president of the State Council in 1967. In power he openly challenged the Soviet dominance of Romania, but his secret police kept rigid controls over his own people. His regime collapsed when he ordered security forces to fire on antigovernment protesters in 1989, whereupon the Romanian army defected to the demonstrators and captured, tried, and shot both Ceausescu and his wife.

1989 Emperor Hirohito dies

Above: Nicolae Ceausescu in April 1989, shortly before he was shot. Below: George Bush winning the US presidential election. Right: John Major replaces Margaret Thatcher as prime minister of Britain.

HIROHITO succeeded his father Yoshihito as Emperor of Japan in 1926. His reign was marked by rapid militarization and the wars against China (1931–32, 1937–45) and the US (1941–45), which ended with the two atomic bombs on Hiroshima and Nagasaki. Under American occupation in 1946, Hirohito renounced his legendary divinity and many of his powers to become a democratic constitutional monarch. A keen scholar of botany and zoology, he wrote books on marine biology. He died in 1989, having been the longest-reigning emperor of the longest-reigning dynasty in the world. His era is known as the Showa era. He was succeeded by his son Akihito, born in 1933.

1989 George Bush becomes US president

REPUBLICAN George Bush was director of the Central Intelligence Agency (CIA) from 1976 to 1981 and the US vice-president from 1981 to 1989 under Ronald Reagan. He succeeded Reagan and became the 41st US president in 1989. While president his initial response to Soviet leader Gorbachev's initiatives in the arms race was considered inadequate but he raised his popularity with success in the 1991 Gulf War with Iran. He signed the Strategic Arms Reduction Treaty in July 1991 and began unilateral reduction in US nuclear weapons two months later. However, Bush's reneging on his election pledge of "no new taxes" cost him the 1992 presidential elections, when he lost to Democrat Bill Clinton.

1990 John Major becomes UK prime minister

JOHN MAJOR was Britain's foreign secretary (1989) and chancellor of the exchequer (1989–90). Following Margaret Thatcher's resignation in 1990 he became leader of the Conservative party and prime minister. He gained support over his handling of Britain's efforts in the Gulf War (1991) and was re-elected in 1992. Following this, he faced mounting public dissatisfaction over several issues including Britain's withdrawal from the ERM, drastic pit and hospital closures and past arms sales to Iraq. His success in organizing a ceasefire in Northern Ireland (1994) improved his standing, but a number of senior minister scandals and party divisions over Europe paved the way for his defeat in the 1997 elections.

1990 Nelson Mandela freed

FROM 1964 to 1982 Nelson Mandela was imprisoned at Robben Island Prison, off Cape Town. He was then kept at the maximum security Pollsmoor Prison until 1988, at which time he was hospitalized with tuberculosis. Mandela had continued support among South Africa's black population and his quest for release became a major issue in countries worldwide that disapproved of apartheid. Many countries banned the import of South African goods. The South African government, led by President F. W. de Klerk, released Mandela (aged 71) from prison on February 11, 1990 after the ban on the ANC had been lifted. He entered into negotiations with the government about a multiracial future for South Africa.

1990 Shevardnadze resigns

EDUARD SHEVARDNADZE became a member of the central committee of the Communist Party of the Soviet Union in 1976 and in 1985 was promoted by Gorbachev to be a member of the Politburo and Soviet foreign minister. He helped implement the withdrawal of Soviet troops from Afghanistan (1988) and the negotiation of the arms treaty with the US. He was one of Gorbachev's closest colleagues and one of the staunchest proponents of *perestroika* and *glasnost*. Shevardnadze resigned suddenly in December 1990 in protest against the growing influence of anti-reform members in Gorbachev's government. After the failed coup in 1991 he returned briefly as foreign minister until the Soviet Union collapsed.

1990 Lech Walesa wins elections in Poland

POLISH TRADE union leader Lech Walesa founded the independent trade union, Solidarity, in 1980. A series of strikes drew wide public support and substantial concessions from the Polish government until Solidarity was outlawed in 1981 and Walesa arrested, following the imposition of martial law by General Jaruzelski. He was released in 1982 and awarded the Nobel Peace Prize (1983). After leading more strikes during 1988 he

negotiated an agreement with Jaruzelski (1989) in which Solidarity once more became legal and a new "socialist democracy" was founded. The coalition government elected in September 1989 was dominated by Solidarity and Walesa went on to be elected president by a landslide in 1990.

Nelson Mandela celebrates his freedom with wife Winnie, after 22 years of imprisonment.

1992 Denmark votes against the Maastricht treaty

THE EUROPEAN Economic Community (EEC) was founded in 1957–58 to oversee the economic integration of the nations of western Europe. The EEC joined with European fuel communities forming the European Community or EC (1967). Success of the trade policies sponsored by the EC made its members more receptive to greater economic and political union, which yielded the Treaty on European Union (Maastricht treaty) in 1991. In a 1992 referendum on EC policies the Danish people soundly rejected the treaty. Denmark had joined the EC in 1973, triggering referendums and debates elsewhere in the Community. The Danish government then proposed modifications to the treaty and a second referendum (1993) approved it.

1993 Bill Clinton becomes US president

BILL CLINTON served as governor of Arkansas in 1979–81 and 1983–93 and established a liberal and progressive reputation. He won the 1992 presidential campaign focusing on domestic issues and the ailing economy. In 1993 he became the 42nd US president and the first Democrat in the White House for 13 years. As president he brought in a variety of anti-crime measures and helped pull America out of recession. In foreign affairs he backed the Israeli-PLO peace accord in Washington in 1993 and withdrew US peacekeeping forces from Somalia in 1994. Although his party suffered a huge defeat in the November 1994 mid-term elections, he was himself re-elected as president in 1996.

Above: *Bill Clinton gives his inaugural address after being elected US president.*
Right: *Nelson Mandela is elected president of South Africa—his reforms later earned him the Nobel Peace Prize.*

1994 Labour party leader John Smith dies

BRITISH LABOUR politician John Smith was born in 1938 and first entered parliament in 1970, serving under both Harold Wilson and James Callaghan. He was secretary of state for trade 1978–79, and from 1979 held various shadow cabinet posts including shadow chancellor 1987–92. Following Labour leader Neil Kinnock's humiliating defeat in the 1992 election—Labour's fourth consecutive defeat—and his subsequent resignation, John Smith was elected Labour leader in the same year. A well-respected politician and a powerful opposition leader, he left the country shocked by his sudden death from a heart attack in May 1994. Tony Blair was elected the new leader of the party in July 1994.

1994 Nelson Mandela becomes president of South Africa

A YEAR AFTER his release from prison Mandela was chosen as deputy president of the ANC (the president Oliver Tambo being ill) and he replaced Tambo as president in July 1991. His wife, Winnie, however, had not escaped controversy. In 1989 she was involved in the abduction of four youths, one of whom, Stompie Seipei, was later murdered. Winnie Mandela was convicted of kidnapping and assault and, in 1991 was given a six-year jail sentence with the right to appeal. In April 1992 she and Nelson separated after 33 years of marriage. In the same year she

resigned from her ANC leadership posts. In September 1992, Mandela and President de Klerk agreed to speed up the creation of an interim government under which reforms could take place, agreeing, in 1993, to the formation of a government of national unity after free, non-racial elections. Mandela and de Klerk were awarded the Nobel Peace Prize in 1993, for their efforts to end apartheid, and in April 1994 Mandela was elected president and introduced many new initiatives to improve standards for the black population. Winnie Mandela was given the post of deputy arts and science minister in Mandela's 1994 government but was expelled in 1995. She and Nelson were divorced in 1996.

1995 Rabin assassinated in Israel

HAVING SERVED as Israel's ambassador to the US, Yitzhak Rabin became minister of labor under Labour prime minister Golda Meir, and leader when she resigned in 1974. Rabin ordered the raid at Entebbe, Uganda, in 1976. He stepped down as leader (1977) when it was revealed he had held unlawful US bank accounts. Regaining leadership and becoming prime minister in 1992, he undertook successful negotiations

with the PLO (1993), signed a full peace treaty with King Hussein of Jordan (1994) and won the Nobel Peace Prize in 1994. The territorial concessions he had granted angered many Israelis and during a peace rally in 1995 he was assassinated by a Jewish extremist.

1997 Tony Blair becomes UK prime minister

TONY BLAIR entered parliament in 1983 and was given the shadow cabinet's energy portfolio in 1988, employment in 1991 and home affairs in 1992. Leadership victory after John Smith's death made him the party's youngest leader. By mid-1995 he had revamped the Labour party platform with commitments to free enterprise, anti-inflation policies, and a hard line on crime. Despite criticism from the left of the party he successfully won the voters' favor, heavily defeating the Conservatives in the 1995 council elections. Having led a highly successful "New Labour" campaign in the run-up to the 1997 general elections, he achieved a landslide victory on May 1st, ending 18 years of Conservative government for Britain.

Tony Blair with his wife Cherie addressing an ecstatic British crowd after the Labour Party defeated the Conservatives by a landslide in May 1997.

Business & Economics

I think that capitalism, wisely managed, can probably be made more efficient for attaining economic ends than any alternative system yet in sight, but that in itself is in many ways extremely objectionable.

John Maynard Keynes, 1926

1901 US goes on Gold Standard

THE GOLD STANDARD was first adopted by Great Britain in 1821. This meant that gold could be exchanged for equal weights of gold coinage, coins could be melted down and bullion could be exported or imported freely. The Gold Standard, in effect, operated from about 1870 to the outbreak of World War I. The US adoption of the Gold Standard added extra weight to its importance. Although by this time gold coins were no longer in general circulation, extensive use could be made of the gold-exchange standard, which finally collapsed in the Depression of the 1930s. By 1937 not a single country remained on the full gold standard.

1923 Hyperinflation in Germany

FOLLOWING THE FAILURE of the Allies to agree the level of reparations due from the defeated Germans after World War I, the German currency began a disastrous collapse from June 1923. The currency fell from 20 Marks to the pound to 20 trillion by November. A loaf of bread was valued at 200 billion Marks. The German situation was further complicated by the French and Belgian occupation of the Ruhr, its major source of coal. Trade unions demanded that the government seize all food and clothes in an attempt to ration them and ban the manufacture of all luxury goods. Only a loan from the USA in the following year to help pay for the reparations and stabilize the Mark managed to control inflation and effectively re-value the currency.

1929 Black Thursday – the Wall Street crash

FEAR, CONFUSION, AND PANIC triggered the frantic sale of 13 million shares on October 24th. Thousands of small investors lost everything. Many companies had been overvalued, buoyed by the easy profits to be made and general over-confidence from investors and speculators. Eleven of the latter took their own lives when their fortunes were wiped out in minutes. Brokers, desperate to offload over-valued shares, hunted for anyone who would buy. As the sheer volume of sales increased, the shares plummeted, reaching rock bottom before noon. Prices rallied after lunch but not before police riot squads had been called in to cope with the hysterical crowds in Wall Street. Governments throughout the world would have to cope with the horrors of economic depression over the next few years.

Overleaf: Lech Walesa, who played a significant part in the process of democratizing Poland (see page 71). Right: the Industrial Giant—Franklin D. Roosevelt's New Deal, part of a plan to lift the US from Depression.

1933 US New Deal unveiled to lift the country from Depression

FRANKLIN D. ROOSEVELT announced his New Deal of 13 major measures to beat the Depression in the US. In the three months after his swearing-in ceremony, the new president effectively took control over industry by regulating wages, working hours, and production. Some $3 billion were ploughed into public works to boost the economy, the Prohibition laws were repealed and money was found to bail out penniless farmers and mortgage holders. By the end of the first 100 days, just under 2 million new jobs had been created. $75 million was allocated to feeding and clothing the poor over the winter. With over 3.5 million American families on welfare, another $700 million was found to provide federal relief. Without doubt, this rapid and effective program was instrumental in ending the Depression.

A sign of the times after the Wall Street Crash, which destroyed the American dream of wealth and prosperity.

J. M. Keynes, who revolutionized theories of employment and economics, which had significant influence on the British government.

1936 Keynes writes "The General Theory of Employment, Interest, and Money"

THE BRITISH ECONOMIST and pioneer of the theory of full employment was greatly influenced by the cycles of unemployment he witnessed. Although his *General Theory* initiated a revolution in economic thought, he wrote two other major texts that support his reputation. Arguing that full employment was not an automatic condition, he strongly disagreed with successive governments' policies. Unemployment was curable, he suggested, if the government fine-tuned its monetary and fiscal policies to suit the circumstances. Keynes not only influenced the British government, but his theories were also incorporated into Roosevelt's New Deal. Keynes was also instrumental in setting up the International Monetary Fund and the International Bank for Reconstruction and Development. The 30-year boom after World War II has often been referred to as the "Age of Keynes."

1936–37 General Motors strike in Detroit

ALTHOUGH FORD ESTABLISHED the first car-production plants in the city, the emergence of mass-production techniques attracted many companies to Detroit. The car industry suffered greatly during the Depression, but began to recover quickly. The labor movement was far more active than before and numerous strikes at the huge General Motors plants in Flint resulted in the recognition of the United Automobile Workers of America. This industrial action was by far the most significant of all strikes in the century. Over the course of the dispute it affected thousands of car workers across America. During World War II, the city earned the name of "Arsenal of Democracy" for its production contributions to the armed forces.

1946 The Soviet Union's five-year plan

ON FEBRUARY 9, 1946 Stalin announced his fourth five-year plan since taking power. Previous plans had covered 1928–32, 1933–37, and the wartime 1938–42. By regulation, control, and planning Stalin used these plans to carry forward his own program of socialism. He collectivized

agriculture, forcing up the crop yield, developed industrialism, and made Russia a manufacturing state. He was keen to eradicate illiteracy and was a strong supporter of the sciences. Within the confines of the state apparatus, a wealthy and privileged new class emerged, bound to the state by virtue of their office and power. His plans were not always successful, but in many cases they proved to be the right policy for Russia.

1973 Arab–Israeli War triggers oil embargo

WHILE ISRAELIS CELEBRATED Yom Kippur, the Egyptians stormed across the Suez Canal and surged into the Sinai desert. The Arab States, responding to the US financial and political support of the Israelis, increased oil prices by 70 per cent and announced a rolling cut in oil production of 5 per cent per month. Western Europe would suffer too from the price rise and the production cut, leading to gasoline shortages and rationing. Hundreds of gas stations closed as refined petroleum

became ever more scarce. In the UK, the government imposed a road speed limit of 50 MPH. Idi Amin announced the "Save Britain" campaign as Arab oil producers doubled the price. By January 1974, the war was over and Britain had discovered oil in the North Sea.

1980 The birth of Solidarity

AFTER THREE MONTHS of strikes and demonstrations Polish workers, led by dockers and the strike leader Lech Walesa, wrung concessions from the hard-line Polish government. The agreement signed on August 30th allowed independent trade unions the right to strike, the release of political prisoners and the easing of government censorship. The defeat of the Polish government sent tremors throughout the Eastern Block. Arguably, the defeat of the Communist government in Poland was the first step in the collapse of the Russian domination of Eastern Europe. Lech Walesa would become the leader of his country and General Jagielski would face criminal charges before the end of the

decade. Although the Polish press condemned the strikers, they represented a democratizing movement that would sweep the Communist government from power.

1986 Oil prices plummet

AT THE END OF 1985 the Organization of Petroleum Exporting Countries (OPEC) announced that it was abandoning its official pricing structure based on restricting production. From now on, it would sell oil at whatever price it felt was right. In November 1985 oil prices were set at $27 a barrel, but by the end of January 1986 it had fallen to $15. Prices continued falling up to March, reaching a price under $10 a barrel. In August, the OPEC members announced that they would restore the old restrictions on production. As a consequence, the prices began to stabilize at $13–$14 per barrel. By the end of the year, despite arguments between the OPEC members, the price had fixed at $18 based on a 7 per cent cut in production.

Lech Walesa set Poland on the path to democracy after his support of workers on strike overturned the strict government policies about trade unions.

1987 Black Monday stock exchange crash

IN JUST ONE DAY £50 bn was wiped off the value of UK quoted companies. Panic gripped the stock market as it mirrored the Friday falls in Wall Street and Tokyo. Hong Kong closed their market for a week. Although this was the sharpest fall in stock market history (10 per cent), twice as bad as the worst day of the Great Crash of 1929, it did not rival the massive losses in America. The market had been expanding for five years with share values rising by almost 400 per cent. The root cause of the collapse has been much debated, but the probable reason was the huge US trade deficits and rising interest rates.

1989 High inflation world-wide

UK INFLATION RATES began to spiral upwards from 1989, reaching a peak in 1990 at 10 per cent. The main cause of the UK inflation problems during this period stemmed from the cuts in government spending, which led to tax cuts. As a result consumers had more to spend. Earlier inflation problems in the 1970s, which peaked at over 20 per cent, could be attributed to oil price increases. Rises in the 1980s have been linked to excessive pay claims. Although inflation rates were high around the world during this period, some countries still face the problems of spiralling costs. In 1992, Brazil could boast an annual inflation rate of over 1,200 per cent. This is known as hyperinflation.

1990 The Guinness scandal

HINTS OF A SCANDAL involving several major business personalities hit the headlines as early as 1987. During the Guinness bid to buy Distillers, individuals had invested in Guinness to inflate the value of the shares. Ernest Saunders, the Guinness chairman, was sacked, charged with perverting the course of justice, ordered to repay £5 million to Guinness and later jailed. Gerald Ronson, head of the Heron International Group, was charged with stealing £6 million from Guinness, and merchant banker Roger Selig of Morgan Grenfell charged with the theft of £2.95 million. The ripples of stock market manipulation and illegal share dealings led to a major Department of Trade & Industry investigation aimed at clamping down on insider dealing. The disgraced head of Guinness would, in time, have his own story to tell.

1990 Michael Milken pleads guilty to fraud

OPERATING FROM HIS X-shaped desk, Michael Milken and his associates pocketed hundreds of millions as the "Junk Bond" market became the main source of capital to fund takeovers in the US. Junk Bond companies are essentially good businesses that have fallen on hard times and cannot obtain loans from traditional sources. He managed to raise billions of dollars for deserving companies who were willing to pay investors high levels of interest. The Junk Bond market collapsed in 1989, but by then Milken was in trouble. He served two prison sentences for "insider dealings," after being found guilty of making profits from privileged information regarding the business plans of various companies. He also faced lawsuits amounting to $1.3 billion, which he managed to settle. After his experiences in business, Milken faced prostrate cancer. Once cured, he set up a number of charitable and educational trusts.

1991 World recession

FORMERLY A RECESSION was known as a depression, the effects were very similar. All the major economies in the world suffered a fall or slowing down of their Gross National Product, which measures the size of their economy. Countries experienced increasing unemployment and low investment. Analysts believe that this trend is just a part of the normal cycle of the world economy. During this period a number of developing countries, in particular, suffered from a lack of support from the developed world. Notable UK business casualties during the recession included Polly Peck, Coloroll, and the Canary Wharf development project. In 1992 alone, business failures totalled 62,000.

1996 Walt Disney Company acquires Capital Cities

IN WHAT WAS THEN the second biggest merger in history, Walt Disney paid $19 billion for Capital Cities/ABC Inc. Although there were many complications regarding the sole ownership of television stations in California, the merger went ahead as it did not violate American antitrust laws. At the time, only the Nabisco merger with Kohlberg Kravis Roberts & Co., valued at $25 billion, eclipsed the Walt Disney deal. In many respects, the Walt Disney merger was seen as the first of

several major takeovers and mergers in the US communications business. In 1997, Bell Atlantic Corp. combined with Nynex Corp for $25.6 billion and later the same year WorldCom Inc. beat a $24 billion offer from British Telecom to buy MCI Communications Inc. for a massive $37 billion—the biggest takeover to date.

Opposite: *Black Monday in Britain—the stock market crashed, taking £50 billion with it, in October 1987.*
Left: *Michael Milken is sworn in on Capital Hill as his "insider dealings" come under investigation.*

Arts, Entertainment & Culture

4

In the future everyone will be famous for fifteen minutes.

Andy Warhol, 1960s

1900 Chekhov's play "Uncle Vanya"

Overleaf: Snow White— "Disney's folly" that became his greatest break- through (see page 85). Below: Sigmund Freud, the founder of psychoanalysis. Right: a view of Paris at the time of the Universal Exhibition.

ANTON CHEKHOV, a Russian dramatist and storyteller, developed a new kind of theater. All the major events take place off-stage and the audience's attention is focused on the inner life of the characters. Dramatic events are replaced by close emotional observation, and each gesture of the character is full of intimacy, pessimism, and tension. In *Uncle Vanya*, he uses these techniques brilliantly. Set on an estate in nineteenth-century Russia, the four-act play explores the interaction of characters with conflicting interests and desires. Although it focuses on the emotional upheaval of Vanya, Sonya, and Serebryakov, the play finishes in a kind of deadly stasis.

1900 German philosopher Nietzsche dies

FRIEDRICH NIETZSCHE lived as an ascetic, struggling through bad health and mental illness to continue his work as a philosopher. He was passionate about promoting independence of the mind: he wanted to stimulate his readers to think for themselves; to stir their minds into activity and productivity; to encourage them to take flight with ideas. He discussed the value of truth in *Beyond Good and Evil*, the nature of religion and morality in *The Anti-Christ*. They are difficult texts compressing "in ten sentences what everyone else says in a book—what everyone else *does not* say in a book." He died in 1900 in his family's care, following a mental and physical collapse.

1900 Sigmund Freud writes "The Interpretation of Dreams"

SIGMUND FREUD invented a new way of looking at ourselves, and it was a vision that was to have a profound impact in the twentieth century. The founder of psychoanalysis, Freud mined deep into the unconscious mind in an attempt to find the causes of neurosis and anxiety. His study *The Interpretation of Dreams* (1900) deals with the puzzling problems of dreams and is the key text to his theories. Freud studied all the previous literature on the subject and then presented his views on the function of dreams and their sources. He also described a method of interpreting them. He stated that dreams can reveal things which we have hidden— "repressed" from ourselves in our conscious mind. Freud believed that the stimulus for a dream is always an unconscious wish that had its origin in childhood. He threw a light on the inner nature of a child's mind that startled and repelled his contemporaries. He main- tained that the hidden layers in a child's mind were full of sexual and hostile attitudes to its parents, the Oedipus complex being an example. Freud considered dreams to be "the royal road to the unconscious" and the interpretation of dreams is still an important method used by today's psychoanalysts in the treatment of patients.

1901 World Exhibition opens in Paris

THE 1889 EXHIBITION unveiled the Eiffel Tower, which had been described as a "ridiculous tower dominating Paris like a gigantic, black chimney." The 1901 exhibition was more whimsical and retrospective in tone. At the front gate stood a statue of La Parisienne wearing a tight skirt and a charming hat of the latest style, symbolizing Paris as the fashion capital. Also featured were "palaces" from every major country, which were dotted along the Rue des Nations and the Quai d'Orsay. The Electrical Illuminations and the Hall of Illusions were the most popular attractions of the year. The French hoped to restore the international image of their Empire in the Exhibition.

1904 Premiere of Puccini's opera "Madam Butterfly"

LTALIAN COMPOSER GIACOMO PUCCINI was gifted with a vivid sense of the stage and a talent for beautiful harmonies and fine orchestration. It made him popular in the theater, where his music seemed as brightly colored and flowing as the drama taking place before the audience's eyes. In the summer of 1900, Puccini saw David Belasco's one-act play, *Madam Butterfly*. He was immediately drawn to the character of the little geisha and her tale of love and abandonment. He built an opera around it, using his melodic gifts to heighten the passion, tenderness, and despair. *Madam Butterfly* premiered at La Scala in February 1904, and was revised in May with astounding success.

1902 Tiffany designs the Lotus Lamp

ART NOUVEAU was the western world's major decorative style of the early twentieth century. The emphasis was on curved patterns, based on natural forms, but its practitioners were unconcerned with creating the illusion of reality. In the United States Louis Comfort Tiffany combined metal with opalescent colors of glass to make beautiful jewelry, windows, bowls and, in particular, the Lotus Lamp of 1902. Tiffany was born in New York, the son of a jeweler, but, instead of entering the family business, he established a glass-making plant. He invented a type of glass which made him famous; it was glowing and iridescent. He called it Favrile, but it is known best by his name, Tiffany.

1904 Opening of J. M. Barrie's play "Peter Pan"

PETER PAN was a boy who never grew up; the leader of the Lost Boys who lived in Never Never Land somewhere in the starry skies. He landed on the London stage in 1904. J. M. Barrie based his play on an earlier, less successful one, *The Little White Bird*, but the preparations for *Peter Pan* were shrouded in secrecy. The actress playing Wendy was alarmed to receive a notice saying "Flying, 10:30 A.M.," along with a request for her to insure her life. The performance would involve the actors sweeping upwards on specially designed wires as they followed Peter beyond the clouds. It was a hit then and it is still a Christmas pantomime favorite.

Left: *the Eiffel Tower was the highlight of the 1889 Paris Exhibition.* Above: *Puccini drew his inspiration for* Madam Butterfly *from the play by David Belasco.*

1907 Braque and Picasso and the birth of Cubism

CUBISM LITERALLY changed the perspective of art. Until 1907, artists had experimented with color, depth, and brush technique, but had represented objects and nature in a fairly straightforward way. Picasso and Braque created a new way of seeing the world. Strange angles, distorted surfaces, and bizzare geometrical planes replaced portraiture and still lifes. Objects were no longer in scale and shapes were crammed on to the canvases seemingly haphazardly. Most startling of all was what happened to people's faces on a Cubist canvas. The major work in the discovery of the Cubist principles was Picasso's savage *Les demoiselles d'Avignon*. Heads, noses, and eyes are seen simultaneously in profile and full face. It is as if the artist were looking at all possible angles at once. Even the air behind them was woven with criss-crossing lines. Braque made jagged shapes of everyday things, like guitars and houses. He shaded them with herringbone lines and used many sources of light. It was his attempt to "materialize the new space," and it was disorientating and explosive. Cubism abandoned all the old ideas about art. The pictures of tables and chairs, newspapers, bottles, and people were selected for their ordinarness, but were made extraordinary by the creative vision focused upon them. The paintings were difficult to understand, which was their challenge.

1907 Victoria and Albert Museum opens in London

THE VICTORIA and Albert Museum houses a rich collection of decorative and applied arts, spanning nearly every period and nation. It was founded in 1852 as the Museum of Manufacture with the mission of "raising standards and improving public taste in contemporary industrial design." On display were objects from the Great Exhibition of 1851. It moved to South Kensington, to became part of the Science Museum, and then became the Victoria and Albert Museum in 1899 when Queen Victoria laid the cornerstone of the new building, designed by Sir Aston Webb. It took some years to complete and was finally opened by King Edward VII in 1907.

1913 Premiere of Stravinsky's "The Rite of Spring"

IGOR STRAVINSKY is one of the colossal figures of twentieth-century music. *The Rite of Spring* was at first a *succès de scandale*, causing a violent outcry when it was premiered in Paris on May 28, 1913. The audience laughed and jeered, at the music and at Nijinsky's choreography for the ballet. But its new treatment of harmony, orchestration, and structure eventually made it one of the most influential works of the century. Its idiosyncratic rhythms, hard-edged and fast-pulsed, were its most outstanding feature, overturning the decorous romanticism of previous years. Stravinsky was born in Russia in 1882, the son of a prominent opera singer. As a student at the University of St Petersburg

Left: *Picasso, the pioneer of the Cubist style, with examples of his work.* Right: *The Adolescents from Stravinsky's* The Rite of Spring, *which paved the way for new forms and styles of music.*

This is the great picture upon which the famous comedian has worked a whole year.

6 reels of Joy.

Charles Chaplin

IN

"THE KID"

Written and directed by Charles Chaplin

he learnt orchestration from the great composer Rimsky-Korsakov, and on graduating he decided to pursue composition as his life's work. In 1909 he met Sergei Diaghilev, the ballet impresario, and was commissioned to write his first ballet score, *The Firebird*. This piece of music had much of the sparky originality and rhythmic drive that would characterize all of Stravinsky's work.

It was the *The Rite of Spring*, with its "scenes of pagan Russia," that made his name. It began with a cluster of pan pipes and revolutionized the world of music with its fierce, primal rhythms and its beautifully inventive harmonies.

1915 Charlie Chaplin stars in "The Tramp"

A PRICKLY MUSTACHE, a bowler hat, and a curious waddling walk made up Charlie Chaplin's character in *The Tramp*. Chaplin became the most popular actor in the days of silent cinema. He fought tyranny and injustice with a melancholy humor and a punchy aggressiveness, and as the figure of the little tramp he was universally loved. The 1915 film of *The Tramp* was a milestone for Chaplin. It was here that he was first seen in the classic fadeout, in which the scruffy, resilient figure scuttles off into the distance. The Tramp may be lost and alone, but he's on the road to a new adventure, heading hopefully towards his future ....

1915 Rupert Brooke – romantic war hero

FOLLOWING HIS untimely death in 1915, Rupert Brooke became the poet hero of World War I. He was beautiful, young, tall, and blond—a "golden boy." He was a fellow at Cambridge University, and traveled in the United States and the South Pacific. When war broke out he immediately enlisted as an officer. He died on a hospital ship, before he could witness the bloodiness of the fighting. Brooke became a symbol of all the gifted youth killed in the conflict. He is best remembered for his patriotic poems, such as "The Soldier" and "Granchester," where his romantic view of the war was reassuring to those not fighting at the front.

1920 Mary Pickford marries Douglas Fairbanks Junior

MARY PICKFORD was "America's Sweetheart" with her head of golden curls and her dimpled beauty. She was the Silver Screen's biggest star and one of its highest-paid actors. She had control over scripts, co-stars and directors and her silent films were immensely profitable. In 1920, "Little Mary" married the swashbuckling hero Douglas Fairbanks Junior. His films were all about movement; he slid down the sails of Spanish galleons, dived off ocean liners and the camera loved him. The ceremony was a lavish affair, befitting the King and Queen of Hollywood, and they moved into "Pickfair," a combination of their last names and a fairy-tale castle of a home.

Charlie Chaplin was the first great movie star, and became universally loved through the characters he played.

Above: *Broadcasting House, the home of the BBC in its early days.*
Right: *poster for the British Empire Exhibition.*
Opposite: *advertisement for the lavish film production of E. M. Forster's* A Passage to India.

1922 BBC formed

AMERICAN RADIO was commercial: advertisers paid the stations for air space, and all the listeners had to do was buy a wireless and tune in. Soon the airwaves were crammed with competing stations, fighting for a share of an audience of 13 million. British broadcasters were not impressed with the American system and formed a consortium, the British Broadcasting Corporation. Advertising was banned and the company was to be financed by an annual licence fee, paid for by the listener. It went on air in 1922 as a "public service." Because it had a monopoly over the airwaves, its attitude to programing was very different from the American system. It was to be a cultural oasis, representing "the best of British" without any of the tacky vulgarisms so popular in the United States. Sports, popular music, comedy, vaudeville, and entertainment were all broadcast, but the manner in which they were presented, like the voices of the announcers, was upper middle class. The first newscasters had to wear dinner jackets when addressing the nation so that they would not slip into casual tones of voice when reporting on important matters. In the early years the BBC did not have regional diversity, but it provided entertainment and education at a very low cost.

1922 James Joyce's "Ulysses" published

ONE OF THE MOST important novels of the twentieth century was published in a small bookshop in Paris in 1922. James Joyce's *Ulysses* told the events of a single day in Dublin. Using a technique that would become known as "stream of consciousness," Joyce positioned the reader inside the minds of the characters, carried along by the flow of their thoughts. The book is rich with puns and word play, symbolism and history. It is also sexually frank and was banned under obscenity laws in America until 1933. The last section of the novel is a long, unpunctuated monologue by Molly Bloom. It ends with the simplest of words: "Yes."

1924 British Empire Exhibition

THE BRITISH EMPIRE Exhibition of 1924 was full of pomp and circumstance. It was set up to show the wealth and resources of the British Commonwealth and it reproduced the whole of the Empire in miniature. The Taj Mahal was created in concrete and other buildings were constructed in wood and mud. The opening ceremony took place in the newly built Wembley Stadium, the largest sports arena in the world. A subterranean reproduction of Tutankhamen's tomb was very popular with the vast crowds who visited. Also, thousands of tons of real diamond-bearing soil had been brought over from South Africa to demonstrate the process by which diamonds were mined, cut, and polished.

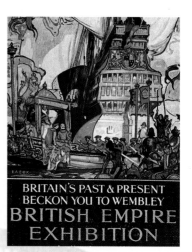

1924 George Gershwin writes "Rhapsody in Blue" and "Lady Be Good"

IN THE TWENTIES the "Jazz Age" was swinging and George Gershwin was right at its center. He composed vibrant, witty songs that had syncopated rhythms and expressive harmonies. The tunes seemed to sparkle and they had "that high attribute of making people fall in love with them." In 1924, Gershwin bridged the gap between classical and popular music with "Rhapsody in Blue," which captured the "tempo of modern living with its speed and chaos and vitality" but was performed as a serious piece of music. In the same year he wrote "Lady Be Good," to which witty lyrics, written by his brother Ira, were set. It marked the advent of *the* Gershwin musical.

1924 E. M. Forster's "A Passage to India" published

E. M. FORSTER came from a wealthy and privileged background; and he went on to study classics and history at Cambridge. He also visited India, which became the setting for his most famous novel, *A Passage to India.*

The playwright George Bernard Shaw, who was well-known for his strong social and moral comments.

Published in 1924, the book is a complex study of human misunder- .
standings in colonial India. Characters find themselves ranged against
each other because of race, religion or personality. The situation is
worsened when Dr. Aziz, a young Indian surgeon, is falsely accused of an
attack on a woman in the Malabar Caves. The incident reveals hidden
hate and distrust. It is a powerful illustration of Forster's theme—the
difficulty of "connection" between people in circumstances of restraint.

1925 Kafka's "The Trial" published

FRANZ KAFKA was a Czech author who died of consumption in 1924.
He published little in his lifetime and had asked for his unpublished
work to be burnt after his death. But his friend Max Brod rescued
and printed his strange and mystifying texts. *The Trial*, Kafka's story
of a man arrested for an unspecified crime, was published in 1925,
earning the author a unique reputation in modern European
literature. His style is crystalline and clear, but the subjects of his
novels are claustrophobic. In all of them a character is involved in a
nightmare situation over which he has no control, but which he must
try to understand.

1925 George Bernard Shaw awarded Nobel Prize for Literature

GEORGE BERNARD SHAW became one of the greatest socialist
thinkers of his day. Although an outstanding speaker and critic, he is
best known for his drama. He used his brilliant, witty plays to show
his concern with social and moral issues, such as the English class
system, prostitution, and slum landlording. He reluctantly accepted
the Nobel Prize in 1925 for *Saint Joan*, a work about Joan of Arc.
It was his greatest and most successful play, making enough money
at the box office for him to decline the prize money, saying it was
"a lifebelt thrown to a swimmer who had already reached the shore
in safety."

1925 Great Paris Exhibition

ART DECO WAS "DISCOVERED" at the huge Paris Exposition
des Arts Décoratifs in 1925. For a while after the war, style and
identity in the artistic world had been hazy, skittering towards
overlavishness or stripping down to the purely functional. Suddenly
there was a new vitality. Simple geometric shapes and sweeping
curves began to be featured on clocks and cigarette lighters, on
coffee tables and cocktail cabinets. Colors were strong,
blazing oranges and golds, green against silver. Chrome tubing
emphasized outlines and glassware was elegant and bright.
Decorative crafts caught the spirit of the Jazz Age,
and millions of visitors came to admire the display of
architecture, interior design, and high fashion.

cartoon would have synchronized sound, Mickey would talk, and he would be the very first cartoon character to do so. Disney came up with the idea of *Steamboat Willie*. The opening featured Mickey whistling as he recklessly steered across the water. The tune "Turkey In The Straw" became a concert, using the livestock cargo as musical instruments. It worked beautifully; critics said: "Clever is a mild word to use. It is a wow." Disney capitalized on the success of Mickey Mouse, and within months hundreds of manufacturers were producing huge volumes of licensed Mickey merchandise. Things would only get bigger.

1926 Rudolf Valentino dies

THE DEATH OF RUDOLF VALENTINO—the "Great Lover"—caused an unprecedented outpouring of public grief. Thousands wept and mourned; heaving crowds threatened to overwhelm his coffin as he was lying in state. The great male screen idol of his time, Valentino was sleek, graceful, and alluringly exotic. With his slicked-back hair and his flashing smile, he made villainy attractive. He had worked as a gardener in Central Park until he became a dancer in New York nightclubs. He played small parts in films but it wasn't until *Four Horsemen of the Apocalypse* that he became a star. His major role was in *The Sheikh*. As prince of the desert, his searing eyes cast such spells of seduction that women fainted in the cinema aisles.

Left: *Rudolph Valentino playing the Sheikh in the film of the same name— the role that earned him world-wide adulation.* Below: Winnie the Pooh *is still one of the most popular children's books.*

1926 Winnie the Pooh is born

WINNIE THE POOH, the plumpish, honey-loving bear, was born in 1926. He was created by A. A. Milne for his son Christopher Robin. The Milne family had lived an the edge of Ashdown Forest in Sussex, which became the setting for the stories about Pooh and his friends. The bear, Piglet, and Eeyore were based on toys that the real Christopher had in his nursery. Rabbit and Owl were entirely imaginary, Kanga, Roo, and Tigger were later presents from Christopher's parents: "carefully chosen, not just for the delight that they might give to their new owner, but also for their literary possibilities." The books are full of warmth and charm.

Ⓜ ## 1926 Mickey Mouse is born in Disney's first film with sound

ONE OF THE WORLD'S biggest global media corporations was built with the help of a mouse. In 1926 things were shaky for Walt Disney, but they were about to change. He was traveling by train from New York to Hollywood, doodling on a drawing pad to pass the time. A shape began to appear on the page in front of him: "out of trouble and confusion stood a mocking, merry, little figure; it grew and grew. And finally it arrived—a mouse. A romping, rollicking, little mouse." He was named Mickey. The trouble was that while Mickey was spirited and funny, there was nothing particularly original about him. Disney decided that his

1926 Yehudi Menuhin begins his career

AT THE AGE of 10, violinist Yehudi Menuhin was already causing a sensation. His effortless performance of *Symphonie Espagnole* was a fantastic technical feat. He was only a young boy, in short pants, but he had a mature vision of music, which gave depth and understanding to his fresh, spontaneous style. He did not abandon his gift as he grew older. During World War II he gave over 500 concerts for American and Allied troops in the theaters of war. Later he conducted many leading symphony orchestras, and established a school for musically talented children in London. Nobody could forget the purity of his style as a violinist.

Below: the brainchild of Belgian artist Georges Remi, Tintin has charmed cartoon fans since his creation in 1929.

Right: book burning in the Opera Square in Berlin.

1929 Tintin is born

TINTIN IS THE BLOND-quiffed hero of a series of comic strips first printed in a Belgian newspaper in 1929. He was created by the Belgian author and artist Georges Remi, who reversed his initials to make up the pseudonym Hergé (R. G.). Tintin is a teenage reporter-cum-amateur detective, cum-explorer, who gets involved in all kinds of thrilling adventures. The books are witty, the dialogue fresh and salty, and the characters much loved. Tintin always has with him his trusty companion, Snowy the dog. Also hanging around are the daffy Thompson Twins, the absent-minded Professor Calculus and the bulky, sozzled figure of Captain Haddock, who has a fine line in nautical swearing, for example "blistering barnacles."

Ⓜ 1933 Nazis burn books

A HUGE BONFIRE of books took place in the square in front of Berlin University on May 10, 1933. Another fire burnt in Munich. Tossed into the flames were books which were considered "un-German" by the ruling Nazi Party. Among them were the works of Thomas and Heinrich Mann, Helen Keller, Jack London, Upton Sinclair, and Erich Maria Remarque who wrote the anti-war classic *All Quiet on the Western Front*. The assembled crowd was told by the Nazi propaganda minister Joseph Goebbels: "The soul of the German people can again express itself. These flames not only illuminate the final end of the old era; they also light up the new." It was a chilling speech. Any books which represented World WarI in an unfavorable light were removed from public libraries and replaced by Hitler's *Mein Kampf* and other works by leading Nazis. It was a horrifically symbolic portent of what was to come. Literature and the arts were already being censored and destroyed in the name of racial purity. German culture was being put into a Nazi straitjacket. Hitler wanted to "cleanse" Germany of its "decadent" art. The Third Reich would not stop at print and page.

1938 Bette Davis wins Academy Award for "Jezebel"

BETTE DAVIS was given *Jezebel* as a consolation prize for not getting the role of Scarlett O'Hara in *Gone with the Wind*. She plays Julie, a perverse Southern belle, who ruins her own chances in love, as well as shaking up America's Old South. It is the Lupas Ball in New Orleans in 1852, and Julie turns up in a scarlet dress, while all the other unmarried women are dressed in pristine white. As she walks across the dance floor, couples shrink away from her. Her defiance threatens all the social conventions. The film is shot in black and white but the dress still seems fiery red, and Davis won an academy award for her colorful performance.

1938 Release of "Snow White"

SNOW WHITE was called "Walt Disney's folly." He was determined to make the first feature-length cartoon, but nobody thought it would work. Disney, however, managed to entrance his animators with his vision of the Grimms' fairy tale, and before long thousands of sketches and watercolors were being produced to make the creation that is so famous now. Disney wanted the characters to be individual, and Snow White to move as a realistic human figure. Everything was discussed in the minutest detail. The film was a masterpiece of imagination and innovation, scary and magical. It made Disney "a hatful of money" and charmed cinema audiences when it was released in 1938.

1939 "Gone with the Wind" released

SCARLETT O'HARA was the role that every actress wanted. *Gone with the Wind*'s producer David O. Selznick used it to launch a publicity blitz of a kind never witnessed before. He created the illusion that any woman in America could win the part of the wilful heroine of Margaret Mitchell's best-selling Civil War novel. He organized talent contests and screen tests throughout the land, mostly to create public interest in his project, with the part always likely to go to one of Hollywood's established stars. After two years of searching, the part finally went to little-known English actress Vivien Leigh. She turned out to be an inspired choice—playing the impetuous, resilient, selfish Scarlett beautifully. The whole production was star-studded, with Clark Gable as the handsome, gambling Rhett Butler, Leslie Howard as Ashley "darling", and Olivia De Havilland as Melanie. The set pieces were theatrical and tremendous: the burning of Atlanta, the carnage at the railway station, full of smoke, fire, and wounded bodies. The film is nearly four hours long, and took a year of filming, editing, and scoring until it reached movie screens in 1939. It had cost almost $4 million, and audiences flocked to it. It won nine Oscars and remains one of the biggest cinema hits of all time.

1941 Virginia Woolf commits suicide

ON THE DAY of her death in 1941, Virginia Woolf dressed herself in a bulky fur coat. She walked along by the Ouse River, put a large stone in her pocket and stepped into the water. It was the end of a life's work of sensitive, beautifully crafted novels and a struggle with mental illness. Her writing is based on the world of women, and she created a poetic language to explore their lives. Her non-fiction—*A Room of One's Own* and *Three Guineas*—are powerful comments on women's need for financial independence. Woolf was an important figure in the Bloomsbury Group. With her husband Leonard they founded the Hogarth Press, which published new and innovative fiction. She was in her late fifties when she died.

Left: *poster for the nine-Oscar-winning film* Gone with the Wind. Above: Snow White, *the pioneering feature-length cartoon that started Disney on the road to movie success.*

Right: *Creator of the "New Look," Christian Dior, at his first show in the Savoy Hotel, London.* Opposite: *poster for the classic Technicolor film* Singin' in the Rain, *which has become famous for its cheerful music and unique choreography.*

1943 Betty Grable's legs are insured for $1 million; she stars in "Coney Island"

ONE OF THE MOST enduring images of Betty Grable is as the "forces' favorite," looking back over her shoulder in a white swimming costume, and displaying her "million dollar legs," the amount that Lloyds of London insured them for. She was trained at Hollywood Professional School from the age of 12, and was in chorus lines before she was 14. She got her break at Fox, where she starred in 18 musicals, high on gloss and Technicolor. *Coney Island* is typical of them; 95 minutes of Betty singing and dancing, with Coney Island as a background and the story of two guys after the same girl to link the routines.

1944 Glenn Miller disappears on flight to France

MYSTERY SURROUNDS Glenn Miller's death. Colonel Miller and two companions were passengers on a routine flight to France in 1944. While in the air the plane vanished, no distress call was made and no wreckage sighted. He was declared missing, but his music lives on. Miller dedicated himself to writing and arranging his own compositions. The sweet swing melodies of "Little Brown Jug" and "Moonlight Serenade" have a distinctive reed section, with the sound of the clarinet sweeping out over four saxophones. He signed up for active service in the US but his war work became his army band playing in the war zones of the Pacific and Europe as a morale booster for the troops.

1950 Christian Dior gives first show at the Savoy

THE "NEW LOOK" caused a sensation. In the war years women had been dressing in utility clothing, short, drab, and uncluttered in style. Material was rationed and suits and frocks were asexual. And then Dior appeared. He said: "I designed clothes for flower-like women, with rounded shoulders, full feminine

busts and hand-span waists." His dresses used yards of fabric, with hems rustling near the floor. The look was opulent and uncomfortable to wear, but a sunburst after years of practicality. Women were enraptured and rushed to buy them. In England, senior politicians were outraged at the thwarting of fabric restrictions, but soon Princess Margaret was wearing the "New Look" everywhere.

1951 Festival of Britain

IN THE POST-WAR YEARS Britain was in trouble, almost bankrupt and faced with shortages and continued rationing. It was a gloomy and austere time, but a ray of hope shone out in the Festival of Britain in 1951. It was a nation-wide celebration of the country's achievements and potential. In London the main exhibition took place in the blitzed-out spaces between Waterloo and Westminster Bridges. The Festival Hall was the first building to be completed, and the areas surrounding it were transformed with temporary pavilions, restaurants, and a Dome of Discovery. It was cheerful by day, but by night it became "a floodlit dream world breathing music."

1952 Gene Kelly's "Singing in the Rain"

SINGING IN THE RAIN has got everything—color, pace, elegance, and above all Gene Kelly's dancing. It is set in the Roaring Twenties, when sound was introduced to movies. The songs are great, the vibrant "Gotta Dance," or the witty "Moses Supposes;" but it is the choreography that captivates, with Gene Kelly swinging through rain-drenched streets, spinning around lamp-posts and jumping for love. In the "Broadway Ballet," co-star Cyd Charisse's "crazy veil," a 25-ft, white, silk scarf streamed about her, kept airborne by three airplane motors whirring in the wings. The scene took a month to rehearse and two weeks to shoot, and cost one-fifth of the film's overall budget.

The 1950s saw the advent of rock'n'roll, a trend started by American musician Bill Haley with songs such as "Rock Around the Clock."

1954 Bill Haley introduces rock'n'roll

BILL HALEY was an unlikely rock'n'roller, with his kiss-curled hair and staid look. But he changed pop music for ever in 1954 with "Rock Around the Clock." It was released as a "novelty foxtrot," but its fast pulse and snapping beat had teenagers jiving in the aisles, and ripping out cinema seats when it featured in the film *The Blackboard Jungle*. The music fizzed with energy; a boogied-up rhythm and blues slapped out by The Comets, with Bill Haley's dance-call vocals over the top. They had a quick succession of hits, but Elvis soon became King, and the Comets were seen as old pretenders to his rock'n'roll throne.

1955 Disneyland opens in Anaheim, California

DISNEYLAND was designed as a place "where the parents and the children could have fun together." A 160-acre site was bought in Anaheim, Orange County, for the ambitious project. The park had mechanically operated figures, fairground rides, waterways, and themed sections: Fantasy Land, Frontier Land, and Adventure Land. Disney was warned that it would be "a spectacular failure." And the opening day almost was. Food and drink ran out, rides broke down, and women's stiletto heels sank into the melting asphalt. But things improved rapidly–just seven weeks after opening, Disneyland welcomed its millionth customer, and within a year over five million people had visited the magical kingdom.

1956 Grace Kelly marries Prince Rainier III of Monaco

THE MARRIAGE of an American movie queen to Europe's sole absolute monarch was the media sensation of the 1950s. Grace Kelly was blonde, cool, and sophisticated. She came from a wealthy family, went to good schools, and was determined to prove that she could work. She modeled and did some work in commercials; and acted in a few Broadway plays before Hollywood beckoned. Her icy regality was spotted by Alfred Hitchcock who cast her with exquisite taste in *Dial M for Murder*, and opposite James Stewart in *Rear Window*. While working on her

third Hitchcock film, *To Catch a Thief*, she met Prince Rainier III, the ruler of the small principality of Monaco. A year later, in 1956, she married the Prince in spectacular ceremony and left Tinsel Town for a royal palace.

1957 Boris Pasternak publishes "Doctor Zhivago"

DOCTOR ZHIVAGO is a novel on an epic scale. It sweeps across three decades of Russian history, including the revolutions of 1905 and 1917, and their violent aftermath. But it is not all blood and guts; threaded through the narrative is a poetic beauty. Pasternak's descriptions of nature and human love, his religious imagery and philosophical reflections celebrate the human spirit and the value of compassion. It was hailed by western writers as a work of genius and awarded the Nobel Prize for Literature. Pasternak was overjoyed. Unfortunately, in Pasternak's homeland, *Doctor Zhivago* was not the unmitigated success it had been in the West. The author was labelled a "traitor" by the Soviet Writers' Union on account of his hero's thoughts of disillusionment. Within a week of winning the prize, he had been expelled from the Union; as a result, he felt he could not accept the honor.

1958 Elvis Presley joins US army after completing "King Creole"

ELVIS PRESLEY brought sex to rock'n'roll. He was young and handsome and had a voice that melted together blues, country, and gospel in a dark swirl. In 1958 he rocked the USA. His suggestive hips were banned from the television screens, and his look–black, quiffed hair and heavy-lidded eyes–turned him into a pop icon. Elvis was born in Tupelo, Mississippi; his first recordings, two teenage ballads, were a birthday present for his beloved mother, Gladys. He cut a few singles for Sun Records and then moved to the media giant RCA Victor for big money just 16 months after his debut release. His records sold in huge quantities and, guided by the infamous Tom Parker, he registered 14 chart hits by the 1960s. His popularity was not confined to America. On January 24, 1958 "Jailhouse Rock" entered the UK charts at Number One. When he was called up to join the US Army, his posting was deferred so he could finish making the film *King Creole*. After a two-year stint in the army, Colonel Parker decided to transform Elvis into an all-round family entertainer and the rock'n'roller who had so shocked America became an establishment figure.

*Elvis Presley took up
the mantle of the
King of rock'n'roll,
becoming the symbol
of youth and musical
rebellion for many
generations to come.*

role of Porgy, Dorothy Dandridge as Bess and Sammy Davis as Sportin' Life. Poitier initially accepted and then backed out because of feelings within the black community that the story was racist, but he was persuaded to do it. The score won an Oscar in 1959.

1959 Marilyn Monroe stars in "Some Like It Hot"

IN THE SMASH HIT and enduring classic comedy *Some Like It Hot* Marilyn Monroe was perfect as Sugar Kane, the breathy, dizzy blonde who likes saxophone players and men with glasses. However, it was during this period that stardom was beginning to take its toll and affecting her work. She was often late, and couldn't remember her lines. Director Billy Wilder took to writing her words on the furniture in the hope that this would get her through the scenes. But magic happened in the cutting room: Marilyn's waywardness transformed into fine comic timing and her luminous beauty glowed from the screen. Wilder said after the difficult shoot: "You have to be orderly to shoot disorder; this was the best disorder we ever had."

1960 Death of Albert Camus

ALBERT CAMUS was born in North Africa in 1913. Before becoming a writer he had many jobs, including goalkeeper for the Algiers football team. He abandoned the pitch for the typewriter and became a journalist in France. He was involved in the Resistance movement, editing a clandestine newspaper called *Combat*. His novels, full of images of the desert, sky, light, and the sea, were an attempt to understand happiness and responsibility in an "absurd world." *The Stranger*, a book about truth and murder, focused attention on his work. Camus was awarded the Nobel Prize for Literature in 1957. Tragically he died in a road accident in 1960.

The Oscar-winning Porgy and Bess *was a love-story set in a black tenement row. The film incited strong reactions, but was an enormous success.*

1959 George Gershwin's "Porgy and Bess" wins an Oscar

PORGY AND BESS was written as an opera in 1934. Based on a novel by Du Bose Heyward, it was a passionate tale of love and revenge in Catfish Row, a black tenement. Gershwin wrote some wonderful, jazzy, and soulful songs for it, including "Summertime," "It Ain't Necessarily So" and "I Got Plenty of Nothing." It was made into a film at Goldwyn studios with Sidney Poitier playing the

1961 Nureyev defects to the West

RUDOLF NUREYEV was a Russian ballet dancer with extraordinary technique and a compelling stage presence, who magnetized audiences with his passion. He trained in Leningrad and was then accepted as a soloist at the Kirov Ballet Company. He was billed as their principal dancer on its European tour in 1961, but he was apolitical, non-conformist, and professionally ambitious. In Paris, he gave a superb performance of *Sleeping Beauty*, and then at the airport refused to depart with the rest of the Kirov Company, seeking asylum in France. He danced with several companies until, in 1962, he became "permanent guest artist" at the Royal Ballet with Margot Fonteyn as his partner.

1962 Publication of Burgess's "A Clockwork Orange"

IN ANTHONY BURGESS'S *A Clockwork Orange*, gangs of disaffected youths roam the streets of a shabby town, causing mayhem. Old people are beaten and young girls raped. It is a chilling and bleak novel, told through the voice of Alex, one of the young criminals. He is morally vicious but mentally alert and he chooses evil as a reaction against the dulled society he lives in. The soundtrack for Alex's life is Beethoven's music and his violence is expressed in the "droog" argot, a kind of gang slang. A complex, imaginative language dominates the texture of the book. Later Stanley Kubrick's film version proved so controversial that Kubrick himself prohibited its public release.

1964 Jean-Paul Sartre declines the Nobel Prize for Literature

EXISTENTIALISM swept through Europe in the wake of World War II, and Jean-Paul Sartre was its intellectual leader. He taught philosophy until he was drafted at the start of the war. Captured by the Germans, he managed to escape and became a leader in the Resistance movement. After the war he devoted himself to writing, expounding in particular the existentialist philosophy. Sartre maintained that life had no purpose or meaning, beyond the goals that each person set for himself. In 1964 he refused the Nobel Prize for Literature, saying that it was unfair to readers to add the weight of such extraneous influences to the power of the writer's words.

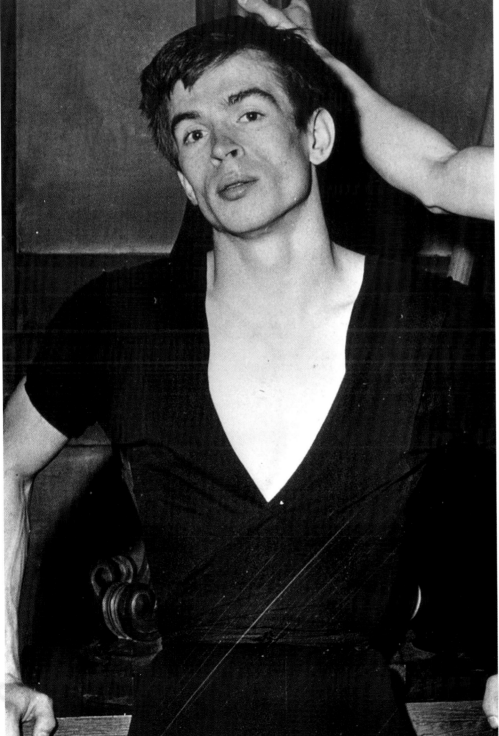

After touring with the Kirov Ballet Company, the world-famous dancer Nuryev defected from Russia and sought political asylum in France.

1967 Andy Warhol's print series of Chairman Mao

ANDY WARHOL returned to his favorite paint medium, screen printing, in 1972. He could quickly make a whole series of icons in glorious, clashing Technicolor. Elvis, Troy Donahue, and Marilyn had already been immortalized; now it was the turn of communist leader Mao Zedong. It was Warhol's first work since being shot by Valerie Solanas. Chairman Mao was an astute choice: the series coincided with Richard Nixon's visit to China. Working from the frontispiece of the famous *Little Red Book*, containing the quotations of Chairman Mao, he made over 2,000 images in vibrant color, squiggled over with brush-strokes. The "hand-painted look" was now "in fashion," stated Warhol.

1969 Woodstock Pop Festival

MONTEREY MAY HAVE been the first, but Woodstock was the biggest. Nearly half a million people gathered in the fields of a farm in upstate New York for a celebration of peace, love, and music. Thunderstorms crackled overhead, and the torrential rain turned the ground into a mudslick, but still the bands played on. A little-known folk singer, Richie Havens, made history when he opened the festival; Sweetwater, who were meant to be first on, had got stuck in one of the 10-mile tailbacks that radiated out from the venue. Sly and The Family Stone, and English rockers The Who were the stars of Saturday. By Sunday, inadequate sanitation and lack of food and drink were beginning to take their toll. Helicopters airlifted supplies to the uncomfortable audience. Joe

Above: the Beatles show off their MBEs. Right: scenes from the Woodstock Festival, the largest pop music event of its time. In keeping with the feeling of the time, the festival became a celebration of love and peace.

1965 Beatles awarded MBEs

THE BEATLES came from Liverpool, and changed the world of music. They started off in black leather, conforming to American rock'n'roll standards, then changing into matching suits and turtlenecks, singing devastating pop harmonies that created hysteria. Headlines were full of "Beatlemania," as their songs took over the charts. They kept a sarcastic edge and a witty irreverence despite the uproar. In 1963 at the Royal Command Variety Show Lennon cracked: "The people in the cheap seats can clap, the rest of you rattle your jewelry." 1965 saw them outside Buckingham Palace posing with their MBEs (Member of the Order of the British Empire), the youngest peace-time recipients of the honor.

Cocker wowed the crowd with his uncoordinated dancing, and Crosby, Stills, Nash, and Young played their second-ever gig in front of that vast crowd. At the end of the evening, Jimi Hendrix played a charged set, which finished up with a twisted, searing "Star Spangled Banner." Max Yasgur, owner of the farm, was impressed that "Half a million kids can get together for three days and have fun and music, nothing but fun and music."

1970 *Janis Joplin dies of drug overdose*

JANIS JOPLIN grew up in Texas listening to Bessie Smith and Leadbelly, and started out singing country music and the blues. In San Francisco she developed a style of her own, a raunchy wail of a voice that ached with vulnerability and power. She got herself a hell-raising image too, glittering in bangles and satins, but going on drinking sprees, and cursing out anyone who crossed her. She was a sensation at the Monterey Pop Festival and her album *I Got Dem Ol' Kozmic Blues Again* was full of hollers and moans. On the day she died from a heroin overdose she was working on her new album. *Pearl* was released posthumously.

1970 *Jimi Hendrix dies of an overdose*

JIMI HENDRIX was born in Seattle, but started roaming after playing in local bands and doing a stint in the army. In London in 1966 he formed the Jimi Hendrix Experience, and set about taking the music

world by storm. His electric-guitar playing was legendary, a kind of innovative buzz of controlled feedback and melodic riffs. He was also a dazzling showman, slinking on stage in velvet and then smashing or burning his guitar. His first album *Are You Experienced?* was a psychedelic blaze of chords with Dylan-inspired lyrics. His later recordings anticipated dub and ambient music. He died of an overdose on September 18, 1970.

1980 *John Lennon murdered*

WHEN JOHN LENNON was shot outside the Dakota building in New York in December 1980, he was one of the most famous men in the world. In the 1960s, as a member of the Beatles, he had made jangly pop an art. Post-Beatles, working with his wife Yoko Ono, he had made music that was more experimental and challenging, the pop chords giving way to primal screams. Meanwhile his political statements and rallying for world peace had made him the voice of a generation. Mark Chapman, although a fan, had decided he was the "anti-Christ." He had asked for Lennon's autograph, and later the same day he gunned the star down outside Lennon's home.

 ## 1985 *Live Aid*

THE WORLD became a "global jukebox" on July 13, 1985, the day of the Live Aid concert. In 1984 musician Bob Geldof had been appalled by pictures of the famine in Africa, and decided to help. He persuaded 40 pop stars to come to a recording studio and the single "Do They Know It's Christmas" was released. The proceeds raised £8 million for famine relief. Live Aid was the follow-up, a 16-hour concert which would take place in England and America simultaneously. It would be broadcast to every country in the world. Once again the stars gathered, appearing for free. They performed for just 17 minutes each, a traffic-light system warning them to get off stage for the next act. Status Quo kicked off with "Rocking All Over The World," Paul McCartney played "Hey Jude" to a massive audience at Wembley Arena, who sang the words for him when his microphone cut out. Phil Collins managed to appear at both venues, thanks to *Concorde.* But it was Queen who stole the show with Freddie Mercury's charismatic performance and their vibrant rock. By the end of the evening an estimated 1.5 billion people had watched the event and $50 million had been raised to help the people in Ethiopia.

Left: *Jimi Hendrix, symbol of the 1960s rock revolution, died from an overdose in 1970.* Above: *a generation mourned after John Lennon was gunned down outside his home.* Below: *icons of the pop world united in the charity event Live Aid, a massive concert to raise funds for the people starving in Africa.*

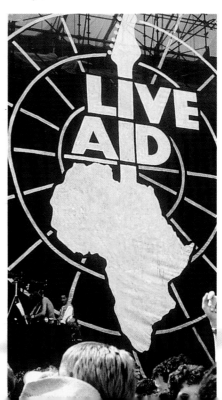

1987 The "Spy Catcher" scandal

PETER WRIGHT'S *Spy Catcher* set off ripples of unease in the Thatcher government of 1986. His memoirs discussed his years as an MI5 officer and included revelations about the illegal activities of MI5 in Britain. The government launched a campaign to stop newspapers from publishing any information received from Peter Wright. A high-court judge agreed, saying that Britain's security forces must be seen to be leakproof. Ironically, the book could be bought in any bookshop in America. In July 1987 an action was brought against *The Times* for publishing an extract. Eventually the government's case was overturned and *Spy Catcher* became a best seller.

1991 AIDS claims Freddie Mercury

FREDDIE MERCURY died of an AIDS-related illness on November 24, 1991. The flamboyant star had been the lead singer of Queen for nearly 20 years. The band's music—basic hard rock glammed over with lush production values—and their outrageous stage shows won them huge popularity. The single "Bohemian Rhapsody" became their best-known song, an operatic pop anthem with falsetto backing, and layer upon layer of vocals, which stayed in the charts for nine weeks. Weeks before his death Freddie Mercury re-released the single and donated all the proceeds to an AIDS charity. The band couldn't continue without him: "Without Freddie there is no Queen."

1993 "Jurassic Park" grosses $500 million

THE MONSTER MOVIE is not dead. In 1993 Steven Spielberg's dinosaurs stalked across the screen with ripping teeth and gripping claws, and into box-office records. *Jurassic Park* grossed $500 million worldwide. Special effects had moved on oceans since the days of *Jaws*, where the shark looked distinctly suspect in close-up. These giant reptiles were hi-tech marvels, huge, menacing, and frighteningly realistic. The film was based on a novel by Michael Crichton, in which a billionaire tycoon biologically engineers dinosaurs from fossilized DNA and decides to open a living museum. The film's gigantic profits made the production budget seem like a snip at $60 million.

Despite efforts to prevent its publication, Peter Wright's Spy Catcher *eventually went on sale in 1987.*

1997 The Spice Girls

"GIRL POWER" stormed the charts in 1997. It was the manifesto of an all-girl band, the Spice Girls. They had four consecutive Number One singles in the UK, three of which went straight in at the top. The songs were pretty and sassy, clean commercial pop, but they became a phenomenon in an industry which had been dominated by the "boy bands." The five girls were called Mel B, Mel C, Geri, Victoria, and Emma but the press quickly dubbed them: "Scary Spice," "Sporty Spice," "Ginger Spice," "Posh Spice", and "Baby Spice." Even campaigning politicians were asked who their favorite Spice Girl was. The band signed several lucrative deals with potato chip and drink manufacturers, so their financial future is assured. Spice Power is also Product Power.

The pop sensation of the 1990s, the Spice Girls took the world by storm with their "Girl Power."

Human 5 Rights & Society

The history of progress is written in the blood
of men and women who have dared to espouse
an unpopular cause.

Emma Goldman, 1908

1901 Roosevelt dines with black teacher—34 die in race riots

ON OCTOBER 16, 1901, President Theodore Roosevelt invited Booker T. Washington (1856–1915) of Tuskegee Institute to a White House dinner. Outraged whites took reprisals against southern blacks, causing riots that resulted in 34 deaths. Washington, an African-American educator, was an important civil rights organizer—in 1881 he was chosen to organize a normal and industrial school for African Americans at Tuskegee, Atlanta, and under his direction Tuskegee Institute became one of the leading African-American educational institutions, emphasizing industrial training as a means to self-respect and economic independence. He was an excellent orator but garnered opposition from many African-American leaders for maintaining that it was pointless for African Americans to demand social equality before attaining economic independence.

1903 Du Bois writes "The Souls of Black Folk"

Overleaf: women working in a munitions factory during World War I (see page 100). Right: Sir Robert Baden-Powell, founder of the Boy Scout movement, and general in the British Army.

WILLIAM EDWARD BURGHARDT DU BOIS (1868–1963) was a lifelong advocate of world peace and a leading champion of the liberation of Africans—in particular, African Americans. Du Bois was the first black to be awarded a PhD from Harvard. In more than 20 books and 100 scholarly articles, Du Bois championed the African-American culture through historical and sociological studies. *The Souls of Black Folk* was a pioneering effort, arguing that an educated black elite should lead blacks to liberation. In 1905 Du Bois founded the Niagara Movement, a forerunner of the National Association for the Advancement of Colored People (NAACP), which he helped organize in 1909.

1904 Helen Keller graduates from Radcliffe College

HELEN ADAMS KELLER (1880–1968) was an author, speaker, and philanthropist whose dedicated work had an extraordinary and wide-ranging influence on the lives of the handicapped. Keller became blind and deaf at the age of 19 months as a result of brain fever and was considered to be beyond help, communicating only with tantrums and wild laughter. She was patiently encouraged and taught by Anne Mansfield Sullivan, and she learned to read Braille and to write by using a special typewriter. The relationship between teacher and child was the subject of *The Miracle Worker*, a 1960 Pulitzer Prize-winning play and 1962 film by William Gibson. In 1904, Keller graduated with honors from Radcliffe College and began a life of writing, lecturing, and raising money for the handicapped.

1907 Robert Baden-Powell founds the Boy Scouts

SIR ROBERT STEPHENSON SMYTH BADEN-POWELL, 1st Baron Baden-Powell of Gilwell (1857–1941), was a British general who founded the Boy Scout and Girl Guide (Girl Scout) movement in the UK. Baden-Powell had written a book on military reconnaissance and scouting that became so popular with younger readers that he wrote *Scouting for Boys* in 1908. The American organization, Boy Scouts of America, was founded on Baden-Powell's model in 1910. Boys attain rising rank within the organization through various accomplishments, each of which earns a rank or merit badge. Locally Cub Scouts are organized into dens and packs and Boy Scouts into patrols and troops.

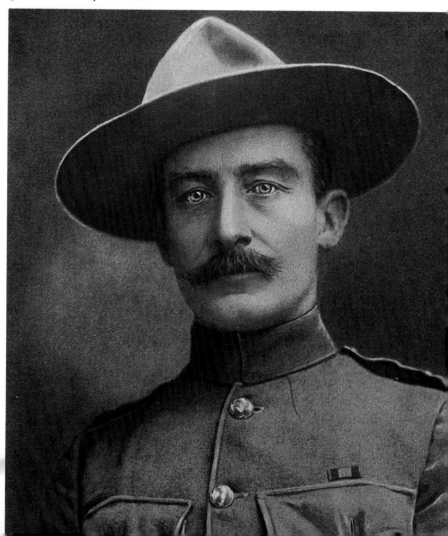

1909 Joan of Arc beatified by the Pope

JOAN OF ARC (Jeanne d'Arc, 1412–31) was a French peasant girl who led the French army against the English during the Hundred Years' War. Called the Maid of Orleans, she is a French national heroine and patron saint. When Joan was about 13 years old she began to hear voices that encouraged her to help liberate the French from the English. In 1429 she left her home in Champagne and led troops under her own command to relieve the city of Orleans, which she did in eight days. She was captured by the Burgundians in 1930, who sold her to the English. Joan of Arc was tried on a charge of heresy, treason, and witchery and on May 30, 1431 she was burned at the stake in Rouen. There are monuments to her memory in many French cities and towns. She was beatified by the Pope on 18 April 1909 and canonized in 1920.

1910 Girl Guides founded

ON MAY 31, 1910 the Girl Guide movement was formed by Sir Robert Baden-Powell and his sister, Agnes Baden-Powell. The Girl Guides was to be run along the lines of the Boy Scouts, with emphasis on discipline, physical fitness, and cleanliness of body and mind. The system included troops with patrols, guide mistresses and merit badges for feminine skills. The Guides were very popular, and within a few short years had troops across the UK. The Girl Scouts of the USA was founded by Juliette Gordon Low in 1912, following the British format. There are now millions of members of both groups around the world.

1912 Women's foot-binding abolished in China

FOOT-BINDING was a traditional Chinese custom in which the feet of young girls were tightly bound with strips of linen in order to discourage growth. The large toe was bent backwards over the top of the foot and the remaining toes were folded underneath and strapped. Foot-binding originated in the Song dynasty (960–1279), after which the custom spread throughout all social classes in China—particularly the upper classes, who deemed it a mark of great beauty and gentility, and proved that women were incapable of physical labor. Girls between the ages of five and 12 were selected to undergo this painful and debilitating procedure. In 1912 the Chinese government officially banned the custom.

Having established the Boy Scouts in 1907, Baden-Powell went on to create a complementary movement for girls. Today both systems still have a large following from young people.

1913 Emily Davison buried

SUFFRAGIST EMILY DAVISON, who had been imprisoned several times and force-fed, was killed on July 14, 1913, when she ran in front of the king's horse at the Epsom Derby, grabbing the reins. She was the first martyr of the British suffragette movement. Emmeline Pankhurst, founder of the WSPU (Women's Social and Political Union), was sentenced on July 8th of the same year to three months in prison. The suffragettes attended Davison's funeral in white, carrying wreaths and banners that pronounced "Fight on and God will give the victory." The demand for the national vote for women had reached a peak in 1914, and the suffragette movement also protested about a range of gender inequalities. In 1928 women were given the vote in Britain.

1914 Women work in factories and other "male" jobs

BEFORE WORLD WAR I (1914–18), women were considered to be largely helpless, weak characters, capable only of light domestic work, shopkeeping and typing. The war, in which Britain lost a large part of a generation of young men, caused women to be successfully engaged in some of the most difficult physical labour, including work on the railways, in service industries, in the arms industry, in factories, in mines, in the fields, and even sweeping chimneys and other traditionally male pursuits. It was a jubilant victory for the suffragettes, for it proved that women were more than capable of doing equal work to men. The domestic effect of the war was to accelerate many social and political developments and as a result, women achieved limited suffrage in 1918 and then full suffrage in 1928.

1918 Women given the vote in the US

THE US WOMEN'S RIGHTS MOVEMENT, which started as early as the 1830s and became involved with the struggle to abolish slavery, resulted in the proposal for the 19th Amendment, introduced in Congress in 1878. This amendment remained a controversial issue for over 40 years, during which the women's rights movement became strongly militant, conducting campaigns and demonstrations for congressional passage of the amendment and then for ratification by the states. This political action, reinforced by the service of women in industry during World War I, resulted in the adoption of the amendment. The 19th Amendment, formally ratified in 1920, provided men and women with equal voting rights.

1919 Nancy Astor becomes Britain's first woman MP

VISCOUNTESS NANCY ASTOR (1879–1964) became the first woman to sit as a Member of Parliament (MP) in Britain. Born Nancy Witcher Langhorne, she married Waldorf Astor, a Conservative Member of Parliament in 1906. When he took over his father's title in 1919, entering the House of Lords, she won his seat in the House of Commons and held it until 1945. Lady Astor was outspoken but enormously popular, and she worked enthusiastically for temperance and for women's and children's welfare. In the late 1930s, doubt was raised about her loyalty to her country, when, at her home at Cliveden, she was the focus of a group that favored an appeasement policy towards Nazi Germany. When Britain declared war, however, she strongly supported the war effort.

World War I saw women taking on many roles traditionally associated with men, including work in munitions factories such as this.

Women world-wide had been struggling for emancipation since the turn of the century; their greatest achievement came with the right to vote in the US in 1918.

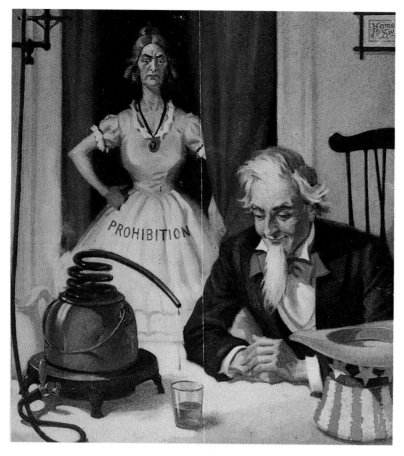

1920 Prohibition begins in the US

PROHIBITION OFFICIALLY BEGAN in 1920, when the 18th Amendment to the US constitution forbade the manufacture, sale, and transportation of alcoholic beverages. Commonly called "the Noble Experiment," national prohibition was the result of a reform movement that had campaigned for more than 100 years. Prohibitionists considered alcohol to be a dangerous drug that destroyed lives and disrupted families and communities, and they argued that it was the government's responsibility to free citizens from the temptation of drink by barring its sale. The law, which was enforced only sporadically, met with widespread opposition. Bootlegging, speakeasies (illegal saloons), and smuggling (known as rum-running) all flourished in a new black-market economy, run by gangsters. Opponents mounted a campaign to annul the law, and were successful in 1933, when the 21st Amendment repealed the 18th Amendment.

1926 General Strike in the UK

FROM 3–12 MAY, 1926 Britain was crippled by a General Strike, in which three million workers rallied to the slogan "Not a penny off the pay; not a minute off the day," in sympathy with coalminers who refused

1920s Ku Klux Klan revived

THE KU KLUX KLAN (KKK) is the name of two groups of American white racists who used violence and subversive methods to preserve white supremacy. From 1866 to 1872 they organized into secret societies that terrorized local white and black Republican leaders and blacks whose behavior violated old ideas of black subordination. Members wore white robes and masks and adopted the burning cross as their symbol. In the 1870s most Americans disclaimed the methods of the Ku Klux Klan but when the story of the KKK was popularized in Thomas B. Dixon's *The Clansman* (1905) and D. W. Griffith's movie *The Birth of a Nation* (1915), the problems increased. The movement reached its height of popularity in the 1920s, preaching anti-Catholic, anti-Jewish, anti-black, anti-socialist, and anti-labor-union "Americanism." At its peak, the Klan had more than two million members and exercised great political power in many states.

Above: *cartoon depicting Uncle Sam and Prohibition—the no-alcohol law was enforced throughout America between 1920 and 1933.* Right: *the white American racist group Ku Klux Klan initiating novices in 1923.*

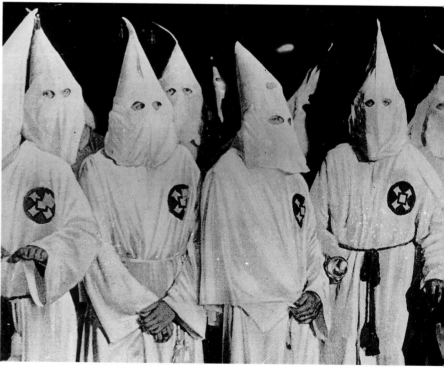

to accept a pay cut averaging 13 per cent and an increased working day. Members of the Trades Union Congress, including railwaymen, printing trade workers, building trade workers, truckdrivers, dock workers, iron and steel workers, chemical industry employees, and some power company workers, walked out in response to a strategy devised by Transport Workers chief Ernest Bevin. Although the strike ground the nation to a halt, it failed, leading to the Trade Disputes and Trade Union Act of 1927, which limited unions' strike powers.

1945 Diary of Anne Frank discovered

ANNE FRANK (1929–45), was a young Jewish girl who hid with her family in occupied Amsterdam between 1942 and 1944. She kept a diary while hiding from Nazi persecution, living in a secret apartment for two years before being discovered. Anne and her family were betrayed to the Gestapo on August 4, 1944, and deported with eight others in the last convoy of cattle trucks to the extermination camp at Auschwitz. Anne was shipped on to the Bergen-Belsen concentration camp, and died there in March 1945. Her three notebooks, left behind at 263 Prinsengracht in Amsterdam, contained her diary, chronicling the period in which she and her family hid from the Gestapo. Her moving diary was abridged in 1947 and became an international best seller, acting as a poignant reminder of the plight of the Jews during the Holocaust.

1945 Goering taken prisoner

HERMANN WILHELM GOERING (1893–1946) was second only to Adolf Hitler in the German National Socialist regime. During the 1930s he had gained enormous power as Prussian minister-president and minister of the interior; chief of the Gestapo (secret police); minister of aviation and, with the rank of field marshal, commander-in-chief of the air force; and economic dictator of the Third Reich, directing the four-year plan. During World War II, Goering was the instigator of many of the atrocities undertaken by the Nazis, but as the war drew to a close, his influence with Hitler was undermined by the failure of the air force against the British and the Soviets. Captured by the Allies in 1945, he was tried as a major war criminal by the International Military Tribunal at Nuremberg. He was condemned to execution but took poison before he could be killed.

1945 US soldiers discover the horrors of Buchenwald

ON APRIL 11, 1945 the American troops overran the East German Buchenwald concentration camp, discovering 21,000 starving survivors and thousands of corpses. It was the beginning of a horrific period when dozens of such camps were discovered throughout Germany and the occupied territories, and it became clear that the mass human extermination that had been the focus of Hitler's "Final Solution" had left more than six million Jews dead. The massacre, known as the Holocaust, began with a Nazi boycott of Jewish businesses, the establishment of quotas in Germany's professions and schools, and a ban on intermarriage between Jews and Gentiles. Jews represented more than half of those exterminated as undesirables in concentration camps.

Left: *the diary of Anne Frank became one of the most revealing insights into the results of anti-semitism in World War II.*
Below: *Auschwitz—one of many concentration camps where millions of people were exterminated in the war.*

1957 *Black and white confrontations at Little Rock, Arkansas*

THE CITY OF LITTLE ROCK, Arkansas, attracted world attention in 1957 when federal troops enforced a US Supreme Court ruling against segregation in the public schools. The 1954 ruling pronounced that segregating black and white pupils in separate public schools was unconstitutional. Arkansas resisted the ruling, and in September 1957 Governor Orval E. Faubus tried to prevent the integration of Little Rock Central High School. President Dwight D. Eisenhower quickly intervened, sending federal troops to Little Rock, and several black students were enrolled at the school. Resistance by whites to school integration continued throughout the 1960s, but by the late 1970s blacks had equal access to virtually all public educational institutions in the state.

1960 *Sharpeville massacre*

ON MARCH 21, 1960 South African police opened fire on a large crowd of black Africans demonstrating outside the police station in Sharpeville, a township on the outskirts of Johannesburg. The newly formed Pan Africanist Congress (PAC) had called for a nation-wide day of protest against one of the fundamental policies of apartheid—the ruling that all blacks had to carry papers or "passes." All over South Africa supporters of the PAC gathered at local police stations without their passes. In Sharpeville some 20,000 demonstrators assembled, and the police started shooting. Sixty-seven peaceful demonstrators were killed and another 178 were wounded. Hendrik Verwoerd's Nationalist government declared a state of emergency and banned both the PAC and the African National Congress. The massacre inspired widespread international condemnation, and trade embargoes ensued. A year later South Africa was expelled from the Commonwealth of Nations.

1964 *Martin Luther King Jr wins Nobel Peace Prize*

MARTIN LUTHER KING JR (1929–68) was a man of profound morality with a powerful belief in the rights of every person, of every race, religion, and class, to have peace. He devoted his life to the fight for full citizenship rights of the poor, disadvantaged, and racially oppressed in the United States. Inspired by the life of Mahatma Gandhi, he traveled widely, lecturing, and writing on his dream for peace and equality. He

organized the massive march on Washington in 1963 where, in his ingenious "I Have a Dream" speech, he "subpoenaed the conscience of the nation before the judgement seat of morality." In January 1964, *Time* magazine chose King as Man of the Year, the first black American so honored. Later that year he became the youngest recipient of the Nobel Peace Prize. *See also* 1968.

1964 *US Civil Rights Act prohibits racial discrimination*

IN RESPONSE TO spiraling violence against black and white civil rights activists, and following the murder of a number of American children and the bombing of dozens of black churches throughout the South, the US government passed several new laws, the most important of which were enacted in 1964 and 1965. The Civil Rights Act (1964) undermined the remaining structure of Jim Crow laws (which had set up a racial caste system in the South) and provided federal protection for those fighting for civil rights. The Voting Rights Act (1965) provided for federal action to put an end to actions by local governments and individuals that interfered with the right of African Americans to register and vote. Both these laws were upheld in challenges before the US Supreme Court.

Martin Luther King, the black Civil Rights leader, who forged the path of equality for American blacks.

*The assassination of
Martin Luther King in
1968 caused widespread
outrage and mourning.
His contribution to the
black cause, however,
will never be forgotten.*

1968 Martin Luther King Jr assassinated

AT THE HEIGHT OF HIS CAREER, Martin Luther King Jr called for a "reconstruction of the entire society, a revolution of value," which gained him widespread support around the world, but also set up a network of conspirators who considered him to be a threat to Americanism. Early in 1968, King began to plan a multiracial march on Washington to demand an end to all forms of discrimination and the funding of a $12 billion Economic Bill of Rights. While organizing the campaign, he flew to Memphis, Tennessee, to offer support to striking sanitation workers. On April 4, 1968, King was assassinated. The violent death of this moral and socially conscious man of peace sent shock waves around the country, and resulted in rioting in black ghettos. James Earl Ray was convicted of King's murder, but theorists believe that his death was planned by more than one man. In 1983, King's birthday was designated a national holiday.

Students rioting at the Sorbonne in Paris; the demonstrations ended in hundreds of injuries as riot police tried to control the crowds.

1968 Students riot in Paris

PARIS BECAME THE scene of violence during the student riots of 1968. With a complex series of grievances, the students, backed by other groups, caused a series of disorders that led to further rioting as workers took up the students' cause. On May 6th 1968, more than 10,000 left-wing students fought CRS riot police, armed with teargas, fire hoses, and batons, in the streets of the Latin Quarter. 600 people were injured, and there were 422 arrests. On May 10th further riots occurred when students dug up paving stones to create a barricade against the violence. The rioting was followed by a five-week student occupation of the Sorbonne University and a general workers' strike. Charles De Gaulle set up a vigorous policy of detaching worker support from the student movement, but his success was short-lived and he resigned the following year.

1977 Death of Steve Biko

STEPHEN BIKO (1946–77) was an influential leader of the Black Consciousness Movement in South Africa who became a martyr to the anti-apartheid cause. In 1968, as a medical student, Biko founded the South African Students Organization (SASO), which actively campaigned against racial discrimination. In 1975 and again in 1976 he was arrested and held for more than 100 days without being charged or put on trial. In August 1977, Biko was arrested for a third time at Port Elizabeth, where he died in custody after being taken by truck while unconscious to Pretoria, 740 miles away. Although the police claimed that he died as the result of a hunger strike, the post-mortem examination disclosed that his death was caused by blows to the head. The police were absolved of blame, leading to public outcry around the world.

1981 Bobby Sands dies

ON MAY 5, 1991, Bobby Sands became the first of 10 Provisional IRA hunger-strikers to die in the H block of Belfast's Maze Prison. Sands, 27, died after 65 days without food. Sands had recently been elected to parliament, in a by-election in the Northern Irish constituency of Fermanagh and South Tyrone, despite the fact that he was serving a 14-year sentence for firearms possession. His hunger strike was in protest against the demands for the reintroduction of special category status for Republican prisoners. He was buried in Belfast's Milltown cemetery on May 7th, in a Republican plot. The nine other hunger strikers died between May and July of 1981, drawing world-wide attention to the Northern Irish cause.

1981 Vietnamese "boat people"

BETWEEN 1979 AND 1981, more than 1.4 million Vietnamese, including large numbers of ethnic Chinese, fled the country by sea, to escape the new Communist regime in Vietnam. They risked death and piracy in order to escape, and as many as 50,000 of these "boat people" may have perished in flight. Partly due to the mass media, who widely publicized their cause, nearly a million settled abroad. The exodus of refugees fled the country in small, unseaworthy craft and sailed to neighboring Thailand, Malaysia, Singapore, Indonesia, the Philippines and Hong Kong. Their plight caused governments world-wide to increase the number of Vietnamese refugees admitted for immigration. In 1981, the US admitted a total of 133,000 Southeast Asian refugees.

1989 Tiananmen Square massacre

IN JUNE 1989, the Tiananmen Square massacre in Beijing brought a tragic end to six weeks of pro-democracy demonstrations by Chinese students and workers. The demonstrations began as a display of mourning for the death of former Communist party leader Hu Yaobang and gathered momentum during a visit to China by Mikhail Gorbachev in mid-May. By that time, more than one million people a day were in Tiananmen Square demanding that government leaders end corruption and instigate political reform. Martial law was declared on May 20th, and the People's Liberation Army was summoned to clear the capital. On the night of June 3–4 PLA units cleared Tiananmen Square and killed almost 1,000 civilians in the immediate area. Thousands of students and others were arrested and executed.

Armed tanks are brought in to control the riots involving Chinese students and workers in Tiananmen Square.

1991 Nelson Mandela freed at last

ON FEBRUARY 11TH, African National Congress leader Nelson Mandela (born 1918) walked free from Victor Verster prison in South Africa's Cape Province, after 27 years in prison for treason. Celebrations around the world were followed by negotiations between the ANC, of which Mandela was elected Deputy President, and President F.W. de Klerk. Mandela became the first black president of South Africa on May 10, 1994. When Mandela was sentenced to life imprisonment in 1964, he came to symbolize black political aspirations. He and de Klerk shared the Nobel Peace Prize for negotiating South Africa's peaceful transition to multiracial democracy. After the ANC victory in the April 1994 elections, Mandela worked to ease racial tensions, court foreign invest-ment and provide services to the black victims of apartheid.

When four white policeman were freed from the charge of beating a black man to death, demonstrations and rioting broke out in the city of Los Angeles.

1991 Kurdish refugees flee

PRESIDENT BUSH'S call for the Iraqi people to overthrow Saddam Hussein was embraced by rebel factions, and the Kurds responded with an uprising in the north that was brutally suppressed by Saddam's

remaining forces. The suppression created an enormous refugee problem, as hundreds of thousands of Kurds fled their homes. International mass media widely publicized the plight of the Kurds, who crowded into the frozen mountains above the Turkish border to escape Saddam's plans for mass genocide. As the death toll among the Kurds mounted, US military forces built camps for them in northern Iraq. The administration of these camps was later assumed by the United Nations. Coalition forces began policing a "no fly" zone for Iraqi aircraft in the south in August 1992.

1992 Race riots in Los Angeles

IN RESPONSE TO the acquittal of four white policemen charged with beating Rodney King, a black motorist, Los Angeles exploded into racial violence in 1992. The Los Angeles riot was the largest and most dangerous since the turn of the century, and more than 60 people were killed and 2,383 injured by the time local and federal law enforcement personnel were able to restore order. The riots cost the city over $800 million in damages, but the issue of greatest concern was the volatility of the black response, which included unprovoked attacks on white civilians, clashes between black rioters and non-black merchants, and widespread looting and arson outside the ghetto area. Two of the four white policemen were later convicted in the Supreme Court.

1994 Hope for Northern Ireland

THE 25-YEAR-OLD Northern Irish troubles were offered some relief when, on August 31, 1994, the IRA announced a "complete cessation of military activities from midnight." The announcement, coming eight months after the Downing Street Declaration between the British and Irish governments, was welcomed by British prime minister John Major. As a result, the government of Britain lifted the broadcasting ban on Sinn Fein, which had been in place since 1981, and Sinn Fein leader Gerry Adams held talks with the Irish Taoiseach, Albert Reynolds, in Dublin. Loyalist paramilitary groups announced their own ceasefire in October. Talks between Sinn Fein and British government officials began at Stormont Castle, Belfast, in December of that year, providing hope for Irish peace.

1996 O. J. Simpson acquitted

IN 1996, American football star Orenthal James (O. J.) Simpson (born 1947) was, in an internationally televised trial, acquitted of the first-degree murders of his ex-wife, Nicole Brown Simpson, and her friend Ronald Goldman. O. J. and Nicole Simpson, who had two children, were divorced in 1992. After midnight on June 13, 1994, the two victims were found stabbed to death outside Nicole Simpson's condominium in the Brentwood section of Los Angeles. O. J. Simpson, who lived 2 miles away, had left late on the previous evening for a long-planned trip to Chicago. On June 17th O. J. was charged with the murders and, after a televised police chase, he appeared before the Los Angeles Municipal Court where he entered a plea of not guilty. He was held without bail in the Los Angeles Prison until trial. The trial was presided over by Judge Lance Ito, and 12 jurors found him innocent of all charges—causing mixed reactions of jubilation and disbelief around the world. The media interest in the trial was unprecedented.

The most controversial court case to date— American football star O. J. Simpson's trial was followed by millions via the media.

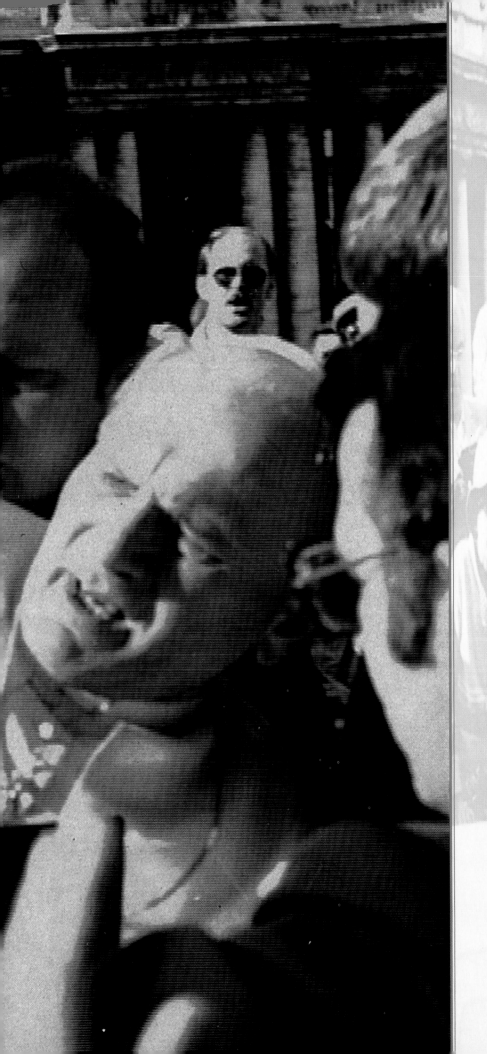

Religion & Cults

"I am appealing to you, who are concerned for the good of your own people and of all humanity. It is very important not to weaken man, his sense of the sacredness of life, his capacity for love and self-sacrifice."

Pope John Paul II in a letter
to the leaders of the world, 1994.

Overleaf: *Pope John Paul II was shot and wounded in St Peter's Square by a Turkish national.*
Right: *Pope Pius X who was canonized in a magnificent ceremony in St Peter's Square in 1954.*

1903 Pope Pius X crowned before crowd of 70,000 in Rome

GIUSEPPE MELCHIORRE SARTO became a parish priest in Venetia and a cardinal of Venice in 1893. He was elected pope in 1903 and crowned before an enormous crowd of 70,000 people. Unlike the previous pope, Leo XIII, he was uninterested in social reforms, instead concentrating on apostolic problems and making the defence of Roman Catholicism his cause. In particular he condemned Modernism, a contemporary intellectual movement seeking to reinterpret traditional Catholic teaching in the light of nineteenth-century philosophical, historical, and psychological theories. He issued a decree in 1907, rejecting Modernist teachings and suggesting remedies to eradicate it, urging immediate compliance with his censorship program. He was canonized in 1954.

1925 Soviet persecution of religious groups

THE RUSSIAN BOLSHEVIK government considered all religion the "opium of the people" and since 1918 the Church had been deprived of all rights including that of owning property. In February 1922 the government decreed the confiscation of all valuable objects preserved in the churches. Tikhon, the head of the Orthodox Church, published a declaration that he "was not the enemy of the Soviet government" but his conformism was to no avail. After his death in 1925 his successors were arrested. Under Joseph Stalin the Church suffered a severe persecution that claimed thousands of victims. By 1939 only three bishops and 100 churches could officially function: the Church was practically suppressed.

1925 John Scopes trial

IN JULY 1925 high-school teacher John Scopes was charged with violating state law by teaching the theory of evolution in Tennessee. A recent Tennessee legislature had declared unlawful the teaching of any doctrine denying the divine creation of man as taught by the Bible. Fundamentalist literal belief confronted liberal interpretation of the scriptures. The judge ruled out any test of the law's constitutionality or argument on the validity of Darwin's theory, limiting the trial to the question of whether Scopes had taught evolution, which he admittedly had. He was convicted and fined $100. An appeal court acquitted Scopes on the technicality of an excessive fine but upheld the law's constitutionality.

1938 Kristallnacht

KRISTALLNACHT (night of (broken) glass) was a night of supreme violence against Jewish people and property carried out by the German Storm Troopers on Novembe 9–10, 1938 in Austria and Germany. It followed the assassination of a German diplomat, Ernst vom Rath, in Paris by a Polish Jewish youth. In all, 91 Jews were killed, hundreds seriously injured and thousands more terrorized. About 7500 businesses were gutted and around 177 synagogues were burnt or demolished. Subsequent measures included legislation preventing Jews from owning businesses or property in Germany and restrictions on schooling, use of public parks and leaving the country. Kristallnacht marked a major escalation in the Nazi program of Jewish persecution.

1959 Dalai Lama goes into exile

THE 14TH INCARNATION of the Dalai Lama, the spiritual and temporal head of the Tibetan state, was born in 1935. Tibetan Buddhists believe each Dalai Lama is a reincarnation of his predecessor and also of Avalokitesvara. Enthroned in 1940, he temporarily fled in 1950–51 when the Chinese overran Tibet. In March 1959 he went into exile in protest at the Chinese annexation of Tibet, escaping from Lhasa to India, then settling at Dharmsala. The Chinese offered to remove a ban on his return providing he would no longer call for Tibet's independence. He was awarded the Nobel Peace Prize in 1989 for his commitment to the non-violent liberation of Tibet.

1978 Mass suicide in Jonestown

THE SELF-STYLED Reverend Jim Jones (1933–78) originally preached his ideas to San Francisco's black community. He established his group, the People's Temple of the Disciples of Christ, in 1974. Jonestown, the commune of the sect, was built northwest of Georgetown, Guyana. Following the shooting of Leo Ryan, a US congressman, and three newsmen performing an unofficial investigation into the group, Jones gave a final sermon, then instructed his followers to imbibe cyanide mixed into a soft drink. In all, 789 people died, according to the official Washington/CIA report, during the mass suicide of November 17–18, 1978. Jones himself died of a gunshot wound to the head.

The aftermath of Kristallnacht—shops were wrecked and synagogues all over Germany were destroyed in the anti-Semitic riots.

1981 Pope John Paul II shot

BORN IN KRAKOW, Poland, Karol Wojtyla took the name of John Paul II when he was elected pope in 1978. The previous pope, John Paul, had died after serving only 33 days. Wojtyla was the first non-Italian pope to be elected since 1522. He is famed for his worldwide trips, his preaching to huge audiences, and his endorsement of traditional Catholic views. He was shot and wounded in St Peter's Square by Mehmet Agca, a Turkish national, in May 1981. It was believed the assassination was attempted because of the pope's outspoken support of the Roman Catholic Church and the Solidarity trade union in Poland. Agca was acquitted for lack of evidence.

1989 Salmãn Rushdie receives death threats following his "Satanic Verses"

SALMÃN RUSHDIE was born in India of a Muslim family, later living in Pakistan before moving to the UK. His novels include *Midnight's Children* (1981), which won him the Booker Prize, and *Shame* (1983) which was a satire and revisionist history of Pakistan.

In 1988 he wrote *The Satanic Verses* (the title refers to deleted verses from the *Koran*), which offended many Muslims with its alleged blasphemy. The book was banned in India in 1988 and in 1989 Iran's Ayatollah Khomeini issued a death threat. Demonstrations followed, in which copies of the book were burnt along with effigies of the author. Rushdie was forced to go into hiding under police protection.

1993 Waco siege

DAVID KORESH formed the Branch Davidian sect in 1959. The sect was a splinter group, formed out of another group which itself had broken away from the Seventh Day Adventist Church. The charismatic leader took his followers to Waco, Texas, and formed a commune. Koresh became more dictatorial as time went on, instructing that he was a messiah and that all the women in the group were his God-given wives. Authorities were alerted over the stockpiling of weapons there and a siege was born. The fiery demise of the compound claimed the lives of Koresh and 74 of his followers, with four federal agents killed in the preceding shoot-out.

Pope John Paul II was shot and wounded in St Peter's Square by a Turkish national, who was later released due to lack of evidence.

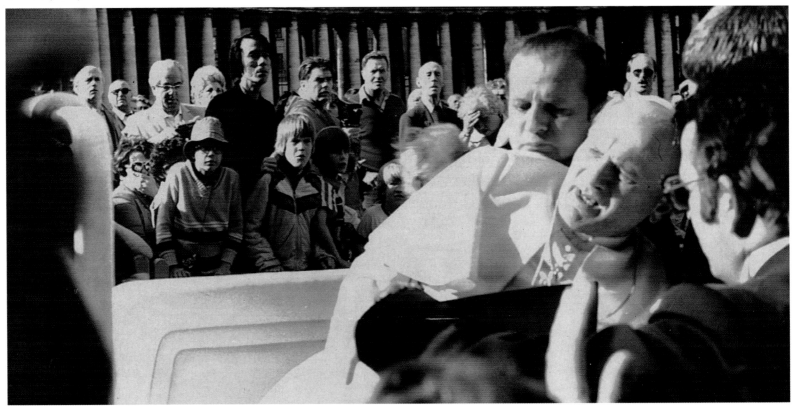

Police were forced to guard author Salman Rushdie after Ayatollah Khomeini issued death threats on the release of The Satanic Verses.

Exploration & Discovery

7

That's one small step for a man, and one giant leap for mankind.

Neil Armstrong, 1969

1902 First Aswan Dam of the Nile completed

THE 1902 ASWAN DAM was built to control the flood tides of the River Nile. It could conserve water in the late summer, so that it could be used for irrigation in the months from February through to July when water was scarce. It was a sensitive project, involving the competing and conflicting claims of the many countries that the Nile passes through: Egypt, Sudan, Ethiopia, Uganda, Democratic Republic of Congo (formerly Zaire), Kenya and many more. The dam was constructed on the lowest waterfall of the river, and built from locally quarried stone. It had a height of 344 ft and was 1.2 miles wide. It successfully allowed the controlled irrigation of vast areas of the Nile Valley and the drought-parched surrounding desert.

Overleaf: *the Pathfinder rover vehicle that supplied the first pictures from the surface of Mars in 1997 (see page 127).* Below: *The ship* Discovery *on which Robert Scott made his pioneering journey to the Antarctic.*

1903 Scott reaches the furthest point south in the Antarctic

ROBERT FALCON SCOTT said, "I may as well confess that I have no predilection for 'polar exploration' " and then set off on a journey to Antarctica. In 1901 the expedition ship *Discovery*, specially built to deal with pack ice, set sail. By January 1902, Scott had made winter camp on Ross Island and was making forays to explore the adjacent ice shelf and the mainland. His first venture towards the South Pole was hampered by the poor performances of the sledges and an outbreak of scurvy. In the summer of 1903, Scott tried again. He sledded up the Ferrar Glacier to the Polar Plateau, in a smooth 59 days. It was the furthest south any person had ever been.

1908 Robert Peary reaches the North Pole

ROBERT PEARY adopted a spartan approach to polar exploration. Traveling with scant provisions, Innuit guides, dogs, and sledges, he managed to cross the treacherous ice fields to the North Pole. His preparation was scientific and meticulous. His traveling companion, Matthew Henson, a black American, spoke fluent Innuit and was invaluable as a conduit for local knowledge. Initially they were delayed by channels of open water. But by April 2nd, Peary and Henson, four Innuit, and 38 dogs were 133 nautical miles away from the Pole and ready to begin the final stage of the journey. By April 6th, he was 3 nautical miles away, and on April 17th additional observations showed that he'd achieved his goal. He and Henson had reached the North Pole.

1911 Bingham finds the lost city of the Incas

HIRAM BINGHAM taught Latin American history at Yale, but he was no armchair traveler. Reckless and adventurous by nature, he became an explorer. His obsession was to find "the lost city in the clouds"—Machu Picchu. It was the last stronghold of the Incas after the Spanish conquest. It is perched high in the Andean Mountains, on a ridge 2,000 ft above the rushing Urubamba River. Bingham crossed over a precarious wooden bridge, just a few logs lashed together, and followed a snake-infested trail until he suddenly found himself "confronted with the walls of ruined houses built of the finest Inca stone." Before him lay the abandoned terraces, temples, and food-storage vaults of the sacred retreat of an ancient civilization.

Cartoon depicting Peary and Scott arguing over who reached the North Pole first.

1912 Remains of the "Piltdown Man" discovered in Sussex

CHARLES DAWSON, a British lawyer and antiquarian, made an archaeological find which would puzzle scientists for some 40 years. In a gravel pit on Piltdown Common in Sussex, he dug up portions of a skull and jawbone. From the animal remains at the site, all indications were that the finds were over 500,000 years old. But strangely the skull was of a modern type, though the jaw was similar to that of an ape. In 1953, chemical analysis revealed that Eoanthropus Dawson was an ingenious fraud. The skull was of a modern man; the jaw, that of an orang-utan. Both had been skilfully stained and aged. Another mystery of human evolution was solved and the need for the careful testing of fossil remains was emphasized.

1912 Scott dies after failed race to the South Pole

"HAD WE LIVED I should have a tale to tell of the hardihood endurance and courage of my companions ... These rough notes and our dead bodies must tell the tale." On January 16, 1912, one of Scott's expedition party spotted a black marker flag left by the Norwegian explorer Roald Amundsen, and knew they had been beaten in their race to the South Pole. They turned back. Ill-equipped, suffering from frostbite and lack of food and warmth, they were trapped in the middle of a snow storm. The tent entombing their bodies was found eight months later by a search party from Cape Evans, though it was not until February 1913 that the news of the tragedy finally reached the British public.

1913–14 Gertrude Bell explores the Arabian Desert

GERTRUDE BELL (1868–1926), English traveler, author, and archaeologist, was one of the foremost explorers of the twentieth century. Her voyage across the Arabian Desert in 1913–14 was an unprecedented document of Middle Eastern culture and archaeology, and brought a new understanding of nomadic tribes. A graduate of Oxford University, she traveled and studied extensively in the Middle East, and during World War I she was a British intelligence

agent in Cairo and Basra, the Turkish province that later became part of Iraq. In 1921 she headed the group that chose Faisal I as first king of the newly independent Iraq. Among her books are *Amurath to Amurath* (1911) and *The Palace and Mosque of Ukhaidir* (1914).

Right: a page from Robert Scott's diary after his failed expedition to the South Pole. Opposite left: the ante-chamber to Tutankhamen's tomb discovered by Howard Carter and Lord Carnarvon. Opposite right: the magnificent death mask of the young pharaoh, wrought from gold and precious stones.

we shall stick it out to the end but we are getting weaker of course and the end cannot be far.

It seems a pity, but I do not think I can write more —

R Scott

Last Entry

For Gods Sake look after our people

1922 Tutankhamen's grave discovered

HOWARD CARTER had been searching for 15 years for the resting place of the Egyptian boy king, Tutankhamen. In November 1922, Carter and his patron, Lord Carnarvon, stood at the bottom of 16 steps in a tunnel in the Valley of the Kings. Before them was a sealed door that bore an ancient royal emblem of the Egyptian Pharaohs. Carter picked up his hammer and chisel, chipped a small hole through the stone and plaster, and looked through. He wrote: "At first I could see nothing, but presently details of the room emerged slowly from the mist, strange animals, statues, and gold—everywhere the glint of gold." After a long and dedicated search the tomb of Tutankhamen had been found.

1924 Mallory and Irvine die trying to reach the top of Mount Everest

EVEREST IS THE highest mountain in the world, reaching up two-thirds of the way into the earth's atmosphere, where the oxygen is thin. Powerful winds and freezing temperatures make it difficult to climb. In 1922, George Mallory had struggled to within 3,200 ft of the summit, and in 1924 he returned with Andrew Irvine to try again. They were less than 1,000 ft from the summit and "going strong for the top," when appalling weather came down and the support team lost sight of them as they disappeared into a swirling snowstorm. Before leaving for Nepal, Mallory was asked why he was so desperate to climb the world's highest mountain. He replied, famously: "Because it's there."

1926 Bennett and Byrd fly to the North Pole by airplane

ON MAY 9, 1926, Admiral Richard E. Byrd (1888–1957) and Floyd Bennett (1890–1928) became the first men to fly to the North Pole by airplane. With the explorer Byrd as navigator, Bennett piloted a plane non-stop from Spitsbergen to the North Pole and back. Both men were awarded the Congressional Medal of Honor for their achievements. In 1928, on a flight to rescue stranded flyers in the Gulf of St Lawrence, Bennett was stricken with pneumonia; from which he later died in Quebec. The same year, Byrd organized an expedition to Antarctica, establishing a base called Little America on the Ross Ice Shelf near Roosevelt Island, and a year later he flew with three companions to the South Pole and back.

1929 Charles Lindbergh photographs Mayan ruins in Yucatan

THE AMERICAN AVIATOR Charles Lindbergh (1902–74) first achieved international fame in 1927 as the first person to fly alone across the Atlantic. He made the daring expedition in the *Spirit of St Louis*, his single-engine monoplane, traveling from New York to Paris in 33 ½ hours. In 1929 he married Anne Spencer Morrow, daughter of the US ambassador to Mexico, and she became his co-pilot and navigator on many subsequent expeditions, including the 1929 flight over the Yucatan peninsula, during which he photographed Mayan ruins. His photographs made an important contribution to the study of the Mayas and to the field of archaeology.

1930 Amy Johnson is first woman to fly from UK to Australia

ON MAY 24TH, British aviator Amy Johnson (1904–41) became the first woman to fly solo from the UK to Australia; she was aged 27. She followed the 19-and-a-half-day flight with a record six-day solo flight from England to India, for which she received international acclaim. Johnson was one of the small, brave group of British women pilots who ferried aircraft from the factory to the airfield during World War II, a mission that held great danger. She was killed ferrying an aircraft in 1941.

Right: *at the age of just 27, Amy Johnson became the first woman to fly half way around the world, from Britain to Australia.*
Opposite: *the Mayan ruins at Yucatan, which were first photographed by Sir Charles Lindbergh in 1929.*

1940 Rock paintings discovered at Lascaux

THE ROCK PAINTINGS and engravings at Lascaux were discovered accidentally in 1940. A group of boys searching for their dog stumbled on some underground chambers connected by passageways. The decorated areas are deep within the caves and stone lamps were probably used to illuminate the area where the artist worked. The paintings are coloured in red and yellow, brown and black, made from ochre ground into powder and mixed with fat. The animal drawings are vivid and beautiful. Bison, rhinos, horses, wolf, and deer are shown running and grazing. Several animals are shown in groups or herds. Some of them have spears or arrows embedded in them, a reminder of their importance as a food source to the artist.

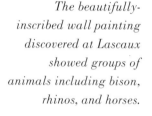

The beautifully-inscribed wall painting discovered at Lascaux showed groups of animals including bison, rhinos, and horses.

1948 Thor Heyerdahl publishes "The Kon-Tiki Expedition"

THOR HEYERDAHL set out to prove that a voyage across the vast seas from America to Polynesia was possible centuries before motorized travel. With the help of an engineer, he built a raft, made from nine huge balsa wood logs bound together with rope, and named it the *Kon-Tiki*. On April 28, 1947, he and five companions set off from Callao Harbour, in Peru. For nearly 100 days they were buffeted by the sea and followed by sharks and whales, but eventually their craft was carried by the trade winds on to a palm-covered island, across the Pacific Ocean. His popular account of the voyage of *Kon-Tiki* was published in 1948, and a documentary film won an Academy Award in 1951.

1950 Tollund Man found

TOLLUND MAN was found in an Iron Age bog on Tollund fen in Denmark. His body was well preserved—and naked except for a well-made leather cap on his head and a hide belt around his waist. Looped around his neck was a leather thong, by which he had met his death, from being hung or strangled.

Radio-carbon dating established that he lived around 210 BC. Analysis of his stomach contents revealed that he had eaten his last meal 12 to 24 hours before his death, a sort of gruel, made from seeds and plants. He had also shaved two or three days before he died. It is less clear why he was killed.

1950 Jacques-Yves Cousteau commands research ship "Calypso"

JACQUES-YVES COUSTEAU (1910–97), the French ocean explorer and pioneer in underwater research, became the foremost authority on oceanography and exploration, inventing (with Emile Gagnan), in 1943, the first scuba-diving device, which he called Aqualung. He commanded the prestigious research ship *Calypso* from 1950, and subsequently wrote a book about his findings, *The Calypso Log*. In 1957 he became head of the Conshelf Saturation Dive Program experiments, in which people live and work for extended periods in deep water along the continental shelves. He also conducted archaeological research, exploring submerged shipwrecks. Cousteau has done much to educate the public about the sea and sea creatures, and his books include *The Silent World* (1953) and *The Living Sea* (1963).

1953 Everest conquered by Sir Edmund Hillary

EDMUND HILLARY was a beekeeper who climbed to the top of the world. In 1953, Hillary and the Nepalese explorer Tenzing Norgay achieved the 29,028 ft summit of Everest. An earlier attempt had been foiled by fierce winds, but on May 29, 1953 at 11:30 A.M. the two men stepped on to the "symmetrical, beautiful snow cone summit." They spent 15 minutes taking photographs and eating mint cake, before leaving the Union Jack, the Nepalese national flag, and the United Nations flag, as well as sweets and biscuits as a Buddhist offering from Tenzing Norgay. Their success was a triumph of scientific planning and lightweight equipment. Hillary was knighted for his achievement, and Tenzing was awarded the George Cross.

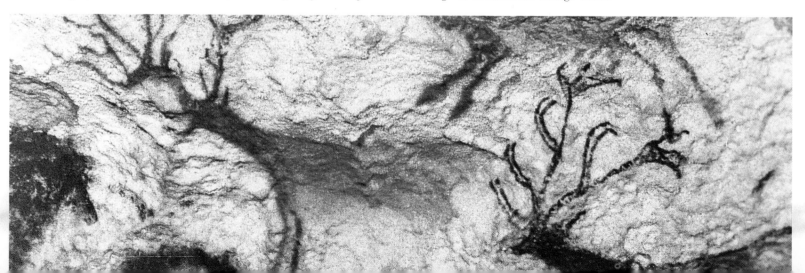

1959 Two monkeys return alive from space trip

THE FIRST ANIMALS to travel in space and return alive were two monkeys. The Jupiter Missile Cone, in which they traveled 1,700 miles and reached a height of 360 miles, was picked up from the Atlantic by the US Navy. Able, a 7-lb rhesus monkey, and Baker, a slight, one-pound squirrel monkey were carefully monitored from the ground to see how they were affected by the stresses of space flight, particularly the weightlessness and the severe acceleration of the launch and then re-entry into the earth's atmosphere. Their performance of trained tasks was also closely observed. The tests were essential preliminaries to the manned space flights which were already in research and development. Seven human astronauts had already been selected.

1960 Piccard and Walsh dive to bottom of Pacific

ON JANUARY 23, 1960, Jacques Piccard and navy lieutenant Donald Walsh descended 35,800 ft into the Mariana Trench of the Pacific Ocean. This is the deepest known point on the Earth's surface, located about 200 miles east of the Mariana Islands. The trench contains a steep-sided gorge called Challenger Deep, into which the two men descended in the bathyscaphe *Trieste*, a pioneering form of submersible craft invented by Piccard's father Auguste. The bathyscaphe was able to withstand the intense pressures of the sea and was capable of measuring currents, temperature, and salinity of the water. It consisted of a compressible, gasoline-filled tank, with a small, pressure-resistant sphere to hold a crew of two. The bathyscaphe undertook a series of record-setting dives, which have proved enduring.

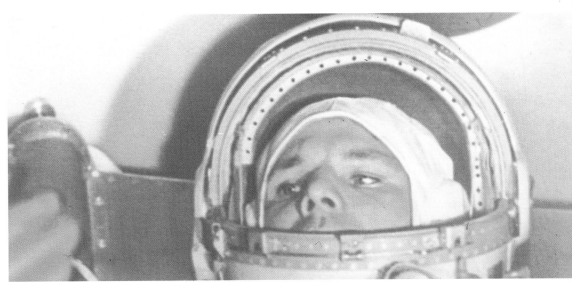

1961 Yuri Gagarin becomes first man to orbit the Earth

ON APRIL 12, 1961, the Soviet cosmonaut Yuri Gagarin (1934–68) became the first man in space as he was launched into orbit in the *Vostok 1* spaceship. Gagarin, an airforce jet pilot, was chosen with the first group of Soviet cosmonauts in March 1960. His ship reached a maximum altitude of 203 miles and circled the Earth once before landing near the Volga River. After the flight, Gagarin became training director of the womens' cosmonaut program and returned to space for the Soyuz program. He was killed in a MiG trainer jet crash in 1968. A crater on the far side of the Moon is named after him.

1965 Russian astronaut walks in space

COLONEL ALEXANDER LEONER of the Soviet Union was the first man to leave his spacecraft and walk in space. Tethered only by a thin cord attached to his craft, the cosmonaut emerged in a bright orange spacesuit and somersaulted against the heavens. Leoner remained outside for about 10 minutes and traveled 3,000 miles in that short time, 300 miles above a small, blue Earth. A few months later, an American, Major Edmund White, climbed out of *Gemini* while it was over the United States. He took photographs and was able to maneuver by using a compressed-oxygen gun to propel himself along. He spent about 14 minutes outside, and had to be persuaded to return to his craft.

Left: *one of the rhesus monkeys that participated in the successful space-travel experiment.*
Above: *Yuri Gagarin, the soviet jet pilot who became the first man in space.*

1967 *"Apollo" spacecraft burns*

VIRGIL "GUS" GRISSOM, Edward White and Roger Chaffee entered *Apollo 1* on January 27, 1967 for a routine countdown test. The command module was filled with pure oxygen, as was usual, and the test proceeded slowly. By 6:30 P.M., the simulated countdown had reached 10. Suddenly Grissom shouted, "Fire in the spacecraft." Seconds later, Chaffee called out, "We've got a bad fire," and flames lashed from the capsule. Technicians tried to reach them, but the heat and smoke drove them back. The hatch, their only escape route, took over a minute to open, but the astronauts were unconscious in seconds from smoke inhalation. After their tragic deaths, the Apollo space program was delayed for 18 months to produce a safer and more reliable craft.

Below: perhaps the greatest scientific accomplishment this century— Buzz Aldrin walks on the moon. Right: the launch of the Columbia space shuttle.

1969 *First man on the moon*

MILLIONS OF TELEVISION viewers from all around the world watched as Neil Armstrong, commander of *Apollo 11* climbed down the ladder of *Eagle*, the lunar module. As he placed his foot on the surface of the moon, his voice crackled through the static: "That's one small step for a man, and one giant leap for mankind." Armstrong was joined by Edwin "Buzz" Aldrin, and the two men in bulky spacesuits walked in the moon's low gravity, leaving their footprints in the dust. The surface was like "a fine powder ... it has a soft beauty of its own." A few hours earlier, the world had heard: "Houston. Tranquillity Base. The Eagle has landed," and now there were men on the moon.

1976 *"Viking" spacecraft sends back first pictures of Mars*

THE *VIKING* SPACECRAFT was launched to find out if there was life on Mars. Previous pictures of the planet's surface had been taken from a distance and had given a generalized impression of the cold, red planet. *Viking* landed on the Plains of Gold in July 1976, and within minutes its camera was sending out clear pictures of the surface of Mars. It looked flat, scattered with small, sharp rocks and a few large boulders. The ground was red, iron-rich clay and the sky a strange pink, probably from the tiny particles of red dust suspended in the air. Over 52,000 photographs were sent back to earth and the planet was observed in greater detail than had ever before.

1981 *First flight of the US "Space Shuttle"*

THE *SPACE SHUTTLE* was the first reusable spacecraft. Until then, creative energy had been focused on winning the race to be first on the moon. Monster rockets had to be developed rapidly. They could be used only once, but they would get you there first. After Neil Armstrong planted the American flag on lunar soil, scientists could turn their attention to smaller, more economical projects. The *Space Shuttle* would be a delivery vehicle, a flying laboratory to repair and recover faulty satellites. The *Space Shuttle* could remain in space for up to eight days on a normal run. With extra supplies, missions could be extended for up to 30 days. The *Shuttle*'s first launch was on April 12, 1981.

1985 Joint French–US team locates wreck of "Titanic"

ROBERT BALLARD of Woods Hole Oceanographic Institution in Massachusetts and Jean-Louis Michel of the Institute for the Research and Exploration of the Sea in Paris headed a joint US–French expedition to locate the fated British ocean liner, *Titanic*, which had been struck by an iceberg and sunk off the coast of Newfoundland in 1912. Ballard's *Argo*—a submersible sled with a camera—photographed the sunken vessel 2 ½ miles under the ocean surface, 400 miles southeast of Newfoundland, preserved almost intact 13,000 ft beneath the ocean's surface. The search had taken 16 days. It was the first sight of the *Titanic* in nearly 75 years.

1986 US "Challenger" space shuttle explodes after take-off

THE 25TH MISSION of the *Challenger* space shuttle had been postponed and delayed four times, before its crew of seven rode out to the launch pad on the morning of January 28, 1986. After a cold night at Cape Canaveral, the launch tower sparkled with icicles, but the countdown went ahead. A few seconds after launch, puffs of smoke emerged from the right-hand booster, but *Challenger* continued to climb normally. Fifty-eight seconds later, a small flame appeared, and then the space shuttle was engulfed in a huge fireball. *Challenger* was torn apart by aerodynamic forces. The fragments, including the crew compartment, continued upwards for another few moments, and then splashed down into the Atlantic Ocean. All seven were killed.

1990 Trans-Antarctica expedition by dogsled

IN 1990, Will Steger and Jean-Louis Etienne completed the first dogsled trip across 3,800 miles of Antarctica. Steger, an American explorer, had previously reached the North Pole accompanied by five American and Canadian explorers in 1986, assisted only by dogs, and they were the first to reach the pole without mechanical assistance since Robert E. Peary planted a flag there in 1909. The Antarctica expedition set out to achieve the same milestone in the South. Explorations of the Antarctic have continued since that time, with satellites showing new and undiscovered areas of the globe still untouched by humans. The continent is of particular interest to environmental scientists because its thick covering of ice—on average 6,500 ft deep—holds the history of the Earth's atmosphere.

1993 US space shuttle launched to repair the Hubble space telescope

THE 1993 launch of the space shuttle *Endeavour*, to repair the Hubble telescope, combined high technology with down-to-earth practicality. On its 11-day mission, the craft reached 360 miles above the earth. Its crew managed the tricky manoeuvre of snaring the $3 billion telescope to replace eight electrical fuses and install two pairs of gyroscopes. They were outside the shuttle for a gruelling eight hours, wrestling with jammed doors on the telescope. Eventually the only way they could get them to close was by tying them together with an improvized luggage strap! They also fitted the telescope with corrective optics, so that it could see to the edge of the Universe, possibly unravelling the secrets of the world's beginning.

1997 First images sent back by "Pathfinder" of the surface of Mars

A ROBOT EXPLORER from the *Pathfinder* mission touched down on the surface of Mars in the early hours of July 5, 1997, and sent back pictures of a planet which is 310 million miles from Earth. The photographs were proof that the *Pathfinder* was on stable ground after hurtling down on to the dusty plains of *Ares vallis*. It was the first time a rover had been put on the Martian surface, and that a craft had landed on a planet without orbiting it. The robot, *Sojourner*, moves at just under half an inch per second, identifying soil and rock samples. The *Pathfinder* will stay in place, sending back pictures and information on Martian weather and its atmosphere.

The Pathfinder *rover vehicle that supplied the first pictures from the surface of Mars.*

Transport

8

Success four flights thursday morning all against twenty one mile wind started from level with engine power alone speed through air thirty one miles longest 57 second inform press home christmas

Orville Wright, 1903

1900 Métro underground rail service opens in Paris

ON JULY 19, 1900, the first 6 miles of the Paris Métro line were opened. Work on the line began in 1898, and its rapid construction was made possible by modified cut-and-cover methods. Vertical shafts were sunk at intervals along the planned route, and from these shafts side trenches were dug. Masonry foundations to support wooden shuttering were then placed immediately under the road surfaces. Construction of the roof arch then proceeded with little disturbance to street traffic. This method of construction is still used in Paris. The Paris Métro became the world's third largest subway (second largest in terms of passenger traffic), carrying more than one billion passengers per year.

1900 Maiden flight of the Zeppelin airship

Overleaf: the Austin Rover Mini, designed to appeal to the masses (see page 138). Below: Ford has become a household name since the company was founded in 1903. Right: the Wright brothers finally make a successful flight at Kitty Hawk, North Carolina.

FERDINAND GRAF VON ZEPPELIN (1838–1917), was the inventor of the rigid airship, or "dirigible balloon," a lighter-than-air flying machine with propulsion and steering mechanisms. Rigid airships, which came to be known as Zeppelins after their founder, were kept buoyant by either hydrogen or helium gas. Zeppelin spent nearly a decade developing the dirigible. He made the first directed flight on July 2, 1900, in the first zeppelin, which was 413 ft in length and contained hydrogen gas in 16 cells. By the year of his death he had built a Zeppelin fleet, some of which were used to bomb London during World War I. The Zeppelin was too slow and explosive a target in wartime and ultimately too fragile to withstand bad weather. The era of the Zeppelin ended after the explosion of the *Hindenburg* in 1937.

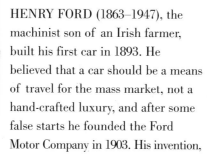

1903 Ford Motor Company founded

HENRY FORD (1863–1947), the machinist son of an Irish farmer, built his first car in 1893. He believed that a car should be a means of travel for the mass market, not a hand-crafted luxury, and after some false starts he founded the Ford Motor Company in 1903. His invention,

and the development of his moving assembly-line technique of mass production (1913), altered the face of the automotive industry. He was backed by a group of Detroit businessmen, who believed that there was potential in a "horseless carriage." Henry Ford was the major figure in the world's automobile industry for the next 15 years, and his company became a world leader in the industry—a position it still holds today. His production methods were intensively studied; in Germany they were called *Fordismus*.

1903 Wright brothers make the first flight

FOR MANY YEARS, attempts had been made to get an aircraft that was heavier than air off the ground, but it took the considerable genius of American aviation pioneers Orville Wright (1871–1948) and Wilbur

Wright (1867–1912) to achieve that dream. They invented the first successful self-propelled airplane after conducting tests with kites and then gliders. Before attempting powered flight, they solved the essential problems of controlling a plane's motion in rising, descending, and turning. The Wright brothers, together with Charles Taylor, designed and built a 12–16-hp engine and propeller for their plane—which was originally named *Flyer I* and commonly called *Kitty Hawk*. On December 17, 1903, on an isolated beach near Kitty Hawk, North Carolina, Orville achieved the first successful flight ever made in a self-propelled, heavier-than-air craft.

1904 New York subway opens line for electric trains

ON OCTOBER 27, 1904, the first permanent New York City subway line opened to the public. The Interborough Rapid Transit (IRT) line ran from Brooklyn Bridge north under Lafayette Street, Fourth Avenue, and Park Avenue to 42nd Street, west to Broadway, and north to 145th Street, completing the run in 26 minutes with a train of five copper-sheathed wooden cars with red-painted roofs, each car seating 56. On the first day, 111,000 people rode the line, increasing to 319,000 on the second, and to 350,000 on the third. For the next 40 years, the city continued to enlarge its subway system, by both extending underground trackage and replacing elevated railroads with subways. It grew to cover more than 842 miles, becoming the largest rapid-transit system in the world.

1904 US Army rejects heavier-than-air flying machines

A YEAR AFTER THE Wright Brothers' landmark flight, they approached the US Army with plans to put aircraft into military use but on September 20, 1904 they were rejected by the army on the grounds that their flying machine was statically unstable—in other words, it needed a pilot to fly it. However, as European inventors began work on more technologically advanced aircraft, the army began to take interest, and in 1907 the Wright brothers were contracted to build a plane capable of carrying two men on flights of up to 124 miles. The plane was delivered and tests were completed in June 1909. On the basis of this, the Army established a small aeronautical division in 1907—a division that was eventually expanded to become the US Air Force.

1905 Trans-Siberian Railway opens

THE TRANS-SIBERIAN RAILWAY—a Russian railroad connecting Moscow with Vladivostok—was finally completed in 1916, making it the longest continuous rail line in the world. During the 1880s, a line had been built as far east as Chelyabinsk, 1,056 miles from Moscow, and the major portion of the Siberian sectors was finished between 1891 and 1900. The completion of the Chinese Eastern Railway in Manchuria, and a short water connection across Lake Baikal, gave Russia a new transportation route across Asia by 1903, and in 1904 a rail loop around the foot of Lake Baikal was opened. With a flurry of enthusiasm, the railway was officially opened on

January 1, 1905, although building work went on until 1916, when the Amur sector was finished. Today, the sparse population of Siberia is concentrated almost exclusively along the route of the Trans-Siberian Railroad.

1906 Alberto Santos-Dumont makes record air flight in France

ON NOVEMBER 12, 1906 Brazilian aviator Alberto Santos-Dumont, made a record flight of 235 yds in his flying machine in France. Santos-Dumont, who began his flying career as a balloonist, began to construct dirigible airships and in 1901 won the Deutsch de la Meurthe prize of 100,000 francs for flying a "lighter-than-air" aircraft for half an hour—the first man to do so. In 1906 he built a heavier-than-air craft on the principle of the box kite, a design that made him one of the pioneers of early flying. In 1932 he committed suicide, depressed by the use of aircraft for military purposes.

A train fitted with a snow-plough on the Trans-Siberian Railway, providing a direct route between Moscow and Vladivostok.

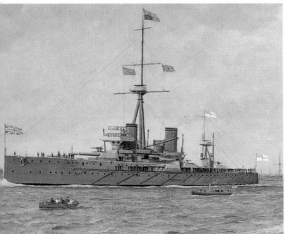

1907 Official launch of HMS "Dreadnought"

CALLED "THE WORLD'S MOST POWERFUL BATTLESHIP," HMS *Dreadnought* was unofficially launched in Britain in 1906, and on February 6, 1907 she clocked the fastest time from Gibraltar to Trinidad. HMS *Dreadnought* was the first battleship in which secondary armament was entirely dispensed with. She was also the first battleship powered by steam turbines. With a maximum speed of 21 knots, *Dreadnought* was a major advance in performance, for she outranged and outgunned every battleship. Remarkably, she was constructed in only 366 days. For these reasons, the name "Dreadnought" was given to this class of ship. HMS *Dreadnought* represented a threat to Germany, which retaliated by accelerating its own naval construction program.

Above: *the HMS Dreadnought, the first battleship powered by steam turbines.* Below: *the Model XI, Bleriot's monoplane that successfully carried him across the Channel.* Opposite: *the New York Grand Central Station which boasted 48 tracks on two levels; it remained the largest rail terminal in the city for nearly 80 years.*

1909 Blériot flies across the English Channel

ON JULY 25, 1909, the French pilot Louis Blériot (1872–1936) became the first man to fly across the English Channel, in a flight from near Calais to Dover Castle. The flight, which he undertook in a single-winged aircraft of his own design—the No. XI tractor monoplane—took just 43 minutes. For this accomplishment, he won the £1,000 prize put up by the London *Daily Mail*. The flight proved that Britain could be reached by airplane from the European continent. During the war, Blériot helped create the SPAD concern, a company responsible for many of the finest French fighters.

1912 "Titanic" sinks on maiden voyage

ON APRIL 15, 1912, the "unsinkable" ship *Titanic* struck an iceberg off the coast of Newfoundland, and sank with a loss of over 1,500 passengers. The ship had been claimed unsinkable because of her 16 watertight compartments, but the collision opened too many of these, and she sank without trace, until 1985 when her wreck was discovered. The ship, the largest and most luxurious built up to that time, was on her maiden voyage from Southampton to New York, carrying more than 2,200 people—many of whom were rich and famous. The death toll was blamed on the shortage of lifeboats, several of which were sent away half-full, and the fact that many passengers opted to stay aboard the ship rather than risk their lives on the icy sea. A nearby unidentified liner failed to respond to the *Titanic*'s distress calls.

1913 Grand Central Station opens in New York

ON FEBRUARY 2, 1913, Grand Central Station was opened in New York City at 42nd Street and Park Avenue, replacing a 41-year-old New York Central and New Haven train shed with the world's largest railway station. Grand Central, which had an impressive 31 tracks on its upper level and 17 on its lower level, was opened to commuters from October 1912. Far bigger than Penn Station, New York's second largest train station, Grand Central remained the city's largest and most important rail terminal for 78 years (until 1991), after which it became a strictly commuter terminal, Amtrak having rerouted its long-distance trains to Penn Station.

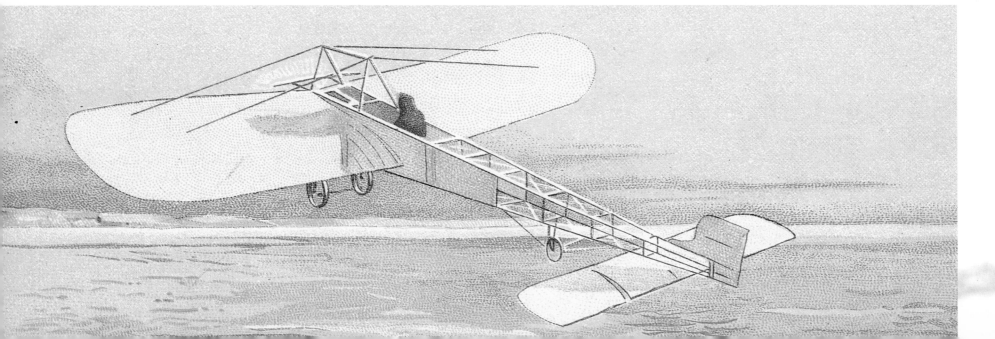

1919 *Alcock and Brown fly the first non-stop flight across the Atlantic*

THE ENGLISH AVIATOR J. W. Alcock (1892–1919) was the pilot of the first non-stop flight across the Atlantic Ocean. Alcock gained fame as a World War I flying ace. In June 1919 he and his navigator, Lt. Arthur Whidden Brown (1886–1948), made their historic Newfoundland-to-Ireland transatlantic flight—a crossing of 16 hours 27 minutes—in a Vickers-Vimy biplane bomber. The plane landed nose-down in Ireland, but both men were unhurt and were later knighted for their accomplishment. Flying to Paris several months afterwards, Alcock was killed when his plane crashed on the Normandy coast.

1924 *Malcolm Campbell breaks world land speed record*

BRITISH CAPTAIN MALCOLM CAMPBELL (1885–1949) broke the world land speed record again and again over his illustrious and unprecedented career, using ever bigger and more powerful vehicles—most of which he called *Bluebird*. Campbell devoted his life to achieving and then holding the land speed record for Britain, and he set new records in 1927 at 74 MPH; 1928 at 206 MPH; 1931 at 245 MPH; 1932 at 253 MPH; 1933 at 274 MPH; and in 1935 at 276 MPH. Later that same year he broke the 300 MPH barrier and clocked up 3,01.1 MPH. His son, Donald (1921–67), took over as world speed champion, carrying on the *Bluebird* name.

1927 *Last Model T car is produced by Ford in the US*

PRODUCTION OF THE FAMOUS Model T Ford, also called the "Tin Lizzie" or the "Flivver," ceased on May 31, 1927, when the 15,007,003rd car rolled off the assembly line. The Model T Ford was introduced in 1908, designed by Henry Ford as the "car for the great multitude," and it was an immediate success. It had a four-cylinder, 20-hp engine, and a simple planetary transmission operated by foot pedals on the floor. To meet the demand for the new car, the Ford Motor Company introduced the moving assembly-line technique for mass production. By 1919 nearly 60 per cent of all US motor vehicles and half of those in the entire world were Model T Fords.

The Model T Ford had a four-cylinder, 20-hp engine, and was immensely popular at the beginning of the century.

1927 *First subway system opens in Tokyo*

IN 1927, Tokyo's Chikatetsu subway was officially opened to the public. The Tokyo system would grow to have eight lines with 102.9 miles of track running to the far reaches of Tokyo's suburbs. From the 1960s, Tokyo lost most of its central city residents to the suburbs, following the trend of cities in most developed countries, and more than 85 per cent of Tokyo's commuters now use the subway system. The volume of commuter traffic on the lines is the highest in the world, and it is not uncommon for office workers in Tokyo to spend two hours or more each day in overcrowded commuter trains.

1928 *First electric traffic signals introduced in the US*

THE FIRST ELECTRIC TRAFFIC SIGNALS were introduced in the US in response to the extraordinary growth in motor vehicle traffic. The system was a simple "stop and go" scheme, and contributed to a significant decrease in traffic-related deaths.

Left: *the crowded subway in Tokyo, where the volume of human traffic is the world's highest.* Below: *the* Flying Scotsman, *the first train service to run directly from London to Edinburgh.*

Today visual control systems are linked to pneumatic vehicle detectors and electronic queue detectors, and signals and television pictures are fed to a central computer control room with human managers, who can take charge in an emergency. Before the 1984 Summer Olympics, Los Angeles installed 3,200 computer-linked sensors in the intersections at 800 traffic signals in its central downtown area. A similar system was installed in New York City in the mid-1990s, and most major cities have plans for implementation soon.

1928 *Express service on the "Flying Scotsman"*

IN 1928, the London and North Eastern Railway offered a revolutionary service, running an express train non-stop from London to Edinburgh—a distance of 392 miles—a landmark in the history of rail travel. Because of its superb speed, the train was nicknamed the *Flying Scotsman.* During World War I the government took control, but not ownership, of the line, and in 1948 all the railways in Great Britain were nationalized and reorganized as British Railways. Increased competition from highway transport has resulted in the abandonment of many branch lines, but the original route of the *Flying Scotsman* is still home to a frequent, popular service.

1934 Diesel-powered passenger trains go into service in the USA

THE INVENTION OF the diesel locomotive made great increases in the operating efficiency of locomotive engines. The diesel engine was invented in the 1890s, and the first diesel-electric locomotive was used by the Central Railroad of New Jersey for switching operations in New York City in the mid-1920s. In 1934 the Burlington and the Union Pacific both used diesel power for their passenger trains, and the new *Burlington Zephyr* train went into service between Chicago and Denver. On May 26th, this streamlined passenger train hit a top speed of 112.5 MPH and averaged 77.6 MPH on a 1,017-mile non-stop run between the two cities. This exciting development heralded the beginning of the end of steam locomotive use in the US.

1935 The first helicopter flight

LEONARDO DA VINCI is generally credited with sketching and describing a helicopter in 1483. But the helicopter—like aircraft of most descriptions—required a lightweight power source, which the gasoline engine supplied. The helicopter was perfected between 1936 and 1941.

Although modest flights had been made prior to this time, it was not until 1935 that a coaxial helicopter constructed by Louis Bréguet and René Dorand in France achieved flights of sustained duration. With the perfection of the single-rotor type by Igor Sikorsky in the United States (1939–41), the helicopter became a practical aircraft capable of carrying a useful load and performing diverse commercial, military, and emergency functions.

1936 Hitler launches Volkswagen, "the people's car"

DESIGNED BY Ferdinand Porsche in the 1930s as the German "people's car"—a small automobile that would be inexpensive enough for the average family—the Volkswagen, with its air-cooled rear engine, was assembled by hand in Nazi Germany. The cornerstone for the first Volkswagen factory was dedicated on May 26, 1936, at Wolfsurb on the Mittelland Canal. The low-cost "Beetle" was commissioned by Adolf Hitler and launched by him in 1936; it would not go into mass production for more than 10 years, but more than 18 million of the "Beetles" would eventually be sold, exceeding the Model T Ford's record. Volkswagen's decision was to concentrate on a single model, to avoid annual model changes.

Right: the first Volkswagen, the "people's car" that would eventually become one of the most popular in the world.
Opposite: The aerodynamic Railton car in which John Cobb broke the land speed record at Bonneville Salt Flats.

1939 New land speed record. for John Cobb

ON AUGUST 23, 1939, British driver John Cobb (1900–52) set a new land speed record at the Salt Flats, Bonneville, Utah, driving his Railton *Red Lion* at 368.85 MPH. The aerodynamically designed car was created by Reid Railton and had a unique system of cooling the transmission brakes with ice. Cobb had previously set a world speed record of 350.2 MPH on September 15, 1938, and he went on to set another official record, on September 26, 1947, clocking 394.19 MPH in his Railton *Mobil Special*. That record wasn't broken until 1964, when Donald Campbell, in a Campbell *Bluebird*, smashed the record at an amazing 403.1 MPH.

1949 De Havilland "Comet's" first flight

BRITAIN INTRODUCED the world's first jet airliner in 1952, the British Overseas Airline Corporation's (BOAC) de Havilland *Comet 1*, which cut the journey time to South Africa by almost half. On July 27th, the *Comet* made its maiden flight from an English airfield with war hero Group Captain John Cunningham piloting. The *Comet* went into service in 1952, running scheduled flights from London to Johannesburg in South Africa, but a series of crashes caused by metal fatigue—an unprecedented problem—forced the company to close for several years while design changes were made. By then, however, the Boeing 747 was in operation and had taken a lead in the world's airlines.

1958 USS "Nautilus" arrives in Portland

IN AUGUST 1958 USS *Nautilus* was welcomed at Portland, Dorset, after a 6,100-mile trip that included the first cruise beneath the polar ice cap to the North Pole. The world's first nuclear submarine, the *Nautilus* was built at the Groton, Connecticut, shipyards, and launched in January 1954. It had been developed primarily thanks to the determination of Admiral Hyman Rickover, who—despite powerful opposition—secured the US Navy's backing for the program. The ship was 322.8 ft long, carried a crew of 105, and traveled at more than 20 knots when submerged. Its 6100-mile journey dramatically

demonstrated the potential of nuclear submarines. However, in later years, when better designed and armed submarines were evolved by the US Army, the *Nautilus* became increasingly costly to maintain. It was decommissioned in 1980.

1959 Austin Rover launches the Mini

ONE OF THE BEST examples of post-war design was Austin Rover's Mini, which became the motorcar of the 1960s in the UK and all over Europe. Designed by Alec Issigonis (1906–88), a Turkish designer, the Mini was marketed as the ultimate car of a new generation, and considered to be "classless." It offered front-wheel drive, "audacious handling" and high speed to an avid market, and cleverly provided a great deal of space in a very small car. "Fun" was the keyword in Austin Rover's campaign, and as a catchword of the 1960s, the car epitomized a generation of hedonistic youth. The size of the Mini precluded its sale in the US, where drivers favored larger cars, such as General Motor's Cadillac, launched a few years earlier. The Mini was Britain's best-selling car, and is still selling today.

Above: *the Mini reached the height of its popularity during the 1960s, its affordability and fun design appealing to the masses.* Opposite: *the ocean liner* Queen Elizabeth II, *a replacement for the original* Queen Elizabeth *which had been destroyed by fire during refitting works.*

1959 Hovercraft is tested in England

THE FIRST AIR-CUSHION VEHICLE, or hovercraft, stemmed from work done in the 1950s by the British electronics engineer Sir Christopher Cockerell. He constructed a model from two coffee tins and a hair dryer and measured its lift with kitchen scales. The idea was patented in 1955, and in 1959 the first full-scale ACV, the SR.N1, was successfully tested at Cowes, England. One of the largest of today's ACVs is the SR.N4, a class of vehicle that is used for ferry service across the English Channel. Hovercrafts cruise at up to 77 knots , making them the fastest class of seaworthy vehicles in the world.

1960 Japan introduces the Datsun to the US

THE DATSUN MOTORCAR, introduced in the United States by Japan's Nissan Motors, was underpowered and hard to start and stop, but would rank sixth among imported US cars by 1966, and third by 1970. By 1980 Japanese automobile production (11 million cars and trucks) would for the first time overtake US production (7.8 million cars and trucks),

which declined by 30 per cent as a result of imports. Imported cars and trucks, 78 per cent of them Japanese, took over nearly a quarter of the US market. In 1981, Japanese makers were forced to placate US industry leaders by voluntarily limiting exports to America to 1.68 million units.

1962 The "Orient Express" goes out of business

ON MAY 27, 1962, after nearly 79 years of operation, the *Orient Express* ended its service. The service was a victim of the airplane, which cut travel time by more than 50 per cent to most European destinations. The *Orient Express* was Europe's first transcontinental train. Its route and the train itself were designed by the Compagnie Internationale des Wagon-Lits et des Grands Exprès Européens headed by Georges Nagelmakers, and included two sleeping cars, an elaborate dining car, a baggage wagon containing a lavish kitchen, and a mail car. The dining car and both sleeping cars were fitted with newly invented four-wheel bogies and superior springing that gave passengers a steady ride even round the sharpest bends at speeds of close to 50 MPH.

1962 Trans-Canada Highway opened

CONSTRUCTION BEGAN on the Trans-Canada Highway in 1949, and it was officially opened in 1962, although work was not finally completed until 1965. The highway is a 4,890-mile road across southern Canada, from St John's, Newfoundland, to Victoria on Vancouver Island, British Columbia. It is the longest national highway in the world. The paved, occasionally divided road, which passes through all Canadian provinces, was jointly financed by the federal and provincial governments, and acts as the major link between cities across the country, contributing enormously to the development of many of the areas along its route.

1967 "Queen Elizabeth II" launched

IN 1967, the *Queen Elizabeth II* was launched, making its maiden voyage in 1969. Nicknamed the *QE2*, the ship was a replacement for the original *Queen Elizabeth*, a British ocean liner driven by steam turbines and weighing 85,000 tons. The original ship was launched in 1938 and used as a troop ship during World War II, later becoming the most opulent of the great passenger liners during the era of transatlantic

The first flight of the revolutionary Concorde *in 1969; the plane was designed to fly at twice the speed of sound.*

ocean travel. In 1969 the ship was sold to investors, who planned to use it as a floating university, but the liner was destroyed by fire while being refitted in Hong Kong. The *Queen Elizabeth II*, its smaller replacement (at 70,000 tons) continued to make transatlantic crossings but also functioned as a cruise ship.

1969 "Concorde's" first flights

THE *CONCORDE* is the best-known supersonic transport (SST), the result of an initiative undertaken by the governments of Great Britain and France in 1962 to build a civil transport airplane that could fly at twice the speed of sound. The prototype made her first flight from Toulouse on March 2, 1969, and after considerable further development a lengthened and refined model entered service with British Airways and Air France on January 21, 1976. The *Concorde* had the longest and most thorough testing procedure of any commercial airplane. The *Concorde*, which flies at 1,450 MPH, did not achieve its goal of flying at twice the speed of sound until November 4, 1970.

1970 Boeing 747 jumbo jet goes into service

WORLD AIR TRAFFIC quadrupled during the 1960s, leading to the advent of wide-bodied jet airliners, called jumbo jets. The first jumbo jet, the 360-seat, four-engined Boeing 747, began flying on January 21, 1970 for Pan American. Four years earlier Pan Am had ordered 25 Boeing 747 jumbo jets, setting a lead that other carriers were forced to follow. Depending on seat configuration, the new planes carried between 342 and 490 passengers, numbers that taxed the capacities of existing terminal facilities. Few airlines were able to keep their 747 jets filled and many, including Pan Am, suffered financial losses as a result of adopting the unprofitable jumbo jets. Boeing introduced two more wide-body passenger planes in the early 1980s, the 757 and the 767.

1981 TGV train service begins in France

FRANCE'S TGV *(TRAIN À GRANDE VITESSE)* train began
service from Paris to Lyon on September 22, 1981. Powered by electricity and capable of 236-mph speeds, it was Europe's first super-
high-speed passenger line and it was extended to reach Marseilles by
1983. The fastest scheduled passenger train runs in the world are
those of France's TGV Atlantique, which travel between Paris and
various cities in western France, at 186.4 MPH. The TGV uses "dedicated track" over much of its route and has permanently linked cars.
It employs electric-powered locomotives, and its fuel consumption
per passenger is about one-fifth of that used by airplanes. The TGV
has been called the "star train" of the 1980s.

1994 Opening of the Channel Tunnel

AFTER MORE THAN SIX YEARS OF construction and at a cost of
more than £10 million, the English Channel Tunnel was officially opened
on May 6, 1994, by Queen Elizabeth II of Britain and President François
Mitterrand of France. The Channel Tunnel, or "Chunnel" as it is some-
times called, consists of two single-track tunnels and a service tunnel
between them. The tunnels run for 31 miles at an average
depth of 131 ft beneath the Channel seabed from terminals in
Folkestone, England, and Calais, France. With 24 miles of the system
running under the sea, it is the world's longest underwater tunnel. The
Channel Tunnel connects the railway networks of British Rail (BR),
French Railways (SNCF), and Belgium Railways (SNCB). The railways'
new Eurostar trains carry passengers and freight directly between Britain
and continental Europe.

*The Channel Tunnel
was finally opened in
1994 after years of
planning and construction
and at a cost of more
than £10 million.*

Science & Technology

People must understand that science is inherently neither a potential for good nor for evil. It is a potential to be harnessed by man to do his bidding.

Glenn T. Seaborg, 1964

1901 *First disposable razor launched by Gillette*

THE IDEA OF using sharpened metallic blades to remove facial or body hair has been with us for most of our history. Although versions of razors have been in use since the Bronze Age, it was not until 1847 that the safety razor was patented by William Henson. At the turn of the century a traveling salesman and inventor, King Camp Gillette from Wisconsin, developed a safety razor with disposable blades. He began to market this money-saving invention in 1901 and the Gillette name is still a household one. A Utopian socialist, King Gillette, set up a "World Corporation" in Arizona in 1910 to advocate a world planned economy.

1901 *First transatlantic radio transmission by Marconi*

IN RADIO TRANSMISSIONS a microphone converts sound waves into electromagnetic waves, which are picked up by a receiving aerial and fed to a loudspeaker, which converts them back into sound waves. The theory of electromagnetic waves was developed by James Maxwell in 1864 and confirmed practically by Heinrich Hertz in 1888. After experimenting with devices to convert electromagnetic waves into electrical signals, Italian Guglielmo Marconi succeeded in transmitting radio waves over a mile in 1895. In 1898 he transmitted signals across the English Channel and in 1901 established transatlantic communication with St John's, Newfoundland, from Poldhu in Cornwall. He shared the Nobel Prize for Physics in 1909 with Karl Braun.

Below: Marconi, the first man to succeed in transmitting radio waves across the Channel, seen with one of the earliest wirelesses. Right and overleaf: French scientists Marie and Pierre Curie in their laboratory.

1903 *Pierre and Marie Curie share Nobel Prize for work on radioactivity*

POLISH-BORN SCIENTIST Marie Curie studied in Paris from 1891. Impressed by Antoine Becquerel's experiments, Curie decided to investigate the nature of uranium rays. In 1898 her husband Pierre abandoned his own researches to assist in her investigations of a new radioactive element in pitchblende ores, which proved to be polonium and radium. Both scientists refused to take out a patent and they were jointly awarded the Nobel Prize for Physics, for the discovery of radioactivity in 1903 with Becquerel. After Pierre's death in 1906, Marie continued their work and in 1910 she succeeded in isolating pure radium, for which she won the Nobel Prize for Chemistry in 1911.

Petit Parisie
SUPPLÉMENT LITTÉRAIRE ILLUSTRÉ
DIRECTION: 18, rue d'Enghien (10°), PARIS

UNE NOUVELLE DÉCOUVERTE. — LE RADIUM
ET Mme CURIE DANS LEUR LABORATOIRE

1910 *Crippen caught by first police use of radio telegraphy*

TELEGRAPHY IS the transmission of coded messages along wires by means of electronic signals and was devised by Charles Wheatstone and William Cooke in England in 1839. Marconi's later experiments in radio telegraphy helped open up the world. In 1910 Hawley Harvey Crippen was trying to flee from the UK with his mistress Ethel le Neve. He had murdered his wife and buried her remains in the cellar of his London home. The suspicious captain of the Atlantic liner contacted Scotland Yard by radio telegraphy (its first use for police purposes) and a detective was dispatched in a faster boat and later arrested the couple. Crippen was executed at Pentonville.

1914 Ford develops moving assembly line at plant in US

US INVENTOR Eli Whitney pioneered the concept of industrial assembly in the 1790s when he employed unskilled labor to assemble muskets. The modern assembly line method of mass production, where a product is built up step-by-step by successive workers, each adding one part, was introduced for the car industry by Ransome Olds of the US in 1901. Henry Ford, who set up the Ford Motor Company in 1903, further refined the principle and introduced the moving conveyor belt in 1913. The design was improved and used for the production of the famous Model T Ford, 15 million of which were produced by this process between 1908 and 1928.

1923 Early TV pictures in US

IN 1873 it was discovered that the electrical properties of the element selenium varied according to the amount of light it received, making it possible to transmit pictures over a distance. The practical idea of television was born and in 1884 a system was patented by Paul Nipkow in Germany. Experimenters in the UK and US were working with the neon gas-discharge lamp produced by D. Moore in 1917 in the US. Using this,

both J. Baird and C. Jenkins experimented with mechanical methods, with Jenkins showing early pictures in the US (1923). In 1926 Baird gave the first demonstration of true television by electrically transmitting moving pictures in halftones.

1927 Wallace Carothers of Du Pont develops plastics, synthetics and nylon

AMERICAN INDUSTRIAL CHEMIST Wallace Hume Carothers taught at various universities before researching polymerization at the Du Pont Company at Wilmington. Discovering that some polymers are fiber-forming, he produced the first successful synthetic rubber, Neoprene, finding it to be much more resistant to light, heat, oxidation, and petroleum than ordinary rubber. He followed this with the development of nylon and plastics. Nylon was the first all-synthesized fiber, made from petroleum, natural gas, air, and water. It was found to be much stronger and more elastic than natural materials. Despite his achievements, however, he committed suicide in 1937, and the patent for nylon, awarded posthumously, was given to the Du Pont Company.

1933–36 British and US engineers develop enhanced TV

ALTHOUGH THE first true television system had been demonstrated in 1926 by John Logie Baird it was the ideas of fellow Brit A. Cambell-Swinton that helped to advance television further. In 1908 Cambell-Swinton had pointed out that cathode-ray tubes would best effect transmission and reception, and cathode-ray tubes were used experimentally in the UK from 1934. In 1932 the Radio Corporation of America demonstrated all-electronic television using a camera tube called the iconoscope (patented by Vladimir Zworykin in 1923) and a cathode-ray tube in the receiver. In 1929 the British Broadcasting Company began broadcasting experimental TV programs using Baird's system and in 1936 it began regular broadcasting from Alexandra Palace, London.

Left: the Model T Ford, one of the 15 million built by means of the assembly line.
Below: the Ekco-Scophony Television Receiver, one of the earliest of its kind.

The Enigma Decoder,
an early forerunner
of the computer, was
used during World
War II to decipher
German messages.

1940 *Alan Turing cracks Enigma code at Bletchley Park*

ALAN TURING was a brilliant English mathematician and logician. In 1936 he described a "universal computing machine" that could theoretically be programed to solve any problem capable of solution. This concept, now called the "Turing Machine," foreshadowed the computer. During World War II he worked with the Government Code and Cypher School at Bletchley Park, where he played a significant role in cracking the German "Enigma" codes. After the war he worked in the construction of early computers and the development of programing techniques. He also championed the idea that computers would eventually be capable of human thought (Artificial Intelligence) and he suggested the Turing test to assess this capability.

1946 *Eckert and Mauchly produce ENIAC, the first general-purpose computer*

THE VERY FIRST electronic digital computer, known as the ABC computer, was built by J. Atanasoff and C. Berry between 1937 and 1942. A special purpose-built computer with vacuum tubes was built independently at Bletchley Park; it was known as the Colossus and was designed to decipher the "Enigma" code during World War II. The major breakthrough in computing came when J. Mauchly and P. Eckert in Pennsylvania built the high-speed electronic digital computer known as the ENIAC (Electronic Numerical Integrator and Computer). In primitive form the ENIAC contained virtually all the circuitry used in present day high-speed computers. It was used by the US Army for military calculations.

1947 *Invention of the transistor*

THE TRANSISTOR was invented in 1947 by John Bardeen, Walter Brattain and William Shockley at the Bell Telephone Laboratories in the US. Transistors, along with subsequent developments such as integrated circuits, are made of crystalline solid materials called semiconductors, which have electrical properties that can be varied over a wide range by adding small quantities of other elements. Early transistors were

"Strictly between you + me...."

CARELESS TALK COSTS LIVES

"Careless Talk Costs Lives"—a propaganda poster from World War II, one of the periods of great scientific progress this century.

produced using germanium but during the 1950s research on the purification of silicon allowed this to be used instead. The properties of silicon soon enabled the creation of tiny transistors that rapidly supplanted the use of vacuum tubes in computers by 1960, as they were smaller and more reliable.

1951 Remington Rand introduce the UNIVAC computer for use by businesses

AFTER THEIR WORK on ENIAC, Eckert and Mauchly established a computer manufacturing firm in 1948. A year later they introduced BINAC (Binary Automatic Computer), which stored data on magnetic tape rather than on punched cards. Eckert remained in an executive position in his company when it was acquired by Remington Rand Inc in 1950. Designed to handle business data, UNIVAC I (Universal Automatic Computer), Eckert and Mauchly's third computer found many uses in commerce and effectively started the computer boom. Between 1948 and 1966 J. Eckert received 85 patents for electronic inventions. Grace Murray Hopper, also from Remington Rand Company, invented the compiler computer program in the same year.

1952 H-bomb tested

THE H-BOMB, or hydrogen bomb, works on the principle of nuclear fusion. A large-scale explosion results from the thermonuclear release of energy when hydrogen nuclei are fused to form helium nuclei. Edward Teller, a Hungarian-born US physicist, is known as the father of the hydrogen bomb. He worked on the H-bomb after taking part in the atom bomb project at the Los Alamos research center in New Mexico between 1946 and 1952. The H-bomb was first tested at Enewetak atoll on November 1, 1952. The USSR first tested a hydrogen bomb on August 12, 1953, followed by the UK in May 1957, China in 1967, and France in 1968.

The ball of fire resulting from the first tests of the H-bomb at Enewatak Atoll in the Pacific Ocean.

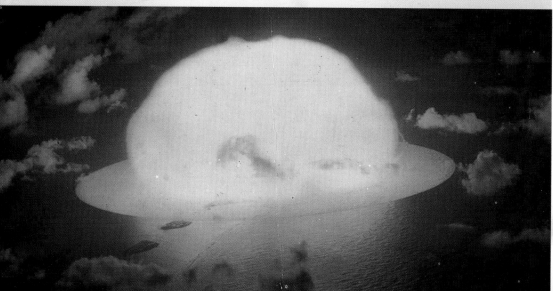

1954 Maser invented by US physicist Charles Townes and others

MASER IS AN ACRONYM for "microwave amplification by simulated emission of radiation." It is a high-frequency microwave amplifier or oscillator in which the signal to be amplified is used to stimulate unstable atoms into emitting energy at the same frequency. Atoms or molecules are raised to a higher energy level, then allowed to lose this energy by radiation at a precise frequency. This amplifier can be used for diverse purposes such as for cooking food in a microwave or as a receiver for satellite communications and radio astronomy. The ammonia-gas maser was suggested by Charles Townes, and independently by Nikolai Basov and Alexsandr Prokhorov in the USSR in 1954.

1955 Albert Einstein dies

ALBERT EINSTEIN was born in Bavaria in 1879. He later became a Swiss citizen and was appointed an inspector of patents in Berne. He published theoretical papers on physics and achieved fame with his special and general theories of relativity (1905 and 1916). His theories attempted to rationalize many unexplained aspects of physics, showing that in the case of rapid relative motion involving velocities approaching the speed of light, phenomena such as decreased size and mass are to be expected. He received the Nobel Prize for Physics in 1921. After Hitler's rise he emigrated to the US (1933). He died in 1955 before he could complete his unified field theory.

1957 Largest radio telescope unveiled at Jodrell Bank

AFTER WORLD WAR II the British astronomer Alfred Lovell began working at the University of Manchester's botanical site at Jodrell Bank with war-surplus radar equipment. Researching into radio and radar astronomy, he began to construct the Lovell telescope, a fully steerable radio telescope with a reflector that measures 250 ft in diameter. Operation began in 1957 shortly before the launch of *Sputnik I*, and the satellite's carrier rocket was tracked at Jodrell Bank. Most operational time there is devoted to astronomy rather than tracking and communication, but the telescope has been part of the tracking network for the US program of space exploration and monitored most of the Soviet accomplishments.

Albert Einstein, whose discoveries about the laws of physics revolutionized twentieth-century scientific thinking.

1957 "Sputnik I," first artificial satellite, launched by Russians

SPUTNIK I, the first satellite launched by man, was an 184-lb capsule. It was launched by the Soviet Union on October 4, 1957 and so heralded the Space Age. It achieved an Earth orbit with an apogee (farthest point from Earth) of 584 miles and a perigee (nearest point) of 143 miles, circling the earth every 96 minutes and staying in orbit until 1958, when it fell back and burned up in the Earth's atmosphere. A month later, on November 3rd, the Soviets launched *Sputnik II*, weighing 1,121 lb and carrying the dog Laika, the first living creature put into space orbit. The flight proved that animals could exist in weightless conditions for an extended period of time, and placed the Soviet Union at the forefront of the international race to develop a space program that included human flight. Eight further Sputnik missions with similar satellites carried out experiments on a variety of animals to test spacecraft life-support systems.

1960 First lasers demonstrated

LASER IS AN ACRONYM for "light amplification by stimulated emission of radiation." They are devices for producing a narrow beam of light, capable of traveling over vast distances without dispersion, and of being focused to give enormous power densities. Operating on a principle similar to a maser, it is unsurprising that it was invented by US physicists Charles Townes and Arthur Schawlow in 1958. The demonstration of the world's first practical laser was by the US physicist Theodore Maiman in 1960. The use of lasers includes communication (a laser beam is capable of carrying more information than radio waves), cutting, drilling, welding, satellite tracking, medical and biological research, and surgery.

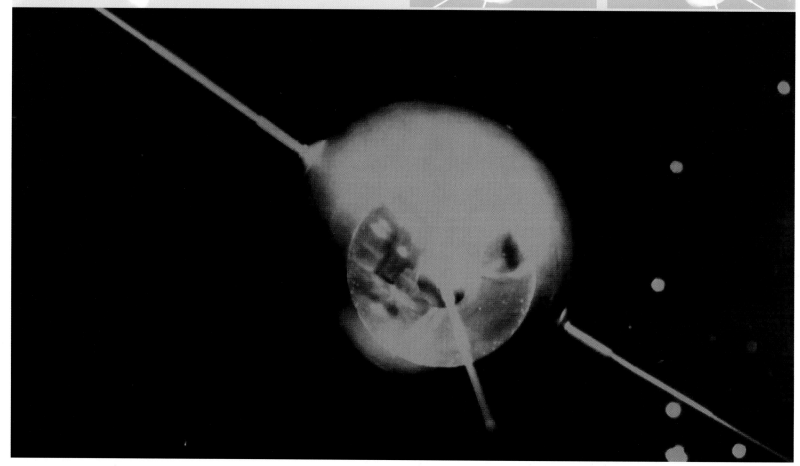

The Soviet Earth Satellite Sputnik, *the first step towards the new "space age," which eventually saw man walk on the moon.*

1962 Watson and Crick discover DNA's molecular structure

DEOXYRIBONUCLEIC ACID (DNA) is the complex giant molecule that contains, in a chemically coded form, all the information required to build, control, and maintain a living organism. In 1949 British molecular biologist Francis Crick and US biologist James Watson began to research the molecular structure of DNA, trying to crack the code of nucleic acids within that molecule that enable characteristics to be passed down through generations. During the 1950s they realized that the molecule was two strands wrapped around each other in a spiral or helix, each strand carrying a sequence of bases which carry the code of life. They were awarded the Nobel Prize for Medicine in 1962.

1980 The rise of Microsoft

WILLIAM HENRY GATES III was born in 1955. In 1975, when he was 19, Gates dropped out of Harvard and joined his schoolfriend Paul G. Allen to establish Microsoft. They began by adapting the computer language BASIC, which was used on large computers, for use on the earliest commercially available microcomputers. In 1980 Microsoft began its domination of the computer industry when Gates licensed an operating system called MS Dos to IBM for use in the personal computer (PC) that it was planning to develop. IBM's PC came on the market in 1981 and by the mid 1980s MS Dos had become the major operating system for American PCs.

1996 The Internet helps in aprehending a criminal

AFTER MUCH CRITICISM of the Internet for its poor content, it hit headlines in May 1996 when, for the first time, the FBI captured one of the "10 most wanted fugitives" using the Internet. A netsurfer in Guatemala saw Leslie Rogge's picture on the FBI homepage and reported seeing him to American officials. In response, Guatemalan national police and US Diplomatic Security launched an extensive search which ended on May 18th when Rogge surrendered at the US Embassy in Guatemala City. Rogge was a convicted bank robber who had escaped custody by bribing a guard in 1985. He was charged with bank robbery, interstate transport of stolen property and wire fraud.

The Internet page which contains pictures of fugitives in the hope that the public will help in their apprehension.

Medicine & Health

10

Nothing in life is to be feared. It is only to be understood.

Marie Curie

Overleaf: *Florence Nightingale, who revolutionized ideas of nursing during the Crimean War (see page 156).* Right: *Robert Koch, the German bacteriologist who won the Nobel Prize for Medicine in 1905.*

1902 Karl Landsteiner discovers blood groups

IN 1902 Austrian immunologist Karl Landsteiner first discovered that blood could be classified by the activity of its antigens. He realized that there are two main antigens (A and B) which give rise to four different blood groups; those having A only (A), having B only (B), having both (AB), and having neither (O). Landsteiner went on to help in the discovery of the Rhesus blood factors (1940) and he was awarded the Nobel Prize in 1930. His work made successful blood transfusions possible and aided forensic medicine. In 1936 he wrote *The Specificity of Serological Reactions*, which helped establish the science of immunology. He also developed a test for syphilis.

1902 Nine thousand die of cholera in Egypt

CHOLERA IS an acute infection of the small intestines, caused by the bacterium *Vibrio cholerae* and characterized by violent diarrhoea and vomiting with rapid and severe depletion of body fluids and salts. As dehydration increases the person becomes comatose and may die in shock. In the period from 1898 to 1907 cholera caused at least 370,000 deaths in India. The severest single outbreak occurred in Egypt in 1902, which caused the death of 9,000 people. Today the formerly high death rate has been significantly reduced by the invention of antibiotics, treatments to prevent dehydration and an effective vaccine. However, outbreaks still occur, such the one in Peru in 1991 where 258 people died.

1904 Ivan Pavlov awarded Nobel Prize for work on digestive system

IVAN PETROVICH PAVLOV was a Russian physicist who became professor and director of the Institute of Experimental Medicine in St Petersburg. He worked on the physiology of circulation and digestion, discovering in some part how food is broken down by physical and chemical means. He is most famous for his work on "conditioned" or acquired reflexes associated with parts of the brain cortex. These animal experiments included the famous dog experiments in which a bell, rung when food is given, will eventually trigger salivation in the dog's mouth even when it is rung with no food being offered. He was awarded the Nobel Prize for Medicine for his work in 1904.

1904 "Ladies' Home Journal" launches exposé of US patent medicine business

THE *LADIES' HOME JOURNAL* was an American monthly magazine, one of the longest running in the US, and for many years it set the style among women's magazines. The *Journal* brought in a strict advertising code to eliminate fraud and overtly extravagant claims by its advertisers, and it was well known for its attention to many social causes. In 1904 it refused to advertise patent medicine, and its subsequent probing and muck-raking campaign against those types of products did much to help bring about the passing of the US Federal Food and Drugs Act in 1906, which brought to an end misleading advertising and placement of patent medicine products.

1905 Robert Koch wins Nobel Prize for Medicine

GERMAN BACTERIOLOGIST Robert Koch and his assistants devised techniques that enabled them to culture bacteria outside the body. Together they formulated the rule system determining if a bacterium is the cause of a particular disease or not. They won the Nobel Prize for Medicine in 1905. Koch's work on wounds, septicaemia, and splenic fever won him a seat on the imperial board of health. His researches in microscopy and bacteriology allowed him to identify the bacteria responsible for diseases such as anthrax, cholera, and tuberculosis. His attempts at a lymph inoculation for tuberculosis were a failure, but his pioneering work meant that cures for these diseases were subsequently discovered.

Professor Ivan Pavlov, whose work made breakthroughs in understanding the human circulation and digestive systems.

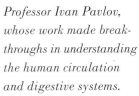

Below: *a Marie Stopes mobile family planning clinic.*
Right: *Florence Nightingale, the philanthropist and nurse who became the first woman to receive the Order of Merit.*
Opposite: *eleven years after Fleming discovered penicillin, scientists Florey and Chain finally discovered a way of producing it as a drug.*

1907 Florence Nightingale awarded Order of Merit

FLORENCE NIGHTINGALE trained as a nurse in Kaiserswerth and Paris and in 1853 became the superintendent of a hospital for invalid women in London. She volunteered for duty in the Crimean War and took 38 nurses to Scutari in 1854. She organized the barracks hospital after the Battle of Inkerman and her rules of discipline and sanitation reduced the Crimean War hospital death rate from 42 per cent to 2 per cent. She founded the Nightingale School and Home for Nurses in London (1856). She also devoted many years to the improvement of nursing and public health in India. In 1907 she was given the Order of Merit, the first woman to receive it.

1921 Marie Stopes opens first birth-control clinic

AFTER STUDYING AT University College, London, and taking her PhD in Munich, Marie Stopes made history by becoming the first female science lecturer at Manchester in 1904. Initially specializing in fossil plants and coal mining, she changed direction after the annulment of her first marriage to R. Gates in 1916. She now turned her attention to marital unhappiness caused by ignorance and began a crusade to spread the word about contraception. In 1916 her book *Married Love* caused a furore and was banned in the US. She married the aircraft manufacturer Humphrey Roe in 1918 and together they opened the first British birth-control clinic in North London in 1921.

1928 Fleming discovers penicillin

SCOTTISH BACTERIOLOGIST Alexander Fleming qualified as a surgeon at St Mary's Hospital in Paddington, London, where his career was spent. As a researcher, he became the first to use anti-typhoid vaccines on human beings and he pioneered the use of salvarsan against syphilis. As a medical officer in France during World War I, he discovered the antiseptic powers of lysozyme, which is present in tears and mucus. In 1928 he made a chance exposure of a culture of staphylococci and noticed a curious mold, penicillin, which was found to inhibit the growth of bacteria and to have outstanding antibiotic properties. Unfortunately he had insufficient chemical knowledge to produce the drug alone.

1941 Antibiotics first used

AFTER FLEMING'S DISCOVERY OF penicillin it took 11 years before two brilliant experimentalists, Howard Florey and Ernst Chain, managed to perfect a method of producing the volatile drug. The three of them shared the Nobel Prize for Medicine for the discovery in 1945. The first antibiotics, all derived from penicillin, came into use from 1941 and were quickly joined by chloramphenicol, the cephalosporins, erythromycins, tetracyclines, and aminoglycosides. Each type of antibiotic acts in a different way and is active against varying types of disease-causing agents. Unfortunately bacteria have the ability to develop immunity following repeated doses of antibiotics so more advanced antibiotics must constantly be discovered to overcome them.

1943 Waksman discovers tuberculosis treatment

RUSSIAN BIOCHEMIST Selman Abraham Waksman became a US national in 1915 and professor of microbiology at Rutgers University in 1930. While researching the process of breaking down organic substances by microorganisms and antibiotics he discovered streptomycin, an antibiotic drug derived from a soil bacterium, in 1943. He coined the word antibiotic to describe bacteria destroying chemicals derived from microorganisms. Streptomycin was found to be useful in treating tuberculosis, influenzal meningitis, and other infections unaffected by penicillin. Tuberculosis is an infectious disease where inflammation and abscesses can rapidly spread through the lungs and into the bloodstream and brain. He was awarded the Nobel Prize for Medicine for this discovery in 1952.

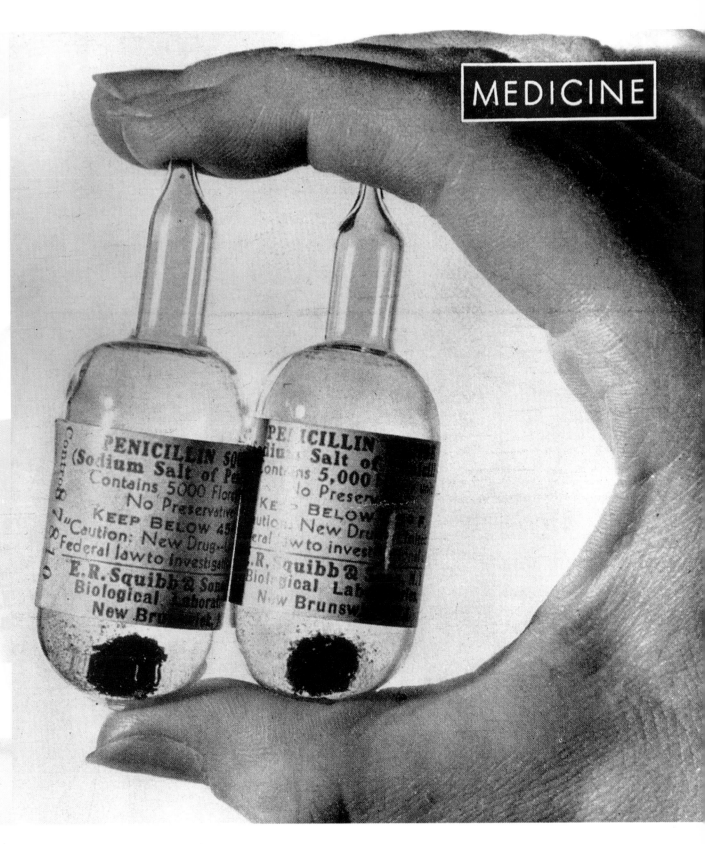

MEDICINE

1961 Female pill launched

GREGORY PINCUS was an American endocrinologist who in 1944 founded the Worcester Foundation for Experimental Biology. This became an important center for the study of steroid hormones and mammalian reproduction. In 1951 he began to look at the anti-fertility properties of steroids. This led on to using synthesized hormones to inhibit ovulation and thus prevent pregnancy in laboratory animals. He combined the female hormones of estrogen and progesterone and found that this inhibited the production of eggs and made the mucus produced by the cervix hostile to sperm. From this research he was able to perfect an oral contraceptive for women, which was launched in 1961.

1967 Barnard performs human heart transplant

NORMAN SHUMWAY achieved the first successful heart transplant in a dog in 1958 and spent the next decade refining the technique and improving immune suppression in animal models. However, it was South African surgeon Christiaan Barnard who performed the first human heart transplant, on December 3, 1967 in Cape Town. The patient, 54-year-old Louis Washkansky, lived for 18 days. His success was followed by numerous attempts at other medical centers, with 101 heart transplants undertaken around the world within 12 months. Despite problems with immune rejection and poor survival rates, Shumway and Barnard continued developing their methods until 50 per cent of patients lived at least five years after surgery.

1973 Hounsfield and Cormack launch the CAT scan

GODFREY HOUNSFIELD, the British electrical engineer, headed the team that pioneered the development of computerized axial tomography (CAT). Inadvertently, his team was working on the project at the same time as American physicist Allan Cormack. They both shared the Nobel Prize for Medicine for the CAT scan device in 1979. The CAT scan enables detailed X-ray pictures of "slices" of the human body to be produced and displayed as cross-sections on a viewing screen. Using views taken from varying angles, a three-dimensional picture of any organ or tissue irregularities in the body can be analyzed and used as an aid in diagnosis without the need for surgery.

1978 First test-tube baby

IN VITRO FERTILIZATION (fertilization in glass) is the process allowing eggs and sperm to unite in a laboratory to form embryos. The embryos produced are then implanted into the womb of an otherwise infertile woman. The work was pioneered by an English obstetrician and gynaecologist, Patrick Steptoe, who, with his colleague Robert Edwards, was the first to accomplish the successful implantation of an egg fertilized outside the human body into the uterus. The first "test-tube" baby was Louise Brown, who was born by Caesarean section in 1978. Since then the field has been extended to the birth of a baby from a frozen embryo and from a frozen egg.

1981 First cases of AIDS in the US

NEWS REPORTS FROM the US in December 1981 told of a worrying new sexually transmitted disease prevalent among a small population of homosexual men. Acquired immunodeficiency syndrome (AIDS) is the progressive destruction of the immune system by the human immunodeficiency virus (HIV). Research carried out between 1982 and 1984 proved that AIDS had spread beyond its originally supposed risk group and now included heterosexual men and women with multiple sex partners, haemophiliacs, and habitual intravenous drug users. HIV is generally spread by exchange of infected blood or sexual fluids. The virus was thought to have originated in Africa. By 1991, 323,378 cases had been reported to the World Health Organization.

Liberace was one of the first famous figures to succumb to AIDS; a cure for the disease still eludes scientists and doctors.

War & Peace

11

What did you do in the Great War, Daddy?

Recruiting Poster, 1914–18 War

1901 Vickers launch Britain's first submarine

BRITAIN'S FIRST submarine was launched at Barrow in October 1901. The 63-foot Holland Class vessel, powered by a gasoline engine with nine crew, was armed with torpedoes. The Admiralty was unsure of the vessel's worth, despite the fact that the Americans had shown considerable interest in it. Submerged, the submarine ran on an electric motor powered by batteries capable of seven knots. The submarine could maintain this for four hours with the crew breathing compressed air. The hull, streamlined to prevent the submarine from being caught by underwater obstacles, also helped progress through the water by reducing resistance. There was a lack of real interest in the project at the time.

Overleaf: helmets of the Argentine armed forces after they surrendered to British Falklands Task Force troops.
Below: a century of warfare: recruitment poster from World War I showing Lord Kitchener.

1902 Peace of Vereeniging ends Boer War

AFTER NEARLY THREE YEARS of conflict, the Boer leaders signed the terms of surrender just one hour before the deadline. The Boers had held out as long as possible in the hope that Germany would come to their aid. In a last-ditch attempt, the Boer leader Paul Kruger went to Germany but the Kaiser refused to meet him. The Boers met at the Transvaal border town of Vereeniging and voted to accept British rule. In return for the promise of future self-rule, the British agreed to provide a grant of £3 million for reconstruction of the region. The architects of the Boer defeat were Lord Kitchener and Lord Milne.

1903 Colombian rebels declare Panama's independence

A WIDESPREAD and popular revolt plunged Colombia into civil war in 1902. The government's General Marjarres defeated the rebels under Uribe-Uribe in October and limited the revolt to Panama. Initially refusing the US offer concerning the building of the Panama Canal, Colombia later relented, but it was too late. By November, the US had no option but to send three gunboats to Panama in support of the rebels. The gesture appeared to work, as later in the same month the Republic of Panama was created, with the US as one of the first countries to recognize it. Within days of the recognition, the US had signed a deal that would lead to the building of the Panama Canal.

1903 Turks massacre 50,000 Bulgarians and 10,000 in Macedonia

AS A RESULT of the Macedonian Central Revolutionary Committee mounting a revolt against the Turks, the Turkish military built up a force of 300,000 to retaliate. In September, the Turks moved into Monastir and massacred 50,000 Bulgarian men, women, and children. Later in September, the Turks struck against Kastoria in Macedonia, slaughtering another 10,000. The fragility of the Balkan region was a grave cause of concern for all the major European powers. Kaiser Wilhelm II visited Emperor Franz Josef of Austria who, in turn, conferred with Czar Nicholas II in Vienna. Meanwhile, the British also pledged their support for the Russian and Austrian plans to settle the problems in Macedonia.

1904 British troops massacre 1,000 dervishes in Somaliland

IN 1900, the British Deputy Commissioner, Jenner, was murdered in an uprising. The rebel leader, Mohammed bin Abdullah, claimed to possess supernatural powers and masterminded countless attacks on tribes friendly to the British. By 1902, the British had already defeated him in battle, but he persisted with his mission of bringing the Islamic faith to the unbelievers. He became known as the "Mad Mullah" and had his base across the border in Italian Somalia. In 1903, General Manning, supported by 10,000 Abyssinians, attempted to trap the Mad Mullah. It was not until January 1904 that the 5,000-strong rebel force was found by a small detachment of British soldiers and pursued for 12 miles. The massacre that ensued claimed 1,000 Somali lives.

YOU ARE THE MAN

1905 Russians surrender Port Arthur to Japanese

THE WAR BETWEEN THE Russians and the Japanese began in January 1904. The Japanese had territorial ambitions in Korea and the Russians wanted Manchuria. The Russians, however, were very active in Korea, which led the Japanese to land 80,000 men to aid the Korean government. The war was a disaster for the Russians. They lost numerous warships and thousands of troops were killed, wounded or captured. Port Arthur was their major base in the area and was cut off. After a seven-month siege, the 20,000 strong Russian garrison (originally 40,000) surrendered in January 1905. 58,000 Japanese were killed or wounded.

1906 Theodore Roosevelt awarded Nobel Peace Prize

WHEN STOCKHOLM awarded Theodore Roosevelt the Nobel Peace Prize in December, this capped an impressive year for the American President. Only a month before, Roosevelt had been the first American leader to leave the US while still in office. His visit to the site of the Panama Canal construction was seen as a key part of his foreign policy initiatives. America was beginning to flex its muscles in world affairs and was already having a great influence on events around the globe. Although wounded by a gunman in 1912, he continued his presidential campaign, losing to Woodrow Wilson in November. Roosevelt, still an influential figure during the war, died in 1919.

Japanese woodcut depicting the Russo-Japanese War, fought over rights to Korean land.

1912–13 Collapse of Balkan territories ignites Balkan war

WAR SEEMED INEVITABLE when the Balkan League turned on their former rulers, the Turks. Serbia, Bulgaria, Montenegro, and Greece were determined to drive the Turks out of Europe. Despite feverish European attempts to dampen down the disputes, Albania declared independence in November 1912 and the Serbians occupied Durazzo. The Bulgarians laid siege to Adrianople and moved on Constantinople. Although the Turks signed a treaty ending the war in May 1913, Bulgaria and Serbia were in dispute over Macedonia. Bulgaria turned on Serbia, Greece, Montenegro, and Romania, with Turkey taking the opportunity to reclaim Adrianople. Finally, in August, the Treaty of Bucharest brought an end to the Second Balkan War.

1914 Assassination of Franz Ferdinand triggers World War I

THE EVENTS THAT triggered the bloodiest war in history are complex, but when Archduke Ferdinand of Austria was assassinated in Bosnia, the Serbians were blamed. Austria declared war on Serbia; Russia mobilized in Serbia's defence, dragging Austria's ally, Germany, into the conflict. Russia was allied to France and Great Britain. Turkey decided to side with Germany and Austria. The Germans realized that a direct attack on France would fail, so they had prepared themselves to deliver a sweeping move through neutral Belgium and then turn southeast behind the French defences. In August, 750,000 German soldiers were launched in a major offensive, forcing the French back with heavy losses. The French, outnumbered two to one, were saved by the timely arrival of the 100,000-strong British Expeditionary Force led by Sir John French. The allies fought hard, slowly retreating towards Paris. The German advance wavered against the stiffening defense, and then the allies delivered a counter-offensive which drove the Germans back. Although it was not realized at the time, the Battle of the Marne had prevented the Germans from winning the war. By the end of 1914, the Germans had dug in and further offensives were beaten back. From this point on every offensive from either side would cost thousands of lives.

1914 Lille falls

GERMAN TROOPS took the cities of Lille and Ghent on September 12th following a fluid battle that saw the fall of Mons after a bitter struggle. The British Expeditionary Force had only landed in France shortly before being thrown into the line in Belgium. After suffering heavy casualties, the British pulled back, allowing the Germans to sweep across the Sambre and the Meuse rivers. On September 5th the Germans took Rheims and with it 12,000 prisoners. The major decisive battle on the western front was fought on the Marne, where the French retaliated against the German attacks, driving them back to Aisne. This battle managed to save the French capital.

1915 Gallipoli

THE ALLIES HOPED both to capture Istanbul and link up with the Russians with a bold move against the Turks. Some 75,000 men under General Hamilton were landed on the Gallipoli Peninsula, 35,000 at Cape Helles and a similar number further west. The Turks, under

Colonel Kemal (later Kemal Ataturk), held their positions and by November 1916 the allies decided to withdraw. The campaign was typified by tremendous courage of the Empire troops and by the ineptitude of the allied commanders. Australian and New Zealand troops suffered immense losses. The only success in the campaign was the bloodless withdrawal. Both the allies and the Turks are believed to have lost in excess of 250,000 men.

Opposite: *conflict had been brewing in Europe for some time and in 1914 armies from Britain and France mobilized to defend neutral Belgium against the German invasion.*
Above: *the fallen city of Lille after the German invasion.*
Left: *soldiers in the trenches watching the effects of a catapult bomb at Gallipoli.*

1916 Battle of Verdun

IN FEBRUARY 1916 German General Falkenhayn launched the one million strong 5th Army against the French-held city of Verdun. National pride forbade the French to lose the city despite the new policy of all-out attack against the Germans. The outer ring of French defences fell, but accurate artillery fire checked the German attack. The village of Vaux fell on June 6th, but the main thrust on Verdun failed on July 11th. Up to this point the Germans had lost 280,000 men against the French casualties of 315,000. In October the French counter-attacked and took back much of the ground lost. By the end of the campaign the French losses were 542,000 compared with German losses of 434,000.

1916 First day of the Somme claims 57,000 British casualties

THE BRITISH and the French attempted a breakthrough between Arras and St Quentin from July to November 1916. After a week's shelling, the British attacked over a 15-mile front with 18 divisions and the French with 16 divisions. The massive British losses were made for just 1,000 yds of land. A breakthrough was impossible and the campaign was reduced to attrition. By the end of the campaign, the allies had advanced just 7 miles along the front at a cost of 418,000 British soldiers and 195,000 French. The Germans had lost a staggering 650,000 killed or wounded. The campaign is also significant for the first use of tanks in warfare.

1917 Lawrence of Arabia helps Arabs take Jerusalem

AFTER THREE ATTEMPTS by three different generals, the British and their Arab allies took Gaza in 1917. In doing this, Jerusalem surrendered after being in Muslim hands for over 700 years. These victories and many more were made possible by the brilliance of T. E. Lawrence, sent as an adviser to Feisal, the third son of the Grand Sherif of Mecca. Success began in 1916 with the capture of Hejaz and Taif, culminating in the capture of Damascus in October 1918. Using Lawrence's tactical genius, the Arabs had harassed the Turks all the way to the most important city in the Arab world. Lawrence would die in a motorcycle accident in 1935.

Manfred von Richthofen (right), the Red Baron, who was killed during the second Battle of the Somme in 1918.

1918 Black day of the German Army

BRITISH, Canadian, American, French, and Australian troops spear headed by 400 tanks smashed the German front around Amiens on August 8th. With the Germans in full retreat back to the old Hindenburg line, leaving some 30,000 prisoners, they were utterly defeated. The massive weight of the attack and the poor state of the German soldiers made the victory possible. Ludendorff described the defeat as "the black day of the German army." In many respects the defeat was inevitable as the German frontline had been stripped of heavy weapons. But although the commanders may have anticipated the retreat, they could not have predicted the scale of the defeat.

1918 Flying ace Baron von Richthofen shot down behind British lines

JUST MONTHS BEFORE the end of the war one of the conflict's greatest celebrities, Manfred von Richthofen, became another casualty of the second Battle of the Somme. Even at this late stage of the war, it was a high tide for the Germans. Only the month before Ludendorff had launched 3 million men (now released from the Russian front) against the western allies. The Red Baron and members of his Flying Circus had been giving the ground troops air cover when he was shot down. His red Fokker triplane burst into flames as it hit the rear trenches of the British. In just two years, he had claimed 80 allied kills. He was buried with full military honours at the site of the crash.

French soldiers counterattacking the German onslaught at the Battle of Verdun, which saw nearly one million men die from both sides.

*Celebrations in Britain
as the Armistice is
announced, ending over
four years of conflict.*

1918 Armistice ends World War I

THE END OF THE World War I came unexpectedly with the German surrender on November 11th. Foch had been planning a new offensive to be launched on November 14th, but it was Ludendorff who had hastened the decision to end the conflict. The German front, he had argued, was in immediate danger of utter collapse. Kaiser Wilhelm agreed and dispatched Chancellor Prince Max of Baden to plead with President Wilson for an armistice. Shortly before dawn on the 11th, in a railway carriage just outside Compiègne, Germany admitted defeat and signed. The Germans were required to surrender 5,000 heavy guns, 30,000 machine guns, 2,000 aircraft, and their entire submarine and surface fleet. In addition, the allies demanded 5,000 locomotives, 150,000 wagons, and 5,000 lorries. Allied troops would occupy the Rhineland, at Germany's expense, and the blockade of Germany would remain intact. The 15th was set aside as Victory Day, with church bells ringing and London's Big Ben joining in for the first time in four years. Thousands cheered Prime Minister Lloyd George in Downing Street, and the King and Queen attracted huge crowds as they drove through the capital. Towns and cities throughout Britain celebrated by tearing down the blackout curtains and drinking the pubs dry. The war had cost 10 million lives.

1919 Treaty of Versailles

IT TOOK FIVE MONTHS to construct the massive 200-page document that officially ended the Great War. The Germans were obliged to pay 20 billion gold marks as reparations, surrender 33.5 sq miles of territory with 7 million inhabitants to their neighbors and suffer an allied occupation of the Rhineland for 15 years. The Germans were also required to accept sole responsibility for the outbreak of the war in 1914. After the final signatures had been obtained, the Germans returned home to transform their government given the vacuum created by the abdication of the Kaiser and the absence of formal rule. The new republic came into existence in July with the adoption of the Weimar Constitution.

1931 Japanese bomb Manchuria railway

THE VIOLENT and desperate war between the Japanese and the Chinese was sparked off by an unprovoked attack on the Chinese garrison at Mukden. It was claimed that the Japanese-owned railway was under threat from the Chinese and the execution of a Japanese spy was the final straw. Certain Japanese officers plotted to seize the whole of Manchuria for the empire. Mukden fell to the Japanese, signaling a full-scale invasion of Manchuria and other key areas of China. Jiang Jieshi's Nationalist party, undermined by the Communists and divided by civil war, was in no position to prevent the Japanese from creating a puppet regime in February 1932.

1935 Mussolini invades Abyssinia

THE LONG-AWAITED Italian invasion of Abyssinia finally took place in October. Despite the massive differences in the sizes of the armies and the technology available, it took the Italians until June 1936 to conquer the country. The Italians suffered a number of reversals and the Abyssinians fought with great courage. The outcome of the conflict was never really in doubt. Notably, the Italians used poison gas on the Abyssinians in direct violation of the Geneva Convention of 1925. The country, formerly known as Ethiopia, was renamed Abyssinia by the Italians. Emperor Haile Selassie became a puppet of the Italians, until the British liberated the country in 1941.

1936 Military uprising inspired by Franco triggers Spanish Civil War

POLITICAL UNREST and a lack of direction prompted right-wing military factions to revolt against the Spanish government. General Sanjurjo, who was to lead the uprising, died in a plane crash, leaving General Franco to take command. After seizing Morocco, he landed in Cadiz at the head of Spanish foreign legionaries. After a series of sharp clashes, the rebels moved on Madrid. By 1937, with the capital still under siege, many European countries had become entangled in the war. Although the Nationalists continued to enjoy popular support, the better-trained Republicans continually outfought them. Spain provided a useful training ground for many European troops.

1938 Chamberlain signs Anglo-German accord

DISORDER IN CZECHOSLOVAKIA, instigated by Sudeten Nazis, gave Hitler the excuse to demand the protection of the German population of 3.5 million. Faced with the prospect of war over the issue, Chamberlain flew to Germany and signed a deal with Hitler that would give the Nazis control over the region. At the time, it was believed that this "peace with honour" would mean that war had been averted. Chamberlain was roundly criticized for caving in to Hitler and many thought that he had been fooled. On October 5th the Germans occupied parts of Czechoslovakia, other areas being taken by Poland and Hungary. The Czechs received nothing from the deal.

Left: a propaganda postcard from the Spanish Civil War. Above: Japanese and Chinese troops fighting at Manchuria; the Japanese were eventually victorious.

Above: *German troops invading Polish territory in 1939. Right: a British battleship lying wrecked after the evacuation of Dunkirk.*

M 1939 Germany attacks Poland

AT 6 A.M. on Friday, September 1st German troops crossed the Polish border. The 1.25 million men, spearheaded by tank divisions, swept all resistance before them. Within hours, the Polish air force had ceased to exist and the railway system was in tatters. This new form of warfare, called "Blitzkrieg," was seen as a determined attempt to avoid the trench warfare stalemates of the previous war. The Germans had claimed the port of Danzig and the Polish Corridor, but peaceful attempts to resolve the situation had failed. Britain and France declared war on September 3rd and by September 8th the Germans were at the gates of Warsaw. On September 17th, following a pre-agreed plan, the Russians invaded Poland. The partition of Poland was complete by September 30th, the Germans taking the west of the country and the Russians absorbing the east. Over 60,000 Polish troops died and 200,000 were wounded. The Germans took 700,000 prisoners. Although the League of Nations and the majority of states around the world condemned the action, Poland had ceased to exist. Poland would suffer many indignities over the next six years and beyond. If nothing else, this "lightning war" should have proved to be ample warning to the western allies: a similar fate would face France within a year.

1940 Evacuation of Dunkirk

HOLLAND surrendered on May 14th, leaving the French, British, and Belgians to stem the German attacks. After Guderian's tanks broke through between Namur and Sedan and captured Calais and Boulogne on the 25th and 26th, British communications were cut in France. A withdrawal was ordered by the Admiralty, code-named Operation Dynamo. The BEF (British Expeditionary Force) and the French 16th Corps were positioned around Dunkirk. Amid an inferno of bombardment, 338,226 men (including 120,000 French) were evacuated over a nine-day period. An armada of 860 vessels, of which 240 were sunk, took part in the operation. Despite this success, more than one million allied prisoners were taken by the Germans.

M 1940 The Battle of Britain

AS A PRELUDE to Operation Sealion, the proposed invasion of Britain, the Germans pounded Channel shipping from July 10th. The RAF, commanded by Dowding, had just 600 fighters against the Germans' 3,000. The Germans switched their attacks to the Channel ports and airfields in the south of England, reaching a peak on August 15th with a 940-bomber attack. The last week in August and the first of September were the most critical, with the RAF losing 25 per cent of their strength and the Germans losing 50 per cent of theirs. Unable to defeat the RAF, the Germans switched to daylight terror raids on British cities. The Battle of Britain is said to have ended on October 12th when Hitler canceled Operation Sealion. The RAF had given the Germans their first defeat at a cost of 915 aircraft and 481 pilots. The Germans admitted losing 1,733 aircraft, while the British claimed the figure was closer to 2,698. Churchill is credited with two of the most memorable quotes of the period. On August 20th at the height of the battle he said of the RAF, "Never in the field of human conflict was so much owed by so many to so few." After the cancellation of the invasion he taunted the Germans with, "We are waiting for the long-promised invasion. So are the fishes."

— HITLER

What do YOU say, AMERICA?

1940 German Blitz on UK cities

SOME 900 GERMAN AIRCRAFT, followed by another 250, launched a series of raids against London on September 7th. The massive daylight raids reached a peak on the 15th when Goering sent over 400 bombers. He lost 60 of these to the RAF and flak guns. The Germans were forced to resort to night attacks and for 57 nights an average of 200 bombers appeared over the capital. On October 15th 400 bombers dropped 380 tons of explosives and 70,000 incendiaries; Fighter Command responded, supported by 2,000 mobile flak guns. The Luftwaffe attacks continued into 1941 on a diminished scale, the last big raid occurring on May 10th just before Barbarossa.

1941 Hitler launches Barbarossa

ON JUNE 22ND the Germans launched one of the biggest invasions of the war, violating the Russian border on a 1,800-mile front. The Germans massed 100 divisions, reaching Minsk, halfway to Moscow, in just eight days. On July 16th Smolensk fell, followed by Novogorod on August 25th. The Russians launched a disastrous counter-offensive at the end of the month, which only managed to isolate more Russian troops. Leningrad was under siege by the end of September and Kiev fell on the 19th. By the end of the year Moscow itself was in danger of capture. Ultimately, the weather and the tenacity of the Russian people would defeat the Germans.

1941 Japanese bomb Pearl Harbor—US join the war

WITH BRITAIN largely occupied elsewhere, the Japanese only had to deal with the US Pacific Fleet based in Hawaii to leave the zone open to their territorial ambitions. An armada of 350 aircraft launched from the Japanese carrier fleet hit the ill-prepared American base. Despite the loss of several battleships and other warships, the Americans were fortunate that their own aircraft carriers were out on exercises. America declared war on the Japanese and later on the Axis. The American lack of battleships in the Pacific caused them to center much of their operations on the carriers which proved to be the undoing of the Japanese.

1941 Amy Johnson dies ferrying an aircraft

AMY JOHNSON had been flying aircraft from factories to RAF bases since 1940. As she flew over the Thames Estuary, her aircraft's engines cut out and the craft plunged into the sea. A search of the area revealed the wreckage, but her body was never found. Amy was the daughter of a Hull fish merchant and was the first woman to fly solo from Britain to Darwin in Australia. The 10,000-mile journey took her 19 days. At the time she had had only 100 hours' flying experience. Her second-hand aircraft cost her just £600. In May 1936, she completed a return trip to Cape Town in a record 12 days and 15 hours.

Left: the results of the Blitz—a London bus lies in a bomb crater.
Above: an American recruitment poster—the US entered the war after the Japanese bombing of Pearl Harbor in 1941.

1943 Battle of Stalingrad

HITLER launched an attack on Stalingrad using the 22 divisions of the 6th Army commanded by von Paulus. The Russians clung to every building, knowing the strategic and psychological importance of the city. A final German attack on October 29th yielded a mere 50-yd gain. It was now the Russians' turn to counter-attack. Beginning at the end of November, the Russians struck at the flanks of the 6th Army, overrunning the Germans and their Romanian allies and encircling the city. By January 1944, some 300,000 Germans had been killed and von Paulus was forced to surrender. This battle proved to be the real turning point in the war in the east.

1943 Allies win in Africa and invade Italy

ON MAY 12TH all organized Axis resistance on the continent of Africa ceased with the fall of Tunisia. The allies captured 110,000 Germans and 40,000 Italians. The door to Europe had swung open. By July the allies were ready and landed along a 100-mile front in Sicily. The two allied generals, Montgomery and Patton, raced for the prize of Palermo, which would trap the 45,000 Axis troops on the island. By August, Messina had fallen and the allies were able to bombard the Italian mainland. The following month, after the capture of Reggio di Calabria and Salerno, the Italians surrendered. The Germans somehow managed to rescue Mussolini and bring him to Berlin.

1943 Warsaw ghetto uprising

THE NAZIS had created the Warsaw ghetto as a massive concentration area for deported Jews. By June 1942, there were over 600,000 people contained there and the Nazis began the extermination process by killing 50,000 in September. In February 1943, the decision was made to eliminate the ghetto and slaughter the remaining Jews. In response, the inhabitants rose up against the Germans. Stalin offered his verbal support but no more. The revolt continued through to September 1944, with the Poles fighting for their lives against the Germans' superior weapons and numbers. It is strongly believed that the Russians could have broken through, but they were happy to see the strength of Poland ebb away.

Children in Warsaw watch German bombers overhead; the Germans later established the Warsaw ghetto where thousands of Jews were exterminated.

Ⓜ 1944 D-Day– allies invade Normandy

ON JUNE 6, 1944, the allies finally opened the long-awaited second front against the Germans. Landing on a 30-mile stretch of the Normandy coast, they established a bridgehead with ten divisions. Up until the last minute, the Germans had been fooled into believing that the invasion would be targeted at Calais and several key German divisions sat out the early stages of the invasion in the belief that Normandy was just a diversion. Airborne landings protected the five beaches, Omaha, Utah, Gold, Silver, and Juno. At Omaha, the Americans suffered 3,000 casualties on the first day and penetrated just one mile. To the east, the British and Canadians took Arromanches and Bayeux against strong German opposition. The British on Sword Beach failed to take their main objective of Caen, but the Canadians from Juno swept 7 miles inland. The Germans reacted slowly, hindered by the allies' parachutists and superior air cover, not to mention the widespread activities of the French Resistance. Hitler released his panzers too late and by the afternoon of the 7th the battle for Normandy had been won. By June 12th the bridgehead had expanded to 80 miles x 10 miles. D-Day still ranks as the greatest amphibious landing in history.

1944 Germans conscript children

BY OCTOBER 1944, the invasion of Germany itself was imminent. In desperate response, Hitler called up all able-bodied males from 16 to 60 to form a new fighting force called the Volksturm (People's Guard). One month later, in recognition of the turning of the tide, the British Home Guard was disbanded. This "Dad's Army" had in fact 1,701,208 males and 31,824 women in its 1,084 battalions. In Germany, the situation was desperate. Himmler was given command of the armed forces, 20 million Germans were homeless as a result of allied bombing and the last great German counter-offensive in the Ardennes had failed, with crippling losses. The Nazis had less than six months left.

1945 Yalta Conference

WINSTON CHURCHILL, Franklin D. Roosevelt and Stalin met in the Crimea for eight days in February to decide the fate of the world after the war. They agreed on the strategies to finish off Germany and how they would deal with Japan. It was decided that Germany should be

partitioned between the US, USSR, Britain, and France. With Russia's enormous gains on the eastern front, they were in a strong position to make territorial claims. With the allies advancing on all fronts against the Germans and the Japanese, it would not be long until these agreements came into force. Roosevelt was, by now, far more interested in the Pacific campaign.

Above: the allies coming ashore at Normandy in the last great push of World War I. Below: delegates at the Yalta Conference in 1945.

1945 Dresden destroyed by British and American bombers

OPENING WITH a saturation bombing by 900 British aircraft and following with attacks by more than 400 American B-17s, the city of Dresden was reduced the city to a smoking ruin on February 14th. The original population of 600,000 had swelled to one million and civilian casualties were believed to be in the region of 400,000. The industrial center was completely destroyed. The night and day attack managed to level most of the city, the Americans finishing off the parts of the city that had survived the RAF bombing the night before. Bomber Harris, whose "terror bombing" theory led to the attack, has been strongly criticized for his decision to flatten Dresden, which was not a military target.

1945 Allies discover the horrors of the Holocaust

ON APRIL 30TH British troops entered the Buchenwald concentration camp. In it they discovered 40,000 emaciated prisoners, many beyond help. Huge heaps of rotting bodies were found everywhere; it was believed that 30,000 had died there in the last few months before liberation. American troops liberated Belsen, finding another 20,000 prisoners there, including 900 boys under the age of 14. Many SS guards were executed on the spot. The Russians made further discoveries, confirming that the German "Final Solution" was well advanced. Victory had come too late for so many in Europe. In June 1945, many Germans would be forced to witness the reality of the Nazi regime and the mass murders in the camps.

1945 US drop atom bombs on Hiroshima and Nagasaki

WORKING IN intense secrecy, thousands of American workers finally discovered what they had been laboring towards. The Manhattan Project, under Major Leslie Groves, cost $2 billion. On August 6, 1945 the first atomic bomb was dropped on Hiroshima; the second, on the 9th, obliterated Nagasaki. "If Japan does not surrender," President Truman threatened, "atomic bombs will be dropped on her war industries. A rain of ruin from the air, the like of which the world has never seen." The Hiroshima bomb was dropped by the US bomber *Enola Gay*. The Nagasaki bomb alone killed 70,000 outright. Many thousands more would die of radiation sickness and their injuries in the next few weeks and months. The Japanese had no choice but to surrender unconditionally. The bomb, created by the German scientist Otto Hahn, produced a massive explosion following the splitting of uranium 235 atoms. Churchill was prompted to say, "By God's mercy British and American science outpaced all German efforts. The possession of these powers by the Germans at any time might have altered the result of the war." On August 19th the formal occupation of Japan began and MacArthur accepted the surrender of Japanese forces on the deck of the US carrier *Missouri* in Tokyo Bay.

1945 VE Day

ON MAY 13, 1945, the victory in Europe was complete. Hitler was dead, Berlin had fallen at the end of April and German soldiers were surrendering on all fronts. Winston Churchill announced the good news at 3 P.M., stating that all fighting would cease at midnight. The pent-up feelings of many years of suffering exploded on the streets of London. The Royal Family made a number of appearances that day, much to the delight of the crowds. Many of the more notorious Nazis were in allied hands, but for now the civilians could begin to think about the future and how they would rebuild their lives as well as their homes.

Below: Nagasaki, where the second US atom bomb was dropped, killing 70,000 people outright. Opposite: Winston Churchill with the Royal Family at Buckingham Palace on VE Day.

1950 US lead UN coalition in fight against North Korea

KOREA was split after World War II, with the north in Russian hands and the south under the control of the Americans. When communist North Korea invaded the south of the country without warning, it was inevitable that East and West would come into the conflict. The US president, Truman, offering military assistance on the 26th, swiftly responded to the invasion of June 25th. He ordered the 7th Fleet into the area to block further escalation. The UN backed the South and pledged to offer as much help as was needed. The Royal Navy in the Pacific theater was put under the command of MacArthur and by July US ground troops were in action. Britain decided to send troops on July 26th and disembarked the following month. On September 15th the UN made a surprise landing at Inchon, 50 miles west of Seoul, driving the North Koreans inland and taking 125,000 prisoners. They seized Kimpo airfield on the 19th and aimed to liberate the South Korean capital. By October the Chinese had committed nearly 200,000 troops to the conflict and were pushing the UN back. A counter-offensive in January 1951 saw the UN recross the 38th Parallel (the old border), but 350,000 North Koreans and Chinese hit the UN again in April. After heavy fighting the front was stabilized and hostilities ceased on July 10th. An armistice was signed at the end of the month.

First Marine division troops boarding the ship that would take them to war in North Korea.

1945 Clement Attlee announces the defeat of Japan

JUST TWO WEEKS after his surprise election win over Churchill, Clement Attlee was able to announce that "the last of our enemies is laid low." The government declared a two-day holiday following the announcement of the capitulation of Japan. Celebrations mirrored the joy of VE Day and Britain could now start bringing its soldiers home. The defeated Japanese surrendered on August 14th, their 100,000 troops in Manchuria handing over their weapons to the Russians on August 19th. The formal surrender in Singapore to Lord Louis Mountbatten did not happen until September 12th. Four days before that, the Japanese premier, Tojo, attempted to commit suicide. He would hang in 1948.

1952 Albert Schweitzer awarded Nobel Peace Prize

THE GERMAN THEOLOGIAN and missionary was awarded the Nobel Peace Prize for his humanitarian activities. He had founded a hospital in the French colony of Gabon in 1913 and spent much of his life tending to the needs of the inhabitants of the area. He raised considerable sums of money to fund his medical work by giving organ recitals and writing books. His publications of particular note include *Life of Bach* (1905), *The Quest of the Historical Jesus* (1906), *On the Edge of the Primeval Forest* (1921) and *My Life and Thought* (1931). He was also awarded the Order of Merit in 1955. He died in 1965.

1961 US back unsuccessful invasion of Cuba

IN APRIL 1961, a shortlived but potentially dangerous and ill-considered invasion took place in Cuba. Some 1,500 anti-Castro Cuban exiles had been formed into a fighting unit by the CIA and trained to overthrow the Communist leadership. Following a landing in the Bay of Pigs, 90 miles southwest of the capital Havana, the incursion only lasted four days. The project had been authorized by Eisenhower and was carried out during John F. Kennedy's presidency. Cuba had continually been a thorn in America's side and Castro was violently anti-American. Later, in 1962, Soviet missiles were installed on the island and Krushchev, by agreeing to remove them, narrowly averted war.

Ⓜ 1964 US becomes involved in Vietnam War

THE AMERICANS had been embroiled in some way since the French pulled out of the area in the 1950s. But when North Vietnamese torpedo boats attacked a US destroyer in the Gulf of Tonkin, President Johnson ordered a retaliatory strike from the aircraft carriers *Ticonderoga* and *Constellation*. They caused extensive damage to a number of enemy positions along the coast. The US followed up the action by reinforcing their troops and positions in South Vietnam and Thailand. Marines were landed the following year, but the Vietcong struck back and destroyed the US embassy in Saigon. More US troops were flown in, further escalating the conflict. Many of the earlier battles were conventional, but as the war continued guerrilla tactics became the practice by the Vietcong. By 1967, some 11,000 South Vietnamese had been killed, 9,300 Americans and over 38,000 North Vietnamese. The North launched a major offensive in 1968 that reversed the US policy of gradual with-drawal. Although there was a ceasefire in 1973, fighting soon flared up again, which culminated in the fall of Saigon in 1975. The country was reunited once more as the Vietnam Socialist Republic. The war still lives in the minds the American people and without doubt it was one of the most humiliating defeats of a major western power in the century.

A US soldier in Vietnam, one of the most haunting conflicts of modern times.

ⓜ *1967 Arab–Israeli Six-Day War begins*

The Arab-Israeli War was initiated by the Israelis attacking Arab aircraft; for six days battle raged throughout the territories.

THE TENSIONS between the Arab states and Israel finally engulfed the region in war. The Israelis attacked first, destroying the majority of the Arab's aircraft on the ground. On the first day they seized El Arish in the Sinai, fought tank battles with the Egyptians in the desert and attacked the Jordanian army in Jerusalem. By the end of the second day, June 6th, they had reached the Suez Canal and taken the Gaza Strip from the Egyptians and Bethlehem and Hebron from Jordan. The Arabs responded by cutting off oil supplies to the west, claiming that they supported the Israelis. After losing Jerusalem and Jericho, the Jordanians accepted the UN ceasefire. On the 8th, after the failure of the Egyptian counter-offensive, they too accepted the ceasefire. Nasser resigned the next day despite the continued backing of his people. Meanwhile, the Israelis had switched their attacks to the north and had advanced into the Golan Heights and were bombing Damascus. The Syrians accepted the ceasefire terms just in time. In just six days the Israelis had extended their territory to four times its size before the war. Arab casualties were high, in excess of 100,000. The Israeli losses numbered fewer than 1,000 killed on all fronts.

1970 US bombs Cambodia

ON MAY 1, 1970, a task force of South Vietnamese troops and 5,000 US infantry, supported by massive bombing strikes, tanks, and artillery, thrust 30 miles into southern Cambodia in an operation to surround and destroy Vietcong bases. One of the bases was suspected to be the main Vietcong headquarters. This act was a gamble to bring the war to a close. Even though the US had reduced its ground troops by 1971, the bombing continued until 1973, when it officially ceased. For most of the rest of the war, Cambodia remained a relatively safe haven for the Vietcong who extensively used the country for training, transport routes, and supplies.

1973 Yom Kippur War

ON OCTOBER 6TH Syria and Egypt simultaneously launched powerful offensives against Israel. Taking advantage of the Jewish Day of Atonement, they caught the Israelis unawares. The Israelis managed to recover quickly and by the 10th had regained their original lines in the north. By the 16th they were within 24 miles of the Syrian capital, Damascus. The Israeli line in the south had been buckled and thrown back by the Egyptians, but by the 10th the element of surprise had gone and the Israelis counter-attacked. They cut the Suez–Cairo road and entered the outskirts of the city just as the ceasefire was announced. The Arabs lost over 20,000 men to the Israelis' 3,000.

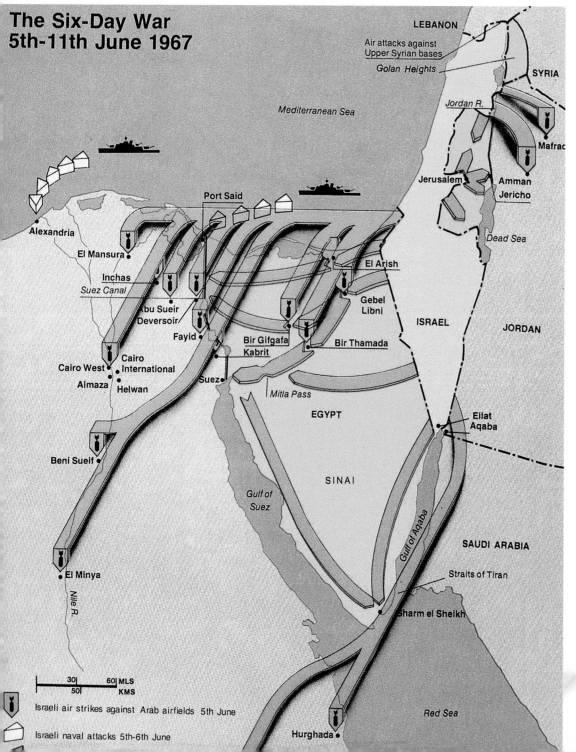

The Six-Day War 5th-11th June 1967

LEBANON

Air attacks against Upper Syrian bases

Golan Heights

SYRIA

Mediterranean Sea

Jordan R.

Mafrac

Jerusalem

Amman
Jericho

Port Said

Dead Sea

Alexandria

El Mansura

El Arish

Inchas

Suez Canal

Gebel Libni

ISRAEL

JORDAN

Abu Sueir
Deversoir

Fayid

Bir Gifgafa
Kabrit

Bir Thamada

Cairo

Cairo West   International

Almaza   Helwan

Suez

Mitla Pass

Eilat
Aqaba

EGYPT

SINAI

Beni Sueif

Gulf of
Suez

Gulf of Aqaba

SAUDI ARABIA

Straits of Tiran

El Minya

Nile R.

Sharm el Sheikh

30	60 MLS
50	KMS

Israeli air strikes against Arab airfields 5th June

Israeli naval attacks 5th-6th June

Red Sea

Hurghada

1978 Camp David accord brings peace between Israel and Egypt

PRESIDENT ANWAR SADAT of Egypt and Menachem Begin, the prime minister of Israel, finally signed an agreement that would lead to the recognition of the rights of the Palestinians. The Israelis agreed to give back the Sinai, held since the Six-Day War in 1967. The architect of the accord was the US president Jimmy Carter. The peace treaty opened diplomatic relations between the two countries, but both leaders knew that their agreement would not be welcomed in their respective countries. The agreement would also lead to the murder of Sadat three years later.

1982 War in the Falklands

ON APRIL 2ND, the Argentinian military invaded the Falkland Islands and neighboring South Georgia. Over 1,000 troops and 40 warships overwhelmed the single company of Royal Marines. The Argentinians had a long-standing claim on the islands which they called Las Malvinas. By April 25th South Georgia was back in British hands and a major task force on its way to evict the invaders. Despite a number of reversals and losses, the British took back the islands on June 14th. The death toll for the campaign was 255 British and 652 Argentinians. Directly after the liberation of the islands, Argentinian president General Galtieri, was ousted.

1983 US invades Grenada

A COUP IN 1979 ousted Grenada's prime minister, Gairy, and the new premier, Maurice Bishop, appealed for calm. By October the island had become independent of the UK and all appeared quiet. In 1983, another coup, backed by the army, murdered Bishop and seized power. The Americans swiftly responded by invading the island. They had been sent to protect the 1,000 or more Americans, including those attending the medical school in the capital, and to stop the building of a fighter base. Resistance was quickly dealt with, despite the involvement of over 600 Cubans. Bishop's body was found with other murdered islanders in November.

1985 Libyan hostages freed

UNDER INTENSE PRESSURE and described as "state sponsors of terrorism" by Ronald Reagan, the Libyan government finally agreed to release four British hostages in February. The four had been held for nine months. Instrumental in the release was Terry Waite, the special representative of the Archbishop of Canterbury. In the following year, Libya clashed with the Americans in the Gulf of Sirte. Also in 1986, the Libyans were implicated in the planting of a bomb on a TWA airliner, which prompted the US to respond by bombing Libya in April. They had hoped to kill the Libyan president, Colonel Gadaffi.

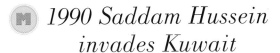 1990 Saddam Hussein invades Kuwait

IRAQ had a historical claim to Kuwait stretching back to 1871 when the country was incorporated into an Ottoman province centered on Basra. On August 2nd Iraqi forces invaded Kuwait. The UN responded immediately, condemning the action and demanding a withdrawal. Saddam Hussein showed no intention of doing so; consequently US troops started to arrive in Saudi Arabia as early as

Left: *Argentine helmets after the soldiers had surrendered to British Falkland troops.*
Below: *the invasion of Kuwait by Saddam Hussain sparked the Gulf War between the UN and Iraq.*

the 9th. On August 28th Iraq declared that Kuwait was to be incorporated as the 19th province. War was inevitable. A 28-state coalition mobilized to enforce the UN sanctions. At first they adopted a defensive posture to protect Saudi Arabia (Desert Shield). The air war began on January 17, 1991, followed by the land attacks (Desert Storm) on February 24th. The campaign, masterminded by the US General Norman Schwartzkopf, succeeded in destroying most of the Iraqi military and much of the country's infrastructure. The war had brought Iraq to the verge of civil war: the Shi'ites and the Kurds took advantage of the situation and rose in revolt against Saddam. Once the coalition forces started their withdrawal, Iraq was free to suppress the rebels. They inflicted many atrocities on the Kurds and viciously dealt with the rebels in the south of the country. Iraq, to this day, remains a constant threat and a thorn in the side of the US and UN.

1993 Israeli–Palestinian peace accord

WITH FUNDS drying up and support withering, the Palestinians realized that the opportunity of a peaceful settlement was their only option. Luckily, a Labour government had come to power in Israel and it was committed to the implementation of Palestinian autonomy within a year. A series of secret meetings were held in Norway between January

and September and on the 13th a historic agreement was signed. Both the Palestinians and the Israelis agreed to recognize each other and over a five-year period the Gaza Strip and the West Bank would be given over to the Palestinians. Self-rule has been a delicate issue and zealots from both sides continue to do their best to derail the agreement.

1995 Destruction and partition of Sarajevo

HEAVY SHELLING OF Sarajevo resumed in April 1995. The Serbian stranglehold over the town could not be broken by the Bosnians. In May the UN Commander General Rupert Smith issued an ultimatum to the Bosnian Serbs and the Bosnian government to withdraw their heavy weapons from Sarajevo. Bombing raids followed, with the Serbs taking 300 UN soldiers hostage. They were released by June and a multinational UN force was flown in to protect the safe areas. Given that Sarajevo had a mix of ethnic backgrounds, there was no alternative but to partition the town, along with most of the rest of the region.

1995 Evidence of ethnic cleansing in Srebrenica, Bosnia

THROUGHOUT THE 1990s the town of Srebrenica was at the center of conflict between the predominantly Muslim population and the Serbs. The United Nations declared the town as one of the safe areas for Muslims, but despite this the Bosnian Serbs laid siege to the town and took control of it in July 1995. Following the siege, the Serbs murdered thousands of Muslims, expelling the rest. When Bosnia and Herzegovina were partitioned in 1995, Srebrenica was included in Serb-held territory. For most of the post-Yugoslavian period, a great deal of the violence was centered on the aim of creating

Below: the effect of the war in Sarajevo—an old man leaves the soup kitchen with his rations. Opposite: a Russian soldier in the ruined capital city of Grozny in the Chechnyan war.

ethnic purity in areas that had once had a mixture of cultures. Ethnic cleansing displaced more than a third of the population of Bosnia and Herzegovina. In July 1995 at the International War Crimes Tribunal for the Former Yugoslavia at The Hague, Radovan Karadzic was indicted for war crimes. He was the leader of the so-called Republika Srpska (Serb Republic) in Bosnia. His military commander, Ratko Mladic, was also charged for genocide and crimes against humanity. Free elections are to be held in the region, but all those indicted as war criminals are barred from standing for public office. Whether the truth about the ethnic cleansing and the fate of many thousands of people will ever be known is impossible to say.

1995 Russians wage war in Chechnya

SECESSIONISTS EMERGED in 1991, taking advantage of the USSR's decline in power. Dzhozkhar Dudayev was elected Chechin president in October, declaring independence the following month. He was a nationalist and extremely anti-Russian. In 1992, Chechnya divided into two republics and by 1993 the economy was in such a bad state that he dissolved the parliament. In 1994 armed pro-Russian rebels attempted to depose him, but they failed. On December 11th the Russians invaded and attempted to seize the capital, Grozny. By March 1995 over 40,000 Russians managed to take Grozny. Casualties were high on both sides. Chechin rebels resisted for some time before a degree of order was restored.

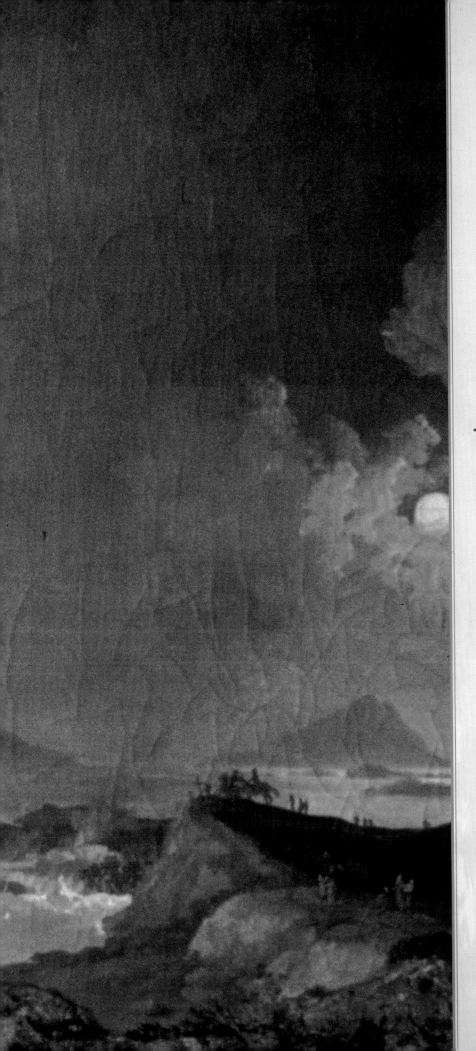

Natural & Environmental Disasters

12

I have never experienced a war but it must be something like this.

Survivor of the 1995 Japan earthquake

1901 400 die in a New York heatwave

UNPRECEDENTED WEATHER conditions in the state of New York throughout the summer caused numerous deaths and massive disruption to the financial capital of the US during 1901. Over a period of weeks the temperature had gradually interfered with the running of the city. The freak weather conditions culminated in the deaths of nearly 400 people when a heatwave struck the city. Temperatures in excess of 110°F were recorded in the shade. Most of the deaths were caused by heat exhaustion as the inhabitants desperately tried to find shelter from the sun. Two months before there had been a total eclipse of the sun, which lasted for six and a half minutes.

1901 81 miners die in Caerphilly pit disaster

JUST AS THE 5:30 A.M. SHIFT was leaving the Universal Mine at Sengenydd, South Wales, three enormous gas explosions entombed the men. The mine had been operating for only 18 months, and was the first to be dug in the Aber valley. The explosions could be heard over 3 miles away. Three bodies were retrieved by rescuers, but the majority of the miners were buried alive. There was no hope of saving the men, as huge rock-falls, cave-ins, and a massive build-up of gas frustrated those who fought to release them. Although this was not the worst pit disaster in British history, it was certainly the first in the modern age, despite new safety measures.

Overleaf: the eruption of Mount Vesuvius (see page 184). Below: a priest blesses the dead after the Martinique disaster when the volcano Mount Pelée erupted, exterminating the entire city of St Pierre.

1902 30,000 die in Martinique volcano

ON MAY 8, 1902 the island of Martinique, a French island in the West Indies, was devastated when the volcano Mount Pelée exploded, unusually through its sides rather than through its peak. Smoke had been seen issuing from Pelée since early April and by April 27th, birds and animals had been asphyxiated by poisonous gases from the ash. The explosion wiped out the entire city and population of St Pierre, a primary port. In all 36,000 people were killed instantly, either incinerated, suffocated by the gas or blasted to death. Every home was blown apart or partially destroyed and the city took four days to cool down enough for rescuers to enter.

1904 Norwegian city of Alesund burns down—12,000 homeless

LOCATED ON the north-western coast of Norway, the town of Alesund was devastated by fire in the early hours of the morning of January 23rd. The furious winter storm spread a blaze akin to an explosion, covering the whole town center in ashes and leaving between 10,000 and 12,000 people homeless. Following exceptional restoration work, including shipments of building materials from Emperor Wilhelm II of Germany, the town was completely rebuilt in the Art Nouveau style. Alesund remains one of the only towns like this in the world and looks very much like an illustration from a fairy tale. It now has a population of 36,000 and is the commercial and industrial capital of its region.

1906 Mount Vesuvius erupts

MOUNT VESUVIUS in Italy has long been one of the most active volcanoes. In this century nearly 2,000 people have been killed by its eruptions in 1906 and 1944. The 1906 eruption began on April 4th when a fissure opened on the cone. Lava began to flow with increasing intensity over the next two days and 105 parishioners were killed in San Giuseppe when a "lava bomb" devastated the local cathedral. The culmination of the eruption came with a great "gas blow-off" on April 8th. So much ash was left by the explosion that "hot avalanches" occurred for days and, when heavy rains fell, mudslides caused extensive damage in Ottaiano.

1906 San Francisco earthquake and fire

THE SAN FRANCISCO quake and fire of April 18, 1906 caused the deaths of an estimated 700 people, obliterated 500 city blocks, and caused $500 million of damage. On that day and for two days afterwards San Francisco was virtually burnt to the ground. The quake measured 8.3 on the Richter scale, its epicenter was a few inches from the Golden Gate Bridge and was created by shifting along the San Andreas Fault. The quake came in two shocks, one of 40 seconds the other of 75. The fire, caused not by the quake but by the bumbling efforts of troops trying to stop it with dynamite, lasted three days.

Magazine cover making light of the earthquake and fire which ravaged San Francisco in April 1906.

1908 Earthquake destroys Messina

ONE OF the most vicious quakes ever began under the Straits of Messina, Sicily, on December 28, 1908. The official death toll was set at 160,000 but other statistics put it at 250,000. The entire city of Messina was wiped out and only one building, an iron-reinforced home built by an eccentric, remained. Only 65,000 out of Messina's population of 147,000 survived. Towns within a 120-mile radius of the epicenter were destroyed, including Reggio de Calabria where 25,000 out of 34,000 people were killed. Earth tremors, a 50-ft-high tornado, hurricane force winds, and driving rain came along with the quake, all in the early hours of the morning.

1935 Dust storms sweep America's mid-west

DURING THE YEARS 1933–35 the American mid-west states were hit by severe heatwaves and drought, with temperatures rising to 120.2°F. Strong winds raked up the unprotected soil, creating swirling dust storms which brought everything to a standstill. A bad storm could send

Below: a family prays for rain to relieve the drought which caused relentless dust storms in America.
Right: buildings wrecked by the tornadoes that hit the United States in 1953.

topsoil whirling 5 miles into the air, making day as dark as night. The storm of March 1935 blew for 27 days without ceasing; roads disappeared; houses were buried to window height; and roofs collapsed with the weight of soil. The worst-hit states were Dakota, Nebraska, Kansas, Oklahoma, and Minnesota. In all, 70,000 refugees fled the dustbowl states, leaving areas with only 40 per cent of the previous population.

1952 Tornadoes hit five US states

OVER 700 TORNADOES lash the US each year, traveling at between 30–40 MPH. When a tornado hit the mid-west on March 22, 1952 it left several states devastated, with 2,000 dead and 2,500 injured. Tornadoes tend to hit the US east of the Rockies, especially in the Mississippi basin,

with around 150 each year in that area alone. The most destructive tornado occurred on April 11, 1965. Although it killed only 271 people, it caused damage in excess of $30 billion. A tornado hit Missouri, Illinois and Indiana in 1925, the death toll this time reaching 689. Tornadoes are violent cyclonic storms with a relatively small diameter. It is the updraft from these that causes the deaths and damage.

1966 The Aberfan landslide

THE WORST LANDSLIDE IN Welsh history occurred on October 21, 1966, when an 800-ft-high slagheap outside the village of Aberfan collapsed. Although some blame was attributed to the colliery that had built the pile up to such a height, it was primarily caused by an underground spring that had established itself beneath the pile. It began when a maintenance man climbed the heap, hoping to pronounce it safe. Once on top he noticed the pile shift. He managed to get to safety, but the two million tons of rock, coal, and mud were moving and directly hit the Pantglas school below. Of the 145 people who were killed, 116 were children.

1966 Floods in Florence

A COMBINATION OF heavy rains, and centuries of human neglect was the cause of the River Arno's overflowing its banks and flooding Florence, Italy, on November 4, 1966, 149 people drowned and over 100,000 citizens were trapped in their homes. Thousands of priceless art treasures were destroyed and thousands more damaged. The 40-mph flood tore through the city, the water rising in some places to 20 ft, submerging sculptures, paintings, mosaics, and manuscripts in the city's libraries. The salvage operations revealed that the municipal treasury was depleted and that, despite flood plans since the 1600s, the city had done little more than replace the riverbanks with high walls.

1967 "Torrey Canyon" disaster

THE MASSIVE tanker *Torrey Canyon* ran aground on a reef between the Scilly Isles and Land's End. Rocks ripped the bottom from the boat, and thousands of gallons of oil immediately began to pour from the jagged hole, causing a slick which covered some 260 sq ft of sea water. On 28 and 29 March, Royal Air Force bombers dropped explosives, aviation fuel and napalm to sink the wreck and burn away any remaining fuel. But it was too late for Cornwall's beaches, which were polluted with a sludgy black mess. Birds' feathers clogged up with the sticky oil, making floating or feeding impossible. The beaches were clean for the summer, but 25,000 sea birds had been killed.

Soldiers help to clear the refuse after the floods in Florence which caused hugely expensive damage to the city.

1972 10,000 people killed in Managua

A SERIES OF earthquakes, measuring 6.25 on the Richter scale, hit Managua, Nicaragua, on December 21, 1972. Managua was levelled and turned into an inferno that killed 7,000 people and made 200,000 homeless. Seventy-five per cent of its buildings were destroyed and another 15–20 per cent were left uninhabitable. The population of 325,000 was reduced to 118,000. There was almost no damage a mere few miles from Managua and the catastrophe was caused because the city was built on a fault line. Had it been just 40 km (25 miles) away the tragedy would not have occurred. The lesson was not learnt, though, and the city was rebuilt on the same fault and suffered more earthquakes.

1973 Volcanic eruption in Iceland

ON JANUARY 23, 1973 a mile-long fissure in the side of the long-dormant Helgafell volcano began to erupt. A rain of ash and cinder buried Vestmannaeyjar, a town in southern Iceland on Heima island, and forced the evacuation of most of the 4,500 inhabitants. A more serious disaster was avoided by residents who managed to divert some of the lava by bulldozing it out of the way and by using hoses to chill the lava. The eruption did not subside until June, when most of the evacuees returned and removed the thick deposits of ash that had covered the town's buildings. Vestmannaeyjar subsequently made a complete recovery from this disaster.

1973 The first famine strikes Ethiopia

AFRICA DEPENDS upon farm products for the survival of the 12 billion people in its 12 countries. The lack of rainfall is a natural phenomenon and consequently drought and famine hold the upper hand over the populace. In Ethiopia the start of the more recent famines was in November 1973 when 100,000 died in one year because of famine and attendant malnutrition. The Western world failed to respond with aid because of the economic crisis caused by OPEC's oil-price increase. Little help arrived until the famine peaked in 1984–86 when millions of Ethiopians were threatened with starvation and hundreds died of it each day.

1974 Cyclone in Australia

ON CHRISTMAS DAY, 1974, cyclone Tracey struck Darwin, north Australia, causing the immediate deaths of 44 people and injuries to many more. Ninety per cent of Darwin's buildings were destroyed, leaving 25,000 out of the city's population of 32,000 without shelter. Relief was made all the more difficult by Darwin's remote location and the fact that it was accessible by only one major road. Civilian and military aircraft were drafted in and shuttled in food and supplies. Prime Minister Whitlam cut short a European tour because of the disaster, flying back to be with his people. He made a firm pledge that the city would be rebuilt.

1975 Famine in Bangladesh

DURING 1974 Bangladesh was devastated by floods, which destroyed the majority of the grain crop. This fell at a time when the country was in turmoil, and a national state of emergency had been called to deal with the public disorder. When President Mujib took power he was granted dictatorial powers to control the situation. He was murdered by the military in August 1975 and Khandakar Mushtaque Ahmed temporarily took control. Abusadat Muhammad Sayem then became president, but it was too late to save the thousands who had died or were dying of starvation. The turbulent political situation did nothing to help the crisis and it was only later that food aid arrived to alleviate the suffering.

Opposite: *lava flow from the Helgafell volcano threatens the harbor on the west coast of Iceland.*
Above: *the famine in Bangladesh was caused by flooding which wiped out the crops. The situation was not helped by political unrest in the area.*

1976 Seveso chemical spill

THE SMALL Italian town of Seveso was once the site of the Icmesa factory, which produced agricultural herbicides. In June 1976, a freak accident occurred, releasing a cloud of deadly chemicals into the air. Within 24 hours, plants and trees had withered, animals had collapsed, and people had developed painful skin rashes and sores. The local government declared that the area had been contaminated with dioxin, an active ingredient in the defoliant that had destroyed huge areas of Vietnam. Dioxin can kill animals in small doses, and may cause cancer or birth defects in people in the long term. The chemical cloud had hung over the town for 10 days before the factory was sealed off for ever and the surrounding houses demolished.

1977 Oil well blow-out in the North Sea

MORE THAN A HUNDRED platform workers were rescued from the Bravo rig in Norway's Ekofisk field. The drilling platform blew out of control, sending oil 150 ft into the air. It was like a geyser of black sludge, and over the next eight days 7,000,000 gallons of crude oil cascaded into the sea, causing a slick of 1000 sq miles. Four attempts to stop the flood failed because insufficient pressure was applied by the hydraulically operated rams. Eventually the rig was sealed and the oil flow stopped, but fish stocks had been badly damaged, poisoned by the mass of floating oil. The Norwegian government regarded it as the worst pollution crisis since oil prospecting began in the North Sea.

1978 "Amoco Cadiz" disaster

THE *AMOCO CADIZ* supertanker hit bad weather on her way to Rotterdam from the Persian Gulf. On the swelling sea, the ship drifted onto rocks and broke apart, releasing her cargo of crude oil straight into the water. Initial mopping-up efforts were ineffectual and 400 miles of the Brittany coast was covered in a sticky black mess. It was too thick to be piped away, and the government would not allow detergent to be used onshore because of the possible damage to oyster beds and crops. Instead "Operation Teaspoon" was launched, in which thousands of people worked every day scooping away at the sludge. Despite their best efforts 22,000 birds died and millions of oysters were badly contaminated.

The nuclear plant on Three Mile Island. Children were evacuated after a problem with the reactor threatened to release radioactivity into the atmosphere.

1979 Three Mile Island disaster

PRIOR TO THE Chernobyl incident, the most notorious nuclear accident occurred at Three Mile Island, Pennsylvania, in the spring of 1979. A potentially explosive bubble of hydrogen gas developed inside a crippled reactor. Valves controlling the flow of cooling water failed to function correctly, so that part of the core was left without cooling water and the exposed fuel melted. It was feared that if the reactor's containment was breached a large amount of radioactivity would be released. The state governor recommended the evacuation of children and pregnant women living within a 5-mile radius of the plant. The accident was brought under control and only small doses of radiation entered the atmosphere, but the reactor building was badly contaminated.

1980 Alexander Kielland oil rig disaster

IT TOOK JUST 15 minutes for the huge Alexander Kielland platform to overturn in stormy seas when one of its five supporting legs buckled and collapsed. It was used as a floating "hotel" for North Sea oil workers, and about 200 men were on board—some 50 of them in the movie theater—when the platform began to topple. A spokesman for Phillips Petroleum, the owners, said: "Men just tumbled into the cold water." Darkness began to fall as helicopters, planes, and 13 ships went to the rescue, from the coast 240 miles away. Dozens of bodies could be seen scattered across the water. A survivor said: "Metal screeched as it began to keel over. Suddenly men were cut and bleeding."

1985 Earthquake in Mexico

TOWNS IN THREE PROVINCES of Mexico were devastated by the earthquake of September 1985. Measuring a huge 8.1 on the Richter scale, the quake was felt in Houston, Texas, 745 miles to the north and Guatemala City 620 miles south. Forty per cent of homes in Ciudad Guzman and one-third of Mexico City were destroyed. The City's central hospital toppled, medical supplies within catching alight. There were 1,000 people in the building and hundreds died, trapped between collapsing floors, some surviving the blast but dying of smoke asphyxiation from the fire. Rescue workers were still digging and finding survivors seven days after the initial blast. The total death toll was 9,500.

1985 Colombian volcano erupts

IN SEPTEMBER 1985 initial rumbles from the 16,200-ft-high Nevada del Ruiz volcano had worried residents of nearby Armero and Chinchina, but government officials played down any dangers, saying that it was only a mudslide down the flank of the mountain and that there was no hazard. This had drastic consequences when the volcano erupted on November 13th. Fireballs were flung from its peak, and millions of gallons of water careered down the mountain, collecting mud and forming into a 150-ft wave that flattened vegetation and set fire to trees. In all, 22,490 residents of the towns were crushed, drowned, and buried beneath the molten mud or were burnt to death.

1985 Bhopal disaster

IN THE EARLY HOURS OF the morning on December 2, 1984, a cloud of yellow gas plumed across Bhopal, in India, and a neighboring shanty town. People breathed it in and woke choking and vomiting, their eyes stinging with tears. The cloud was lethal and people died in their beds and out on the streets. The gas had leaked from a storage tank at the Union Carbide factory in the city and was made of methyl isocyanate, a chemical used in the manufacture of insecticides. Within hours, the hospitals were filled to overflowing, 3,000 lay dead, their faces covered over with white cloths, and 40,000 were seriously injured, with damaged lungs and eyes, and bronchial complications, not to mention severe psychological damage.

Left: *the signs warning of a possible eruption from the Colombian volcano were ignored, resulting in thousands of deaths and mass destruction.*
Above: *Mexico City after the earthquake in 1985.*

1986 Chernobyl

THE RESULTS OF the world's worst nuclear disaster were first detected in Sweden, then in Finland, Denmark, and Norway, where huge increases in radioactivity had been measured. Satellite pictures revealed that the top of a reactor had blown off, and a fire followed. The aftermath of the disaster is well known: the radiation alerts in nearly every European country, children kept indoors, the slump in milk and meat sales because of fears of contamination. In Kiev, 62 miles south of Chernobyl, citizens suffered burns and sickness. Experts differ in their estimates of the number of additional cancers that might be caused by the Chernobyl radiation, but the most conservative is 10,000 in Russia and 1,000 in the rest of Europe.

1987 Gales in the British Isles

ON OCTOBER 16, 1987 a television viewer rang the meteorological office asking if a hurricane was due to hit the British Isles. The question was laughed off but within hours the southern parts of Britain were hit with gusts of winds reaching 110 MPH. By the morning at least 17 were dead and there was an estimated £300 million of damage done. The London fire brigade received a record 6,000 emergency calls in 24 hours. Thousands of homes had collapsed and roads and railways throughout the south were blocked by fallen trees. Kew Gardens lost one-third of its trees and Sevenoaks in Kent lost six of the oaks that make up its name.

Above: checking the levels of radiation after Chernobyl, a disaster that had repercussions for many years. Right: unprecedented gales swept through Great Britain, causing millions of pounds of damage.

1986 Swiss chemical plant fire causes environmental disaster

THE RIVER RHINE has long been a symbol of mythical purity, but in 1986 it became an emblem of pollution. After a fire at the Sandox chemical plant, fire fighters washed about 30 tons of highly toxic, liquid pesticide into the river. The full scale of the disaster became apparent when fishermen began hauling hundreds of thousands of dead fish from the water. Some of the chemicals gradually diluted, but large amounts of non-soluble mercury drifted along almost as a solid mass. Water that was once clear and flowing was silvered over with poison, its fish stocks were depleting and it was becoming undrinkable. A powerful German ecological group demanded tough anti-pollution laws to prevent such a disaster from ever occurring again.

1988 Armenian Earthquake

AN EARTHQUAKE measuring 6.9 on the Richter scale struck Soviet Armenia on December 7, 1988. The worst quake in 80 years, it destroyed two-thirds of Leninakan, Armenia's second largest city, and eliminated 20 villages and towns. Officially 28,854 were killed, 12,000 were injured and 400,000 were made homeless although unofficial reports put the casualties at 55,000. Much of the extensive loss of life was due to faulty construction of the houses. Built cheaply and carelessly in the Brezhnev era, they simply folded and crumbled inwards on their inhabitants. Gorbachev was in New York on a diplomatic mission at the time but rushed home when the news reached him.

1988 Hurricane Gilbert hits Jamaica

HURRICANE GILBERT cut a 2,500-mile-wide path of destruction as it crossed the Caribbean westwards from 12 to 19 September 1988. In all, it wreaked $10 billion worth of havoc and killed more than 350 people, causing winds of up to 200 MPH. First hitting land in Texas and crossing through Mexico and the Dominican Republic, Gilbert had already caused damage and death but squarely in its path was Jamaica. It hit Kingston with winds of 145 MPH and lifted the roofs from 80 per cent of homes,

making 500,000 homeless. Twenty-five people died on Jamaica; the banana and poultry crops of the entire island were wiped out and all communications were lost for several days.

1989 San Francisco earthquake

SINCE THE 1906 earthquake San Francisco had experienced several smaller quakes but these had caused little damage. The 1989 quake, however, reached 7.1 on the Richter scale and shook the San Francisco Bay area for 15 seconds. It claimed 67 lives and caused billions of dollars worth of damage. More than a mile of Interstate 880 (Nimitz Freeway) in Oakland collapsed, with 42 lives lost when the upper deck crushed motorists on the lower deck. A span of the San Francisco-Oakland Bay bridge also collapsed. In the Marina district many three-storey buildings were reduced to one, and there was also a fire caused by a ruptured gas main.

Above: *incredible scenes of destruction followed the San Francisco earthquake of 1989.* Below: *Hurricane Gilbert hits Jamaica after passing through Texas and Mexico.*

1994 Australian forest fires claim 1.5 million acres of land

IN MOST YEARS drought affects some part of Australia. The country also suffers from localized flooding and tropical cyclones. South-eastern Australia (which includes Tasmania) has the highest occurrence of bush-fires in the world. The only other areas in the world that can rival the danger levels are California and parts of the Mediterranean. During 1994 bush-fires swept through New South Wales. The dangers from the fires caused the evacuation of the outskirts of Sydney. This was well-timed, as the fires blazed their way into the suburbs, destroying hundreds of homes. All the southern states are subject to hot, dry winds that can make fires commonplace.

1995 Flooding in Europe—250,000 evacuated from homes

IN LATE JANUARY 1995 relentless, torrential rain caused the century's worst floods of western Europe. The Rhine reached record levels and the flood level in Cologne was 35 ft, putting the Old Town underwater. Many historic towns in Belgium, Luxembourg, Holland, France, and Germany suffered devastation. Spring tides and strong winds added to the problem as the canals of Bruges overflowed and in France at least 40,000 homes were damaged. The Dutch authorities carried out the biggest civilian evacuation for 40 years as rising rivers threatened to burst dykes in the Gelderland province. By January 31st more than 20 people had died and the evacuation total was reaching nearly a quarter of a million.

Above: *fishing among the parking metres in Iowa after the floods.* Right: *torrential rain throughout western Europe caused immense flooding throughout France, Germany, Belgium, and Holland.*

1993 Floods in America

IN 1993 heavy rains caused massive flooding along the Missouri and branches of the Mississippi. All the flood measures failed as swathes of farmland disappeared under water. Hundreds of cities and towns were flooded, thousands of homes and factories were ruined. The estimated cost of the disaster was set at around $12 billion. At its height, the Missouri had risen 49 ft above its banks. The flooding also ruined acres of land beyond the most devastated areas. The situation should never arise again as several dams and locks have been built. 1993 was not a good year for the US: in California 25,000 lost their homes when wild fires got out of hand.

1995 6,000 die in Japanese earthquake

ON JANUARY 17, 1995 the most violent earthquake to have struck Japan since 1948 hit Kobe, Osaka, and Kyoto in Japan's industrial heartland. The 20-second seismic wave reached 7.2 on the Richter scale and ripped through motorways and railway tracks, and hurled concrete from rooftops. More than 600 aftershocks followed the first tremor. Scores of fires caused by fractured gas pipes raged out of control and, with roads blocked, helicopters were used to douse the flames. At least 1,800 people were killed by the initial blast with the death toll finally reaching around 6,000. In Kobe 100,000 people spent the night in shelters and about 650,000 homes were without power.

1997 Forest fires cause blackout across Asia

BURNING TO CLEAR LAND for farming and plantations is common practice in Indonesia and the region, but coupled with a severe drought the situation got desperately out of hand. The hundreds of forest fires swathed the whole region in a yellow smoke, bringing visibility down to 100 yds. Numerous deaths were reported and more than 50,000 people fell ill in the region as a result of the smoke. At least five other countries were affected by the fires in Indonesia: Malaysia, Singapore, Brunei, the Philippines, and Thailand. Thousands of firemen were deployed to contain the fires, but to little effect. Tourism, the electronics industry and agriculture were all affected by the disaster.

Above: *the destroyed highway in Kobe, one of the main cities affected by the Japanese earthquake.* Left: *the forest fires in Indonesia covered cities in a blanket of smoke for hundreds of miles.*

Bibliography

WORLD IN ACTION

Calvocoressi, Peter, *World Politics Since 1945*, New York, 1991

Carruth, Gorton, *The Encyclopedia of World Facts and Dates*, New York, 1993

Clutterbuck, Richard, *International Crisis and Conflict*, London and Basingstoke, 1993

Grenville, J. A. S., *A World History of the Twentieth Century*, Glasgow, 1989

Hobsbawn, *The Age of Extremes, 1914–1991*, London, 1994

POWER & POLITICS

Brogan, Hugh, *The Pelican History of the United States of America*, London, 1986

Pearce, Malcolm and Geoffrey Stewart, *British Political History 1867–1990*, London, 1992

Sabrine, George H. and Thomas L. Thorson, *A History of Political Theory*, Orlando, 1973

Sorrentino, Frank M. et al., *American Government: Power and Politics in America*, Washington, 1983

Woolf, Stewart (ed.), *Nationalism in Europe*, London, 1996

BUSINESS & ECONOMICS

Aldcroft, Derek H., *The European Economy, 1914–1990*, London, 1993

Benson, John, *The Rise of Consumer Society in Britain, 1880–1980*, Harlow, 1994

Chacoliades, Militiades, *International Economics*, New York and London, 1990

Tomlinson, Jim, *Public Policy and the Economy Since 1900*, New York, 1990

ARTS, ENTERTAINMENT & CULTURE

Dixon, Andrew Graham, *The Paper Museum*, London, 1997

Hall, Michael, *Leaving Home*, London, 1996

Honderich, Ted (ed.), *The Oxford Companion to Philosophy*, Oxford, 1995

Hughes, Robert, *The·Shock of the New*, London, 1991

Stringer, J. (ed.), *The Oxford Companion to Twentieth Century Literature*, Oxford, 1996

Ward, Ed, Geoffrey Stokes and Ken Tucker, *Rock of the Ages: the Rolling Stone History of Rock'n'Roll*, Penguin, 1987

HUMAN RIGHTS & SOCIETY

Alonso, Harriet Hyman, *Peace as a Women's Issue: A History of the U.S. Movement for World Peace and Women's Rights*, Syracuse, 1993

King, Martin Luther, *Stride Toward Freedom*, New York and London, 1958

Lutz, Ellen, et al. (eds.), *New Directions in Human Rights*, Pennsylvania, 1989

Macfarlane, L. J., *The Theory and Practice of Human Rights*, London, 1985

Socknat, Thomas, *Witness against War*, Toronto and London, 1987

Wolgast, E. H., *Equality and the Rights of Women*, London, 1980

RELIGION & CULTS

Bocock, Robert and Kenneth Thompson (eds.), *Religion and Ideology*, Manchester, 1985

Dawson, Lorne L. (ed), *Cults in Context: Readings in the Study of New Religious Movements*, Toronto, 1996

Ling, Trevor, *A History of Religion East and West*, London and Basingstoke, 1969

Smart, Ninian, *The World's Religions*, Cambridge, 1992

EXPLORATION & DISCOVERY

Boorstin, D. J., *The Discoverers*, London, 1991

Cavendish, R., et al., *Journeys of the Great Explorers*, Basingstoke, 1992

Day, A. E., *Discovery and Exploration: The Old World*, London, 1980

Day, A. E., *Search for the Northwest Passage*, New York and London, 1986

Hanbury-Tenison, R. (ed.), *The Oxford Book of Exploration*, Oxford, 1993

TRANSPORT

Heskett, John, *Industrial Design*, London, 1980

Hillier, Bevis, *The Style of the Century*, London, 1983

Lucie-Smith, Edward, *A History of Industrial Design*, Oxford, 1983

McCarthy, F., *A History of British Design 1830–1970*, London, 1979

Sparke, Penny, *An Introduction to Design and Culture in the Twentieth Century*, London, 1986

SCIENCE & TECHNOLOGY

Flatow, Ira, *They All Laughed: From Lightbulbs to Lasers*, New York, 1992

Hamelin, J., *Modern Radio Science*, Oxford, 1996

Kenyon, N. D. and C. Nightingale, *Audiovisual Telecommunications*, London, 1992

Messadie, Gerald, *Great Modern Inventions*, Edinburgh, 1991

MEDICINE & HEALTH

Cochrane, Jennifer, *An Illustrated History of Medicine*, London, 1996

Coleman, Vernon, *The Story of Medicine*, London, 1985

Loudon, Irvine, *Western Medicine*, Oxford, 1997

Royston, Angela, *100 Greatest Medical Dicoveries*, Limpsfield, 1995

WAR & PEACE

Brogan, Patrick, *World Conflicts*, London, 1985

Erickson, John, *The Road to Berlin*, London, 1983

Gilbert, Martin, *Second World War*, London, 1989

Messenger, Charles, *The Century of Warfare: Worldwide Conflict from 1900 to the Present Day*, London, 1995

Taylor, A. J. P., *From the Boer War to the Cold War*, London, 1995

NATURAL & ENVIRONMENTAL DISASTERS

Alexander, David, *Natural Disasters*, London, 1993

Dains, Lee, *The Encyclopedia of Natural Disasters*, London, 1993

Erickson, John, *Quakes, Eruptions and Other Geologic Cataclysms*, New York, 1994

Robins, Joyce, *The World's Greatest Disasters*, London, 1990

Smith, Roger, *Catastrophes and Disasters*, London, 1992

Author Biographies and Picture Credits

EITHNE FARRY: *Arts, Entertainment & Culture; Exploration & Discovery*
Eithne Farry graduated from Goldsmiths in 1986 and has made London her home. She has worked as a freelance journalist and reviewer for various publications including *Time Out* and *Melody Maker.* She has also contributed to a series of educational books.

KAREN HURRELL: *Human Rights & Society; Transport*
Karen Hurrell is a well-known author who has written 38 books, as well as numerous articles for a wide range of magazines, both in the UK and in Ireland. Although Canadian by birth, she now lives in London with her two sons.

BRIAN MOYNAHAN:
Introduction
Brian Moynahan is a highly respected historian and former European Editor for *The Sunday Times,* whose books include *The Russian Century, The British Century* and *Claw of the Bear.* His most recent work—a new study of Rasputin—was published in February 1998.

JON SUTHERLAND: *World in Action; Power & Politics; Business & Economics; Religion & Cults; Science & Technology; Medicine & Health; War & Peace; Natural & Environmental Disasters*
Jon Sutherland has written more than 60 books over the past 10 years on a range of subjects including business education, sport and children's adventure stories. He now lives in Suffolk.

The Bridgeman Art Library: 22 (l), Crown Estate Commissioners 43, 48 (r), 51 (r), 101, 118 (l), Portsmouth City Art Gallery 132 (t), Victoria and Albert Museum 163, National Archives Trust Pennsylvania 171 (r). *Mirco De Cet:* Ford 134, 145 (l). *FBI Home Page:* 151. *Ford UK:* 130 (l). *Image Select:* 103 (r), Volkswagen 136, 149, 182-183. *Lebrecht Collection:* 78 (r). *Mary Evans Picture Library:* 15 (l), 17 (l), 42-43, 45, 50, 76 (r), 77 (all), 80 (r), 96-97, 98, 100, 102 (l), 118 (r), 119, 122, 131, 132 (b), 142-143, 144 (r), 147, 152-153, 154, 156 (r), 162, 185. *Pictorial Press Limited:* 19, 44, 79, 81, 83 (r). *Topham Picturepoint:* Press Association 12-13, 14 (all), 15 (r), 16, 17 (r), 18 (all), 20, 21, 22 (r), 23 (all), 24 (all), Press Association 25, 26, 27, 28, Associated Press 29, 30 (all), 31, 32 (all), 33, Press Association 34, 35, Associated Press 36 (l), 36 (r), 37, Associated Press 38 (l), Press Association 38 (r), Press Association 39, 42, 46, Associated Press 47, 48 (l), Associated Press 49, Associated Press 51 (l), 52, Associated Press 53 (all), Press Association 54, Associated Press 55 (l), 55 (r), 56 (all), Associated Press 57, Associated Press 58, 59, Associated Press 60, Associated Press 61 (l), 61 (r), 62 (tl&bl), Press Association 62 (r), Associated Press 64 (all), Press Association 65, 66-67, 68, 69, 70, 71, 72, Associated Press 73, 74-75, 76 (l), Press Association 78 (l), 80 (l), 82, 83 (l), 84 (all), 85 (t), 86, 88, 89, 90, 91, 92 (all), 93 (all), Associated Press 94, Press Association 95, 99, 102 (r), 103 (l),

104, 105, 106, Associated Press 107, Associated Press 108, Associated Press 109, Associated Press 110-111, Associated Press 112, 113, Associated Press 114, Associated Press 116-117, 120, 121 (l), 124, 125 (all), 126 (all), Associated Press 127, 128-129, Associated Press 130 (r), 133, 135 (t), Associated Press 135 (b), 137, 138, 139, 140, 141, 142 (l), 145 (r), 146, 148, Associated Press 150, 155, 156 (l), Associated Press 157, 158, Associated Press 159, Press Association 160-161, 164, 166, 167, 168, Associated Press 169 (r), 169 (l), Associated Press 170 (l), 107 (r), 171 (l), 172, 173 (all), Associated Press 174, 175, Associated Press 176, Associated Press 177, 178, Press Association 179 (r), Associated Press 179 (l), Associated Press 180, Associated Press 181, 184, Associated Press 186 (r), 186 (l), 187, 188, 189, 190, 191 (all), 192 (all), 193 (all), 194 (all), 195 (all). *Travel Photo International:* 123.

Every effort has been made to contact the copyright holders and we apologize in advance for any omissions. We would be pleased to insert the appropriate acknowledgement in any subsequent edition of this publication.

snapshots **in time**

Subject Index

Academy Award, 84
AIDS, 94, 158
Albania, unrest in, 35
Algerian Nationalists, 23
Amritsar, Golden Temple of, 31, 60
ANC (African National Congress), 54, 63, 65, 104, 108
Anglo-French Cordiale, 16
Anglo-Russian Agreement, 43
antibiotics, 9, 157
apartheid, 54, 63, 65
Apollo I, 126
Apollo II, 126
aqualung, 124
Armistice, 168
Art Deco, 82
Art Nouveau, 10, 77
Assam, 31
Aswan Dam, 118
Athens Polytechnic, 29
atom bomb, 9, 174

Balkan League, 164
Bangladesh, famine in, 189
Barbarossa, 171
bathyscaphe, 125
Battle of Britain, 170
Bay of Pigs, 26, 53, 177
BBC (British Broadcasting Corporation), 80, 145
Beatlemania, 92
Beatles, 92, 93
Bedtime for Bonzo, 58
Beetle, 10, 136
BEF (British Expeditionary Force), 164, 165, 170
Belsen, 174
Berlin,
    airlift, 22
    Treaty of, 45
    University, 84
    wall, 26, 33
Bhopal, 191
Bible, 112
Blitz, 51, 171
blitzkrieg, 170
blood groups, 9, 155
Bloody Sunday, 44
Bloomsbury Group, 85
Bluebird, 134, 137
boat people, 107
Boer War, 10, 162
book burning, by Nazis, 84
Boxer Rebellion, 14
Boy Scouts, 98
Brighton bomb, 31
British Empire Exhibition, 80
British Printing Corporation, 35
Brighton bomb, 31
British Empire Exhibition, 80
British Printing Corporation, 35
Buchenwald, 103, 174
Buckingham Palace, 92
Budgie the Helicopter, 32
Burlington Zephyr, 136

Caerphilly pit disaster, 184
Calcutta, riots in, 20
Camp David, 56, 60, 179
CAT scan, 158
Challenger, 127
Channel Tunnel, 141
Chechnya, 10

Checkpoint Charlie, 26
Chernobyl, 10, 190, 192
Chikatetsu subway, 135
Chinese Civil War, 17
cholera, 9, 155
CIA (Central Intelligence Agency), 62, 177
Clockwork Orange, A, 91
Cold War, 36, 49, 51
Concorde, 93, 140
contraceptive pill, 9, 158
CREEP (Republican Committee to Re-elect the President), 56
Crimean War, 156
Crystal Palace, 20
Cuba, revolution in, 25, 54
Cubism, 78
Cyclone Tracey, 189
Cyprus, violence in, 25

Datsun, 138
D-Day, 173
de Havilland *Comet I*, 137
Depression, 68, 70
Discovery, 118
Disneyland, 88
DNA, 151
Do They Know It's Christmas, 93
Dreadnought, 10, 16, 132
Dr Zhivago, 88
Dresden, 174
Dunkirk, 170
Du Pont, 145
dust storms, 186

Eagle, 126
earthquakes, 10, 183, 184, 186, 189, 191, 193, 195
Easter Rising, 45
EC (European Community), 63
EEC (European Economic Community), 24, 63
Eiffel Tower, 77
Endeavour, 127
Enola Gay, 174
Entente Cordiale, 43
ETA (Basque Homeland and Liberty), 56
Ethiopia, famine in, 189
evolution, theory of, 112
Exposition des Arts Decoratifs, 82

Falklands War, 58
favrile glass, 77
FBI, 151
Festival Hall, 87
Festival of Britain, 87
Firebird, The, 78
floods, 187, 194
Flying Scotsman, 10, 135
forest fires, 194, 195
foot-binding, 99
Ford Motor Company, 130, 134, 145
Franco-Russian Alliance, 16

Gallipoli, 165
General Strike, 102
German unification, 35
Girl Guides, 98, 99
glasnost, 61, 63
Gold Standard, 68
Gone With the Wind, 84, 85
Grand Central Station, 132
Great Crash, 71
Great Exhibition, 20, 78
Great Train Robbery, 27
Guangzhou, 20
Guinness, 72

Gulf War, 62

H-Bomb, 148
Harrods, 30, 38
heatwave, 184
helicopter, 136
Heysel Stadium disaster, 31
Hindenburg, 48
Hindenburg, 20, 130
Hirohito, 62
Hiroshima, 62, 174
History of World War II, 50
History of the English Speaking Peoples, 50
Hitler Youth, 58
HIV, 158
Hogarth Press, 85
Holocaust, 103, 174
Hong Kong handover, 38
Household Cavalry, 30
Hovercraft, 138
Hungarian uprising, 23
Hutu, 37
hyperinflation, 72

Incas, 118
Internet, 9, 151
in vitro fertilization, 158
IRA (Irish Republican Army), 30, 32, 37, 58, 107, 109
Irangate, 58, 61
Iran-Iraq War, 61

Jazz Age, 80, 82
Jezebel, 84
Jonestown, 113
Jupiter Missile Cone, 125
Jurassic Park, 10, 94

Kano, 15
Kew Gardens, 192
Khmer Rouge, 30
Killers, The, 58
Kirov Ballet, 91
Kristallnacht, 113
Ku Klux Klan, 102

Ladies Home Journal, 155
landslide, 186
lasers, 150
League of Nations, 45, 170
Little Red Book, 50, 92
Live Aid, 93
London, flooding of, 18
Louise, 16

Maastricht Treaty, 63
Machu Picchu, 118
Madame Butterfly, 77
Malayan independence, 24
Manchester United, 25
Married Love, 156
Mars, 10, 126, 127
Maser, 148
Mau-Mau, 22, 23
Maxwell Communications, 35
MBE, 92
Mein Kampf, 84
MI5, 94
Microsoft, 151
miners' strike, 58
Mini, 10, 188
Mirror Group, 35
Missouri, 174
Monterey Pop Festival, 92, 93

Mount Everest, 10, 121
Mount Pelée, 15
Munich,
    Agreement, 48
    air crash, 25

Nagasaki, 62, 174
National Health Service, 49
New Democracy, 50
New Look, 10, 86, 87
New York subway, 131
Nijinsky, 78
Nobel Prize, 60, 61, 63, 65, 82, 88, 90, 91, 104, 108, 113, 144, 148, 151, 155, 157, 158, 163, 176
Norway, independence of, 16

oil disasters, 190, 191
Oklahoma bomb, 37
Operation Blue Star, 31
Opium Wars, 38
Orient Express, 138

Panama Canal, 15, 56, 162, 163
Paris Metro, 130
Parti Quebécois (QC), 38
Passage to India, A, 80
Pathfinder, 128
Pearl Harbor, 171
penicillin, 156
perestroika, 61, 63
Pergamon Press, 35
Peter Pan, 77
Piltdown Man, 120
polio, 9
Porgy and Bess, 90
Prague University, 28
Prohibition, 68, 102

Queen, 93, 94
Queen Elizabeth II, 138, 140

Red Brigade, 57
Resistance (French), 32, 90, 91, 173
Rite of Spring, The, 78, 79
Robben Island Prison, 63
rock paintings, 124
Royal Ballet, 91
Russian Revolution, 17, 46

Saint Joan, 82
St Valentine's Day Massacre, 18
Sandox, 192
Satanic Verses, The, 57
Seaborg, 143
Seveso, 190
Sharpeville massacre, 104
Showa era, 62
Singing in the Rain, 87
Six-Day War, 178, 179
Sly and the Family Stone, 92
Solidarity, 63, 71, 114
Somme, 166
Sons of the Gestapo, 38
Sorbonne, 106
South Pole, 10
Space Shuttle, 126
Spain,
    civil war, 169
    strikes in, 19
Spice Girls, 95
Spirit of St Louis, 122
Sputnik I, 148, 150
Sputnik II, 150
Stalingrad, battle of, 172

Status Quo, 93
Suez,
　　Canal, 26, 55, 70, 178
　　crisis, 53, 55
suffragette movement, 100
Sweetwater, 92
Symbionese Liberation Army, 29

Taj Mahal, 80
TASS, 28
Tate Gallery, 18
tuberculosis, 9, 155
telegraphy, 144
television, 10, 145
Tiananmen Square massacre, 38, 107
Times, The, 94
Tintin, 84
Titanic, 127, 132
Tollund Man, 124
Torrey Canyon, 187
tornado, 186
Train á Grande Vitesse (TGV), 10, 141
Trans-Siberian railway, 131
Treaty of Rome, 23
Trial, the, 82
Triple Entente, 16
Tutsi Rwandan Patriotic Front, 37
typhoid, 9

Uganda National Liberation Army, 57
Ulysses, 80
UN (United Nations), 26, 49, 108, 124, 176,
　　179, 180
Uncle Vanya, 76
University of St Petersburg, 78
uranium, 144
Uribe-Uribe, 162
US Embassy hostages, 56

VE Day, 176
Verdun, 166
Versailles, Treaty of, 45, 168
Victoria and Albert Museum, 78
Vietnam War, 61, 177
volcano, 10, 184, 189, 191
Volksturm, 173
Volkswagen, 136
Vostok I, 125

Waco, 38
Wall Street, 68, 72
Walt Disney Company, 73, 85
Warsaw ghetto, 172
Warsaw Pact, 36
Watergate, 56
Wembley Stadium, 80
Who, The, 92
Windsor Castle, 36
Winnie the Pooh, 83
Woodstock Pop Festival, 92
World Exhibition, 77, 82
World Trade Center, 37
World War I, 17, 29, 43, 45, 48, 68, 84,
　　100, 120, 130, 134, 135, 156, 161, 163, 164, 168
World War II, 24, 29, 36, 46, 47, 51, 52,
　　58, 70, 84, 91, 103, 122, 138, 146, 148, 176

Yalta, 173
Yeti, 18
Yom Kippur, 70, 178
Yoshihito, 62

Zionist Socialist movement, 28

Index of Names

Adams, Gerry, 108
Agca, Mehmet, 114
Albert, of Saxe-Coburg and Gotha, Prince, 42
Alcock, J. W., 134
Aldrin, Edwin "Buzz", 126
Al Fayed, Dodi, 38
Allen, Paul G., 151
Amin, Idi, 55, 57, 71
Amsberg, Claus von, 58
Amundsen, Roald, 120
Anderson, Terry, 35
Andrew, Prince, 32, 36, 52
Andrew, of Greece, Prince, 22
Anne, Princess, 52
Arafat, Yasir, 36
Arc, Joan of, 82, 99
Armstrong, Neil, 9, 117, 126
Asquith, Herbert, 16
Astor, Nancy, 100
Astor, Waldorf, 100
Attlee, Clement, 21, 49, 50, 176

Baden-Powell, Agnes, 99
Baden-Powell, Robert, 98, 99
Baird, John Logie, 145
Baldwin, Stanley, 48
Ballard, Robert, 127
Barbie, Klaus, 32
Bardeen, John, 146
Barnard, Christiaan, 158
Barrie, J. M., 77
Barrow, Clyde, 9, 19
Barton, Edmund, 14
Batista, President, 25
Battenberg, Prince, Louis of, 22
Beatrice, Princess, 32
Beatrix, Queen, 58
Beethoven, Ludwig van, 91
Begin, Menacham, 60, 179
Belasco, David, 77
Bell, Gertrude, 120
Bella, Ahmed Ben 23
Ben-Gurion, David, 22, 28
Bennett, Floyd, 122
Berchtold, Count, Leopold von, 17
Becquerel, Antoine, 144
Bevin, Ernest, 103
Biggs, Ronnie, 27
Biko, Steve, 107
bin Abdullah, Mohammed, 162
Bingham, Hiram, 118
Blair, Tony, 64, 63
Blanco, Luis Carrero, 55
Blériot, Louis, 132
Bokassa, Jean-Bedel, 56
Bonaparte, Napoleon, 10
Bouvier, Jacqueline Lee, 23, 53
Bowes-Lyon, Lady, Elizabeth,18, 51
Brattain, Walter, 147
Braque, Georges, 78
Braun, Eva, 49
Braun, Karl, 144
Bréguet, Louis, 136
Brezhnev, Leonid Ilyich, 193
Brooke, Rupert, 79
Brown, Louise, 158
Bruce, Robert the, 18
Burgess, Anthony, 91
Burns, John, 42
Busby, Sir, Matt, 25
Bush, George, 62, 108
Byrd, Richard E., 122
Byrne, Roger, 25

Campbell, Donald, 134, 137
Campbell, Malcolm, 134
Campbell-Bannerman, Henry, 26
Campora, Hector, 51
Camus, Albert, 90
Capone, Al, 18, 19
Carlos I, King, Juan, 45
Carnarvon, Lord, 121
Carothers, W. H., 145
Carter, Howard, 121
Carter, Jimmy, 30, 56, 58, 179
Casement, Sir, Roger, 45
Castro, Fidel, 25, 26, 54, 177
Ceausescu, Nicolae, 10, 62
Chaffee, Roger, 126
Chain, Ernst, 157
Chamberlain, Neville, 48, 49, 169
Chaplin, Charlie, 79
Chapman, Mark, 93
Charisse, Cyd, 87
Charles, Prince, 30, 36, 38, 52
Chekhov, Anton, 76
Churchill, Winston, 9, 16, 41, 44, 49, 50, 170,
　　173, 174, 176
Churchill, Clementine (*née* Hozier), 9, 16
Clinton, Bill, 62, 64
Cobb, John, 137
Cocker, Joe, 93
Cockerell, Christopher, 138
Collins, Phil, 93
Connolly, James, 45
Cook, James, 33
Cooke, William, 144
Cormack, Allan, 158
Cousteau, Jacques-Yves, 124
Crichton, Michael, 94
Crick, Francis, 151
Crippen, Dr, Hawley Harvey, 10, 144
Cromwell, William Nelson, 15
Crosby, Stills, Nash and Young, 93
Curie, Marie, 144, 153
Curie, Pierre, 144
Czolgosz, Leon, 43

da Vinci, Leonardo, 136
Daladier, Edouard, 48
Dalai Lama, 113
Davis, Bette, 84
Davison, Emily, 100
Dawson, Charles, 120
de Gaulle, Charles, 52, 106
De Havilland, Olivia, 85
de Klerk, F. W., 63, 65, 108
de Lesseps, Ferdinand, 15
Denktash, Rauf, 25
Diaghilev, Sergei, 78
Diem, President, 27
Dior, Christian, 86
Disney, Walt, 83, 85, 88
Donahue, Troy, 92
Dorand, René, 52
Du Bois, William Edward Burghardt, 98
Dudayev, Dzhozkhar, 181
Dylan, Bob, 93

Eckert, J., 148
Eckhert, P., 146
Eden, Anthony, 53
Edward, Prince, 52
Edward VII, 42, 43
Edward VIII, 18, 48
Edwards, Buster, 27
Edwards, Duncan, 25
Edwards, Robert, 158
Einstein, Albert, 148

Campbell, Donald, 134, 137
Eisenhower, Dwight ("Ike"), 51, 104, 177
Elizabeth II, 18, 22,30, 36, 51, 52, 141
Erlander, Tage, 61
Etienne, Jean-Louis, 127
Eugenie, Princess, 32

Fairbanks, Douglas, Jr, 79
Faisal I, 120
Faubaus, Orval E., 104
Ferdinand, Archduke, Franz, 17, 164
Ferguson, Sarah, 32, 36
Fleming, Alexander, 156, 157
Fletcher, Yvonne, 31
Florey, Howard, 157
Fonteyn, Margot, 91
Ford, Gerald, 56, 58
Ford, Henry, 10, 13, 56, 58, 130, 134 , 136, 145
Forster, E. M., 80
Fortier, Michael, 37
Franco, General, 56, 169
Franco, João, 45
Frank, Anne, 103
Franz Josef, Emperor, 45, 162
Frederick VII, 16
French, John, 164
Freud, Sigmund, 76

Gable, Clark, 85
Gadaffi, Colonel, 31, 179
Gagarin, Yuri, 125
Gagnan, Emile, 124
Gandhi, Indira, 31, 54, 60
Gandhi, Mohandas Karamchand (Mahatma), 44,
　　47, 50, 53, 104, 111
Gapon, George, 15
Gates, William Henry, III, 151
Geldof, Bob, 93
George III, 42
George V, 48
George VI, King, 18, 51, 52
George, Kara, 43
Gershwin, George, 80, 90
Gershwin, Ira, 80
Gheorghiu-Dej, Gheorghe, 62
Gibson, William, 98
Gillette, King Camp, 144
Goebbels, Joseph, 84
Goering, Hermann Wilhelm, 103
Goethals, George, 16
Goldman, Emma, 97
Goldman, Ronald, 109
Gorbachev, Mikhail, 35, 36, 58, 61, 62, 63,
　　107, 193
Grable, Betty, 86
Grissom, Virgil "Gus", 126
Guevara, Che, 54

Haakon VII, 16, 52
Habyarimana, President, 37
Hahn, Otto, 174
Haley, Bill, 10, 88
Hammarskjöld, Dag Hjalmar Agne Carl, 26
Harald V, 52
Hardie, Keir, 42
Harris, Bomber, 174
Hauptmann, Bruno, 19
Havens, Richie, 92
Hearst, Patti, 29
Hearst, Randolph, 29
Heath, Edward, 58
Hendrix, Jimi, 93
Henry, Prince, 30, 38
Henson, Matthew, 118
Henson, William, 144
Hergé, (Georges Remi), 84
Hertz, Heinrich, 144

Heyerdahl, Thor, 124
Heyward, Du Bose, 90
Hillary, Edmund, 124
Himmler, Heinrich, 173
Hinckley, John W., 58
Hiss, Alger, 55
Hitchcock, Alfred, 88
Hitler, Adolf, 10, 48, 49, 84, 136, 148, 169, 170, 172, 173, 174
Hoover, Herbert, 46
Hopetoun, Lord, 14
Hopper, Grace Murray, 148
Hounsfield, Godfrey, 158
Howard, Leslie, 85
Humphrey, Hubert, 54, 55
Hussein, of Jordan, King, 52, 65
Hussein, Saddam, 108, 179, 180

Irvine, Andrew, 121
Issiognis, Alec, 138
Ito, Judge, Lance, 109
Ivanov, Eugene, 27

Jagielski, General, 71
Jaruzelski, General, 63
Jieshi, General, Jiang, 20, 169
John Paul II, Pope, 114
Johnson, Amy, 122, 171
Johnson, Lyndon, 53, 54, 177
Jones, Jim, 113
Joplin, Janis, 93
Joyce, James, 80

Kafka, Franz, 82
Kai-Shek, Chiang *see* Jieshi, Jiang, General
Karadzic, Radovan, 181
Keeler, Christine, 27
Keenan, Brian, 35
Keller, Helen, 84, 98
Kelly, Gene, 87
Kelly, Grace, 88
Kennedy, Edward, 28
Kennedy, John F., 23, 26, 53, 54, 55, 177
Kennedy, Robert, 54
Kenyatta, Jomo "Burning Spear", 23
Keynes, John Maynard, 67, 70
Khomeini, Ayatollah, 30, 57, 114
King, Martin Luther, Jr, 104, 106
King, Rodney, 108
Kinnock, Neil, 64
Kitchener, Lord, 162
Koch, Robert, 155
Kohl, Helmut, 35
Kopechne, Mary Jo, 28
Koresh, David, 114
Kruger, Paul, 14, 162
Krushchev, Nikita, 26, 47, 53, 177
Kubrick, Stanley, 91

Landsteiner, Karl, 155
Lawrence, T. E., 166
Leigh, Vivian, 85
le Neve, Ethel, 144
Lenin, Vladimir Ilych, 46
Lennon, John, 92, 93
Leoner, Alexander, 125
Lerroux, Señor, 19
Lindbergh, Charles, 19, 122
Lindbergh, Charles A., Jr, 19
Lloyd George, David, 16, 46, 168
Lodge, Henry Cabot, 23
London, Jack, 84
Lovell, Alfred, 148

MacArthur, General, 174, 176
MacDonald, Ramsay, 42

Macmillan, Harold, 24, 27, 28, 53,
Maiman, Theodore, 150
Major, John, 58, 62, 109
Makarios, Archbishop, 25
Mallory, George, 121
Mandela, Nelson, 53, 63, 64, 65, 108
Mandela, Winnie, 54, 64, 65
Mann, Heinrich, 84
Mann, Thomas, 84
Marconi, Gugliemo, 144
Margaret, Princess, 18, 51, 87
Marjarres, General, 162
Mauchley, J., 146
Maxwell, James, 144
Maxwell, Sir, John, 45
Maxwell, Robert, 35
McCarthy, John, 35
McCartney, Paul, 93
McGovern, George, 56
McKinley, William, 43
McVeigh, Timothy, 37
Meir, Golda, 65
Melbourne, Lord, 42
Menuhin, Yehudi, 84
Mercury, Freddie, 93, 94
Michel, Jean-Louis, 127
Milken, Michael, 73
Miller, Glenn, 21, 86
Milne, A. A., 83
Milne, Christopher Robin, 83
Milne, Lord, 162
Mitchell, Margaret, 85
Mitterrand, François, 23, 141
Mladic, Ratko, 181
Monroe, Marilyn, 10, 90, 92
Moran, George "Bugsy", 18
Moro, Aldo, 57
Moulin, Jean, 32
Mountbatten, Lord Louis, 21, 29, 176
Mountbatten, Lady, 21
Mussolini, Benito, 48, 169, 172

Nagy, Imre, 23
Neave, Airey, 29
Nehru, Jawaharlal, 53, 60
Nicholas II, Czar, 15, 17, 44, 162
Nichols, Terry, 37
Nietzsche, Friedrich, 76
Nightingale, Florence, 156
Nixon, Richard, 51, 53, 55, 56, 58, 92
Norgay, Tenzing, 124
North, Oliver, 61
Ntaryarima, President, 37
Nureyev, Rudolf, 91
Nyerere, Julius, 57

Obote, Milton, 55
Obrenovich, Milosh, 43
Olav V, 52
Ono, Yoko, 93
Oscar II, 16
Oswald, Lee Harvey, 53

Palme, Olof, 61
Palmerston, Henry, Lord, 42
Pankhurst, Sylvia, 100
Papadopoulos, George, 29
Parker, Bonnie, 9, 19
Parker, Tom, 88
Pasternak, Boris, 88
Pavlov, Ivan Petrovich, 155
Paxton, Joseph, Sir, 20
Pearce, Padraic, 45
Peary, Robert, 118, 127
Peel, Sir, Robert, 42
Pegg, David, 25

Perón, Eva (Evita), 51
Perón, Juan Domingo, 51, 54
Petacci, Clara, 49
Philip, Arthur, 33
Philip, Prince, 22, 30, 52
Picasso, Pablo, 78
Piccard, Jacques, 125
Pickford, Mary, 79
Pincus, Gregory, 158
Pius X, Pope, 112
Plehve, Vyacheslav Konstantinovich, 44
Poindexter, John, 61
Poitier, Sidney, 90
Pol Pot, 30
Presley, Elvis, 88, 92
Princip, Gavrilo, 17
Profumo, John, 27
Puccini, Giacomo, 77
Pu Yi, Henry, 44

Quang Doc, 27

Rabin, Yitzhak, 65
Rachman, Peter, 27
Rahman, Tunku Abdul, 24
Railton, Reid, 137
Rainier, III, Prince, 88
Rath, Ernst von, 113
Ray, James Earl, 106
Reagan, Ronald, 30, 56, 58, 61, 62, 179
Reed, Frank, 35
Remarque, Erich Maria, 84
Reynolds, Albert, 109
Rice-Davies, Mandy, 27
Richthofen, Baron von, 166
Rickover, Hyman, 137
Rimsky-Korsakov, Nikolay Andreyevich, 78
Roberts, Lord, 14
Roe, Herbert, 156
Rogge, Leslie, 151
Ronson, Gerald, 72
Roosevelt, Franklin D., 68, 70, 173
Roosevelt, Theodore, 98, 163
Ruby, Jack, 53
Runcie, Robert, Dr, 33
Rushdie, Salman, 57, 114
Rusk, Dean, 26
Russell, William F., 18
Ryan, Leo, 113

Sadat, Anwar, 60, 179
Sands, Bobby, 107
Santos-Dumont, Alberto, 131
Sartre, Jean-Paul, 91
Saunders, Ernest, 72
Schadow, Arthur, 150
Schumway, Norman, 158
Schwartzkopf, Norman, 180
Schweitzer, Albert, 176
Scopes, John, 112
Scott, Robert Falcon, 118
Seipei, Stompie, 64
Selassie, Haile, 169
Selig, Roger, 72
Shah of Iran, 57
Shaw, George Bernard, 82
Shevardnadze, Eduard, 63
Shikai, Yuan, 17
Shockley, William, 146
Simpson, Ernest, 48
Simpson, Nicole Brown, 109
Simpson, Orenthal James (O. J.), 109
Simpson, Wallis Warfield, 48
Sinclair, Upton, 84
Sirhan, Sirhan, 54
Smith, John, 64, 65

Smith, Rupert, 180
Solanas, Valerie, 92
Spaak, Paul Henri, 49
Spencer, Lady, Diana, 30, 32, 36, 38
Spencer, E., 48
Spielberg, Steven, 94
Stalin, Joseph, 10, 46, 47, 70, 112, 172, 173
Steger, Will, 127
Steptoe, Patrick, 158
Stewart, James, 88
Steyn, Marthinus, 14
Stopes, Marie, 1921
Stravinsky, Igor, 78, 79
Sukarno, Ahmed, 24
Sullivan, Anne Mansfield, 98
Sutherland, Tom, 35

Tahombe, President, 26
Tambo, Oliver, 64
Taylor, Tommy, 25,130
Teller, Edward, 148
Thatcher, Margaret, 29, 31, 58, 62, 94
Tiffany, Louis Comfort, 77
Townes, Charles, 150
Trotsky, Leon, 15, 47
Truman, Harry, 46, 174, 176
Tsafendas, Dimitrios, 54
Turing, Alan, 146
Tutankhamen, 80, 121

Umberto I, 42
Uwilingiyimana, Prime Minister, 37

Valentino, Rudolf, 83
Verwoerd, Hendrik, 54, 104
Victor Emmanuel II, 42
Victor Emmanuel III, 42
Victoria, Queen, 29, 42, 43, 78

Waite, Terry, 32, 179
Wakeman, Selman Abraham, 157
Waldersee, Count von, 14
Walesa, Lech, 63, 71
Walsh, Donald, 125
Ward, Dr, Stephen, 27
Warhol, Andy, 75, 92
Warren, Earl, 53
Washington, Booker T., 98
Washkansky, Louis, 158
Watson, James, 151
Wavell, Earl, 21
Webb, Aston, 78
Wheatstone, Charles, 144
Whelan, Duncan, 25
Whidden Brown, Arthur, 134
White, Edmund, 125
Whitney, Eli, 145
Wilder, Billy, 90
Wilhelm II, 162, 168, 184
William IV, 42
William, Prince, 30, 38
Wilson, Woodrow, 16, 45, 163, 168
Woolf, Leonard, 85
Woolf, Virginia, 85
Wright, Orville, 9, 130, 131
Wright, Peter, 94
Wright, Wilbur, 9, 130, 131

Yaobang, Hu, 107
Yasgur, Max, 93
Yeltsin, Boris, 36, 61

Zedong, Mao, 10, 20, 50, 92
Zeppelin, Ferdinand Graf von, 130